THE BEDFORD SERIES IN HISTORY AND CULTURE

American Cold War Strategy: Interpreting NSC 68

THE BEDFORD SERIES IN HISTORY AND CULTURE

Advisory Editors: Natalie Zemon Davis, Princeton University
Ernest R. May, Harvard University
Lynn Hunt, University of California at
Los Angeles
David W. Blight, Amherst College

The World Turned Upside Down: Indian Voices from Early America
Edited with an introduction by Colin G. Calloway, *University of Wyoming*

The Autobiography of Benjamin Franklin
Edited with an introduction by Louis P. Masur, *City University of New York*

Benjamin and William Franklin: Father and Son, Patriot and Loyalist
Sheila L. Skemp, *University of Mississippi*

Narrative of the Life of Frederick Douglass, An American Slave, Written by Himself
Edited with an introduction by David W. Blight, *Amherst College*

Muckraking: Three Landmark Articles
Edited with an introduction by Ellen F. Fitzpatrick, *Harvard University*

Plunkitt of Tammany Hall by William L. Riordon
Edited with an introduction by Terrence J. McDonald, *University of Michigan*

American Cold War Strategy: Interpreting NSC 68
Edited with an introduction by Ernest R. May, *Harvard University*

The Age of McCarthyism: A Brief History with Documents
Ellen Schrecker, *Yeshiva University*

Postwar Immigrant America: A Social History
Reed Ueda, *Tufts University*

THE BEDFORD SERIES IN HISTORY AND CULTURE

American Cold War Strategy: Interpreting NSC 68

Edited with an introduction by

Ernest R. May

Harvard University

BEDFORD/ST. MARTIN'S   Boston   ♦   New York

For Susan Wood

FOR BEDFORD/ST. MARTIN'S
President and Publisher: Charles H. Christensen
Associate Publisher/General Manager: Joan E. Feinberg
History Editor: Sabra Scribner
Associate History Editor: Louise D. Townsend
Managing Editor: Elizabeth M. Schaaf
Copyeditor: Barbara G. Flanagan
Text Design: Claire Seng-Niemoeller
Cover Design: Richard Emery Design, Inc.

Library of Congress Cataloging-in-Publication Data
American cold war strategy: interpreting NSC 68. Edited with an introduction by
Ernest R. May.
   p. cm. (Bedford books in American history)
Includes bibliographical references and index.
ISBN 0–312–09445–0 (cloth). ISBN 0–312–06637–6 (pbk).
   1. United States—Military policy. 2. Cold War. I. May, Ernest R.
II. National Security Council (U.S.)
UA23.A598   1993   355′.033573—dc20

Library of Congress Catalog Card Number: 92-52524
Manufactured in the United States of America.

6   5   4
k j i h

For information, write: Bedford/St. Martin's, 75 Arlington Street, Boston, MA 02116
(617-426-7440)

ISBN: 0–312–06637–6   (paperback)
ISBN: 0–312–09445–0   (hardcover)

ACKNOWLEDGMENTS

   Dean Acheson. Reprinted from *Present at the Creation: My Years in the State Department* by Dean Acheson. By permission of W. W. Norton & Company, Inc. Copyright © 1969 by Dean Acheson.

   John Lewis Gaddis. Excerpted from *Strategies of Containment: A Critical Appraisal of Postwar American National Security Policy* by John Lewis Gaddis. Copyright © 1982 by Oxford University Press, Inc. Reprinted by permission.

Acknowledgments and copyrights are continued at the back of the book on page 228, which constitutes an extension of the copyright page.

Foreword

The Bedford Series in History and Culture is designed so that readers can study the past as historians do.

The historian's first task is finding the evidence. Documents, letters, memoirs, interviews, pictures, movies, novels, or poems can provide facts and clues. Then the historian questions and compares the sources. There is more to do than in a courtroom, for hearsay evidence is welcome, and the historian is usually looking for answers beyond act and motive. Different views of an event may be as important as a single verdict. How a story is told may yield as much information as what it says.

Along the way the historian seeks help from other historians and perhaps from specialists in other disciplines. Finally, it is time to write, to decide on an interpretation and how to arrange the evidence for readers.

Each book in this series contains an important historical document or group of documents, each document a witness from the past and open to interpretation in different ways. The documents are combined with some element of historical narrative—an introduction or a biographical essay, for example—that provides students with an analysis of the primary source material and important background information about the world in which it was produced.

Each book in the series focuses on a specific topic within a specific historical period. Each provides a basis for lively thought and discussion about several aspects of the topic and the historian's role. Each is short enough (and inexpensive enough) to be a reasonable one-week assignment in a college course. Whether as classroom or personal reading, each book in the series provides firsthand experience of the challenge—and fun—of discovering, recreating, and interpreting the past.

Natalie Zemon Davis
Ernest R. May
Lynn Hunt
David W. Blight

Preface

NSC 68 laid out the rationale for U.S. strategy during much of the cold war.

The cold war was already under way in 1950 when NSC 68 was written. The eminent columnist Walter Lippmann had long since published a book with the title *The Cold War* (New York: Harper, 1947). From the end of World War II in 1945, relations between the West and the Soviet Union had become increasingly hostile. Until 1950, however, the contest remained primarily political and economic. NSC 68 argued that, if it continued so, the West would lose. To check or turn back the expansion of the Soviet Union and communism, the document said, the West needed large, ready military forces.

In the spring of 1950, when NSC 68 was drafted, President Harry S. Truman's budget called for spending less than $13 billion for the Army, Navy, and Air Force. This was not quite one-third of projected federal spending and not quite 5 percent of gross national product (GNP). A year later, after officially adopting NSC 68, Truman asked for more than $60 billion for the armed services—almost two-thirds of the total budget and 18.5 percent of a GNP meanwhile lustily growing. In all subsequent years of the cold war, military power would continue to have paramount claim on U.S. resources. NSC 68 thus provided the blueprint for the militarization of the cold war from 1950 to the collapse of the Soviet Union at the beginning of the 1990s.

This volume includes the complete text of NSC 68, preceded by an essay setting it in context and analyzing the processes by which it came into being. Following the text is another essay, posing several approaches to interpreting the document. The core of the book for students of history or political science is contained in the next six chapters, which comprise commentaries by former officials, specialists on American foreign policy, other American scholars, and foreign scholars. Most of these commentaries were written specifically for this volume and are published here for the first time. They illustrate the many ways in which a single historical document can be remembered, read, or understood.

ACKNOWLEDGMENTS

The editor is grateful to fellow contributors for improving the introduction and chapter notes. He is also grateful to Frederick Adams, Brian Balogh, Robert Dallek, Richard E. Neustadt, Paul H. Nitze, Joseph S. Nye, and Thomas Schwartz for reading some or all of the manuscript and offering helpful advice. Joanne Fraser did a fine job of general editing and Barbara Flanagan of copyediting. Philip Roberts prepared the index.

At Bedford Books, Charles Christensen had the vision to conceive the series. Sabra Scribner, as Bedford's history editor, made the vision reality. Louise Townsend assisted with manuscript preparation and permissions. Elizabeth Schaaf carefully guided the manuscript through the design and production process. Sally Makacynas saw to it that I met their deadline for this, the series' inaugural volume.

Ernest R. May

Contents

8. Afterword   199

Introduction:
NSC 68: The Theory
and Politics
of Strategy

In 1950 the U.S. National Security Council—the NSC—had existed for only three years. It was a cabinet-level committee created to advise the president on issues where foreign policy and defense policy intersected. It had a very small staff. There was no national security adviser comparable to Henry Kissinger or Zbigniew Brzezinski later on.[1] A paper for the NSC came ordinarily from the State Department or, via the Joint Chiefs of Staff, from one of the military services. The council's secretariat then assigned it a number as an NSC paper.

In April 1950 the secretariat received a seventy-page typescript from the Department of State. Stamped TOP SECRET and given the label NSC 68, it was distributed to the president and the council's statutory members and advisers, the vice president, the secretaries of state and defense, the chairman of the National Security Resources Board, the chairman of the Joint Chiefs of Staff, and the director of Central Intelligence.

Entitled "United States Objectives and Programs for National Security," the paper analyzed the ongoing cold war and courses of action open to the United States. After reviewing arguments for continuing on the current course, turning to isolation, or deliberately opening war on the Soviet Union, NSC 68 made a case for an alternative, described in its table of contents as "A Rapid Build-up of Political, Economic, and Military Strength in the Free World." To appreciate this document, you should keep in mind that the cold war was still new. World War II, in which the United States and the Soviet Union had been allies, was less than five years in the past. Most Americans still remembered prewar isolationism. They remembered even more vividly the prewar Great Depression. In fact, few had yet accustomed themselves to a normality that did not include silent smokestacks, soup kitchens, and sidewalk apple vendors.

The cold war had come as a surprise. In 1945, even among Americans who foresaw trouble with the Russians, only a small minority had expected anything worse than diplomatic bickering. The majority assumed that issues would be worked out within the new United Nations organization, the UN. Instead, the UN had turned out to be just one more arena for West-East conflict. There, at endless foreign ministers' conferences and in areas liberated and conquered as a result of the war, the former allies moved more and more toward enmity.

At Fulton, Missouri, in March 1946 former British Prime Minister Winston Churchill spoke of the Soviet Union's having dropped an **"iron curtain"** on Eastern and east central Europe. Early in 1947, President Harry S. Truman proposed aiding Greece and Turkey so that they could combat Communists. He said, "I believe that it must be the policy of the United States to support free peoples who are resisting attempted subjugation by armed minorities or by outside pressures." This came to be called the **Truman Doctrine.**

Later in 1947, Secretary of State George C. Marshall added the **Marshall Plan.** According to this plan, the United States was to underwrite European economic recovery. Despite the recent Truman Doctrine, Marshall held out hope that Communist nations could benefit. The Soviets, however, denounced the plan as a cover for Wall Street imperialism. They and their satellite countries refused to take part. Intentionally or not, the plan then became one to aid only non-Communist nations. By this time, the columnist Walter Lippmann had popularized the phrase "cold war."

Strengthening the "iron curtain" image, the Soviets in 1948 truly sealed off Eastern Europe. A Communist coup in Prague, Czechoslovakia, early in the year did away with the last government in which Communists and non-Communists worked together. After that coup, a Gallup poll reported that 77 percent of Americans were convinced that the Soviet Union was seeking to be "the ruling power of the world."[2] Even though conservative Republicans controlled both the House and the Senate, Congress voted the full amount asked by Truman, the Democratic president, for a four-year **European Recovery Program** to implement the Marshall Plan.

The Western powers began to treat Western-occupied zones of Germany as part of a Western bloc. American aid promoted German economic revival. The Soviet Union treated its occupation zone in Germany as part of an Eastern bloc. In mid-1948 the Soviets closed the border between the two parts of the country. This denied the Western powers access by road or rail to their sectors of Berlin, the former German capital, for Berlin was ninety miles inside East Germany.

The United States mounted a round-the-clock airlift to West Berlin. Though the Soviets could have brought down the planes, they let them through. The Western powers had shown similar restraint when Communist Yugoslavia broke away from the Soviet bloc in April 1948. The United States and Great Britain supplied clandestine aid to the Yugoslavs but otherwise kept their distance.

In 1949 the cold war seemed to thaw. The Soviets suspended the blockade of Berlin. Truman had just been elected president in his own right. With Democrats now in the majority in Congress, he began to shift emphasis to domestic affairs. He pressed for a **Fair Deal,** which involved spending for housing, schools, and national health insurance. To pay for these programs without increasing taxes or running a deficit, Truman trimmed military spending. He proposed $14.3 billion for defense for fiscal year 1950 (July 1, 1949 to June 30, 1950), $13.5 billion for fiscal year 1951.

Truman's defense economies troubled Western Europeans. Military intelligence officers estimated that the Soviets had 175 divisions—five times as many as the United States, Britain, and France combined. Europeans felt threatened by this huge force. Even if the Red Army were only a fraction of that estimate, it could still overrun the feeble American, British, and French occupation forces in Germany and the patchwork armies behind them. To calm the Europeans and to give the Soviets a warning, the United States in 1949 signed the North Atlantic Treaty, promising to treat an attack on Western Europe as an attack on itself. Americans also made much of the fact that they alone possessed atomic bombs.

The North Atlantic Treaty had scarcely come into force, however, when air samples collected by the U.S. Air Force and Navy showed that the Soviets had successfully tested an atomic bomb of their own. Though physicists had long predicted a Soviet atomic bomb, the fact of its existence stirred alarm throughout the West.

Under a pretense of calm, American officials frantically reviewed possible responses. Truman promptly gave the Atomic Energy Commission money to increase capacity for producing atomic bombs. He also was urged to authorize development of a hydrogen bomb. Such a bomb, he was told, could be hundreds of times more destructive than an atomic bomb. A committee of scientists advising the Atomic Energy Commission opposed the hydrogen bomb project. So did a majority of the commission itself. Success was too uncertain and potential costs too high, they argued. Some called it a weapon for genocide. Military leaders and key members of Congress pressed the president to disregard such qualms. Given like advice by his secretary of state, Dean Acheson, Truman decided to go ahead.

To meet objections that he was making such decisions piecemeal, Truman ordered that the National Security Council conduct "a reexamination of our objectives in peace and war and of the effect of these objectives on our strategic plans."[3] The task fell to the State Department, and Acheson passed responsibility to the new chief of his Policy Planning Staff, Paul H. Nitze. NSC 68 resulted.

At the time of Truman's directive, Nitze had just turned forty-three. He came from a German-American academic family, his father having been a professor of linguistics at the University of Chicago. Nitze himself had gone to Harvard University and then to Wall Street. That was in October 1929, just before the stock market crash. Nitze jokes that he was probably the last man hired on Wall Street for many years.[4] He married Phyliss Pratt of the Standard Oil Pratts, and fortunate investments gave him riches of his own. Working in Washington during World War II, Nitze developed such an appetite for government service that he never afterward returned full time to the private sector.

At the end of the war, Nitze had headed the United States Strategic Bombing Survey team that appraised the Pacific war. Though he saw how the atomic bomb had devastated Hiroshima, he noted that the bomb damage had not been paralyzing. Parts of the city had regained electric power within a day. Trains had begun running again a day later. People who managed to get to shelters had survived. Nitze carried away the lesson that nuclear weapons did not necessarily mean no victor or loser in a future war. He also came away convinced of the importance of always being prepared for the worst.

Nitze later helped manage the European Recovery Program. In his travels, he saw how much Europeans feared the Red Army. In 1949, not long after Acheson replaced Marshall as secretary of state, Nitze became deputy director of the State Department Policy Planning Staff under Director George F. Kennan.

Marshall had created the Policy Planning Staff on the model of a military planning staff. He had chosen Kennan to head it probably because he recognized in Kennan qualifications that he himself lacked. As a twenty-year professional diplomat, Kennan knew the foreign service as Marshall knew the Army. Having trained as a Russian specialist and been number two in the U.S. embassy in Moscow from 1944 to 1946, Kennan was an expert on the new antagonist.

As a further recommendation, Kennan had skill as a writer. While he would amend his texts in response to comments, he never let them become committee products. Marshall had had his fill of such products when reading State Department prose in the Pentagon. From Kennan, Marshall expected memoranda written in a vivid, precise, and individual style. He also expected memoranda written with vision, for it was Kennan's strength to see current action issues in broad historical perspective.

In a famous **"Long Telegram"** from Moscow in early 1946, Kennan had diagnosed the developing East-West antagonism. The Soviet Union, he said, was "committed fanatically to the belief that with US there can be no *modus vivendi,* that it is desirable and necessary that the internal harmony of our society be disrupted, our traditional way of life be destroyed, the international authority of our state be broken, if Soviet power is to be secure." The Soviet government and Communist parties worldwide would endeavor, Kennan had predicted,

    a. To undermine general political and strategic potential of major western powers. . . .

    b. On unofficial plane particularly violent efforts . . . to weaken power and influence of Western Powers on colonial backward, or dependent peoples. . . .

    c. Where individual governments stand in path of Soviet purposes pressure will be brought for their removal from office. . . .

    d. In foreign countries Communists will, as a rule, work toward destruction of all forms of personal independence, economic, political, or moral. . . .

    e. Everything possible will be done to set major Western Powers against each other. . . .

    f. In general, all Soviet efforts on unofficial international plane will be negative and destructive in character, designed to tear down sources of strength beyond reach of Soviet control.[5]

In his Long Telegram, Kennan had not recommended action. He had called only for Americans' being made aware of the dangers. "We must see that our public is educated to realities of Russian situation. I cannot overemphasize importance of this," he wrote. After being called back to Washington, he tried to contribute to public education. In the quarterly *Foreign*

Affairs, Kennan published an article that he intended to keep anonymous. Entitled "The Sources of Soviet Conduct," with the author identified only as "X," it was known ever after as the **"X" article.**

Kennan's identity soon became known, and passages in the "X" article were taken as a summary of U.S. policy. Because of questions concerning the originality of NSC 68 and of differences between Kennan's views and those in NSC 68, some of these passages deserve quotation:

> The main element of any United States policy toward the Soviet Union must be that of a long-term, patient but firm and vigilant containment of Russian expansive tendencies. . . .
>
> In the light of the above, it will be clearly seen that the Soviet pressure against the free institutions of the western world is something that can be contained by the adroit and vigilant application of counter-force at a series of constantly shifting geographical and political points, corresponding to the shifts and maneuvers of Soviet policy. . . .
>
> But in actuality the possibilities for American policy are by no means limited to holding the line and hoping for the best. It is entirely possible for the United States to influence by its actions the internal developments, both within Russia and throughout the international Communist movement, by which Russian policy is largely determined. This is not only a question of the modest measure of informational activity which this government can conduct in the Soviet Union and elsewhere, although that, too, is important. It is rather a question of the degree to which the United States can create among the peoples of the world generally the impression of a country which knows what it wants, which is coping successfully with the problems of its internal life and with the responsibilities of a World Power, and which has a spiritual vitality capable of holding its own among the major intellectual currents of the time. . . .
>
> It would be an exaggeration to say that American behavior unassisted and alone could exercise a power of life and death over the Communist movement and bring about the early fall of Soviet power in Russia. But the United States has it in its power to increase enormously the strains under which Soviet policy must operate, to force upon the Kremlin a far greater degree of moderation and circumspection than it has had to observe in recent years, and in this way to promote tendencies which must eventually find their outlet in either the break-up or the gradual mellowing of Soviet power. For no mystical, Messianic movement—and particularly not that of the Kremlin—can face frustration indefinitely without eventually adjusting itself in one way or another to the logic of that state of affairs.
>
> Thus the decision will really fall in large measure in this country itself. The issue of Soviet-American relations is in essence a test of the over-all worth of the United States as a nation among nations. To avoid destruc-

tion the United States need only measure up to its own best traditions and prove itself worthy of preservation as a great nation.

Surely, there was never a fairer test of national quality than this. In the light of these circumstances, the thoughtful observer of Russian-American relations will find no cause for complaint in the Kremlin's challenge to American society. He will rather experience a certain gratitude to a Providence which, by providing the American people with this implacable challenge, has made their entire security as a nation dependent on their pulling themselves together and accepting the responsibilities of moral and political leadership that history plainly intended them to bear.[6]

The "X" article sketched what quickly came to be called a policy of **containment.** The same policy prescription appeared in NSC 20/4, also written by Kennan, which went to Truman in November 1948. It, too, deserves quotation:

> Our general objectives with respect to Russia, in time of peace as well as in time of war, should be:
>
> a. To reduce the power and influence of the USSR to limits which no longer constitute a threat to the peace, national independence and stability of the world family of nations.
>
> b. To bring about a basic change in the conduct of international relations by the government in power in Russia. . . .
>
> Attainment of these aims requires that the United States:
>
> a. Develop a level of military readiness which can be maintained as long as necessary as a deterrent to Soviet aggression, as indispensable support to our political attitude toward the USSR, as a source of encouragement to nations resisting Soviet political aggression, and as an adequate basis for immediate military commitments and for rapid mobilization should war prove unavoidable.
>
> b. Assure the internal security of the United States. . . .
>
> c. Maximize our economic potential. . . .
>
> d. Strengthen the orientation toward the United States of the non-Soviet nations. . . .
>
> e. Place the maximum strain on the Soviet structure of power and particularly on the relationships between Moscow and the satellite countries.
>
> f. Keep the U.S. public fully informed and cognizant of threats to our national security. . . .[7]

In December 1949, Acheson gave Kennan the title Counselor and made Nitze director of the Policy Planning Staff. While this was nominally a promotion, it moved Kennan out of the mainstream of department business. Nitze recalls that Kennan wanted this change so that he could prepare for a retirement career as a scholar. Nitze also recalls, however, Kennan's pique at not being consulted as if he were still chief policy planner.[8]

If Kennan had proposed the change, Acheson probably welcomed his initiative, for Kennan did not complement Acheson as he had complemented Marshall. Having earlier served five years as assistant secretary, then under secretary, of state, Acheson thought he understood the foreign service (at least as well as he wanted to). With the cold war well under way, Acheson could get advice about the Soviet Union from a number of sources, including other State Department Soviet experts such as Charles E. ("Chip") Bohlen and Llewellyn ("Tommy") Thompson. Also, Acheson took justifiable pride in his own ability to conceptualize and his own skill as a writer.

When choosing a successor to Kennan, Acheson picked Nitze probably because he craved a planner who could help him get things done. Alluding to the Renaissance Italian dynasty known for its ruthlessness and treachery, Acheson was to write later that Washington was "an environment where some of the methods would have aroused the envy of the Borgias."[9] Kennan had little talent for political management or intrigue. Nitze had plenty.

Acheson may have picked Nitze for one further reason. Kennan did not share Acheson's belief that containment required substantial military forces. He had misgivings about Truman's recent decisions on nuclear and thermonuclear weapons, and he had begun to criticize the stridency of administration rhetoric. Acheson may have sensed that he and Kennan would eventually disagree about how hard a line to maintain.

At the time, the last thing Acheson needed was to be seen as backing away from the crusading anticommunism of the Truman Doctrine. In China, Communists led by Mao Zedong had just won a long civil war, forcing into exile on the island of Taiwan the Chinese Nationalist leader, Chiang Kai-shek. A State Department white paper had explained Communist success in China as due to shortcomings in the Chinese Nationalist regime. Acts of omission or commission by the United States, said the white paper, had been of little consequence. This had drawn on Acheson outraged criticism from right-wingers convinced that the United States had "lost China," largely because Communists and fellow travelers in the U.S. government had blocked aid to the Nationalists.

In January 1950, a federal jury found former State Department official Alger Hiss guilty of perjury. A congressional committee had turned up evidence of his having been a Soviet spy during the 1930s, but the statute of limitations prevented prosecution for a crime so far in the past. Hiss could be—and was—indicted for lying under oath when he swore that he had not been a spy. For practical purposes, therefore, the jury found him guilty of espionage.[10]

At a press conference, Acheson said that Hiss was an old friend and that he would not turn his back on him. This gave Acheson's critics yet more bait. In February 1950, when NSC 68 was being composed, Senator Joseph R. McCarthy of Wisconsin captured headlines by claiming to have proof that the State Department harbored large numbers of "card-carrying Communists." Within a year, "McCarthyism" would be a household word. In these circumstances, Acheson may have been doubly eager for a policy planning chief more inclined than Kennan to approach the cold war as a war.

NSC 68 was Nitze's first major assignment. He had already questioned Truman's ceiling on military spending. Conversations with Europeans had convinced him that they needed reassurance beyond the mere text of the North Atlantic Treaty. They were afraid of the Red Army. If they had to put more money into military forces, their economic recovery might derail. This could mean gains for Communist parties, many of which remained strong in Western Europe. Nitze thought that the best solution would be additional ready U.S. military strength. His new assignment offered an opportunity to put before the president the case for expanding U.S. military forces.

Though Nitze shared authorship of the document with his staff (as Kennan never would have), the text carries his hallmarks. Nitze leaned toward Cartesian reasoning. He frequently insisted on articulation of first principles. NSC 68 has this characteristic. It begins with quotations from the Constitution defining basic national purposes. It then develops step by step the argument that these purposes require "a build-up of military strength by the United States and its allies to a point at which the combined strength will be superior . . . , both initially and throughout a war, to the forces that can be brought to bear by the Soviet Union and its satellites."

The keynote of the document is its apocalyptic warning: "The issues that face us are momentous, involving the fulfillment or destruction not only of this Republic but of civilization itself." In part because Nitze did not hoard authorship, as Kennan might have, few lines seem quotable for pithiness or elegance. But the style is less that of a bureaucratically produced staff paper than of a committee-written speech. Though Nitze himself thinks the force of NSC 68 came primarily from its logic and persuasiveness, Acheson characterized it as exhortation. "The purpose of NSC-68 was to so bludgeon the mass mind of 'top government' that not only could the President make a decision but that the decision could be carried out," Acheson was to write.[11] Acheson added, "The task of a public officer seeking to explain and gain support for a major policy is not that of the writer of a doctoral thesis."[12]

Whether NSC 68 is primarily a brief or primarily a sermon, it probably could not be what it is if the process of its creation had been different. Nitze himself questions the importance of "bureaucratic games."[13] Looking back, however, one sees a sequence of moves that, if not deliberately planned, appear to be so. Without these moves, it seems unlikely that, in the spring of 1950, Truman could have been presented with the stark choices arrayed in NSC 68.

Truman did not want pressure to increase military spending. He had just appointed a new secretary of defense. The previous secretary, James Forrestal, had nagged the president for more money. Wanting instead a secretary who would help him achieve economies, Truman had replaced Forrestal with Louis Johnson, an ambitious politician from his own home state of Missouri. Though Johnson had championed preparedness before World War II and more recently had headed the largest veterans' lobby, the American Legion, he understood what Truman expected. Also, he believed that a reputation for being a cost cutter and a tamer of brass hats would further his chances of being the Democratic presidential nominee when Truman stepped down. Veteran Washington reporter Robert Donovan was to write later, "Louis Johnson, two hundred pounds of power, competence, acerbity, wile, and bumptiousness, hit the Pentagon like a thunderstorm."[14]

Nitze thus faced a formidable task. He had to try not only to turn the president around but to do so in the face of certain opposition from the cabinet officer who was the president's surrogate for military affairs. Someone else might have felt daunted, but not Nitze. He explains that his family name is derived, appropriately, from Nike, the goddess of victory. At eighty, Nitze would still be playing winning tennis, commenting, "My body does what I tell it to."[15] Courage and determination could not by themselves, however, have made successful the effort that led to NSC 68 and Truman's eventual endorsement of it. Those outcomes also required considerable adroitness in management of the policy process.

Nitze formed a committee consisting of himself, a few members of his staff, a handful of Acheson's intimates, and four Defense officials. One, retired Army Major General James H. Burns, was Defense Secretary Johnson's confidant and chosen liaison with State. But Burns had had a heart attack and could work only part time. Among the other three, the one answerable to Burns was civilian Najeeb Halaby, an open opponent of Johnson's cost cutting. Active-duty Air Force Major General Truman H. Landon sat in on behalf of the Joint Chiefs of Staff, who agreed on almost nothing except desire for more money than Truman and Johnson would allow them. The fourth person from the Pentagon was Robert LeBaron, who handled the arcana of relationships between the military and the Atomic Energy Commission.[16]

For participation in Nitze's committee, a prerequisite was possession of a "Q clearance." This clearance was the ticket to seeing Atomic Energy Commission restricted data concerning nuclear weapons. Since Nitze's mandate came out of debate on the hydrogen bomb, this requirement may have been automatic. In any event, it was helpful for Acheson's and Nitze's purpose. Outside the AEC, Q clearances were scarce, even among generals and admirals. The result of the requirement was to confine the drafting of the document to a very small circle. Only later, when Nitze circulated a version classified *merely* "top secret," not "top secret—restricted data," could most other high officials in the State Department get a crack at the text. Officials in the Treasury and the Bureau of the Budget knew nothing of what was in progress. Nor did most White House staff. The Q clearance requirement meant that Nitze's committee could build a consensus among potential supporters. They could postpone dealing with their natural bureaucratic opponents, the officials who wanted money for nonmilitary programs and those who had the mission of keeping the government in the black.

Nitze's committee produced a first draft in a matter of weeks. Then began a process of constituency building. Nitze arranged meetings with a few outsiders who held Q clearances. They came in one by one. Minutes of the sessions show Nitze and his colleagues indicating broad willingness to accommodate suggestions. Each session ended with the outsider having expressed general approval of the effort, usually with a nonspecific understanding that the existing draft would be amended.[17]

Within a few weeks, the document had blessing from J. Robert Oppenheimer, the scientific coordinator of the wartime atomic bomb project and probably the nation's most influential nuclear physicist. It also had approval from Henry D. Smyth and Ernest O. Lawrence, two other eminent scientists not always in accord with Oppenheimer. James Bryant Conant, the president of Harvard University and a chemist with a distinguished war record, had given it his OK, as had Chester Barnard, president of the Rockefeller Foundation.

Most important, the list of endorsers included Robert A. Lovett. A Wall Street financier a dozen years older than Nitze, Lovett had been a wartime deputy to Secretary of War Henry L. Stimson. He had later been under secretary of state for Marshall, and he was known as the person whom Marshall trusted most. Lovett, a lifelong Republican, was also known to be close to and trusted by Republican Senate leader Arthur H. Vandenberg.

Acheson and Nitze came to their first big test when they presented a draft of NSC 68 to Defense Secretary Johnson. The date was March 23, 1950; the place, Acheson's office on the seventh floor of the State Department. Johnson was accompanied by several others, including Joint Chiefs Chairman General Omar Bradley. Acheson describes the meeting in his memoirs:

> After apparently friendly greetings all around, I asked Nitze to outline the paper and its conclusions. Nitze, who was a joy to work with because

of his clear, incisive mind, began to do so. Johnson listened, chair tilted back, gazing at the ceiling, seemingly calm and attentive. Suddenly he lunged forward with a crash of chair legs on the floor and fist on the table, scaring me out of my shoes. No one, he shouted, was going to make arrangements for him to meet with another Cabinet officer and a roomful of people and be told what he was going to report to the President. Who authorized these meetings contrary to his orders? What was this paper, which he had never seen? Trying to calm him down, I told him that we were working under the President's orders to him and me and through his designated channel, General Burns. . . . But he would have none of it and, gathering General Bradley and other Defense people, stalked out of the room.[18]

After Johnson got back to the Pentagon, he cooled off. It probably occurred to him that he could not challenge the professional qualifications of Burns, Halaby, Landon, and LeBaron. Moreover, he learned that Nitze and his colleagues had already quietly worked the corridors of the Pentagon. All the civilian service secretaries and service chiefs of staff had given Nitze their support. Facing these conditions and the backing of Nitze by the fraternity of physicists and by Conant, Barnard, and Lovett, Johnson was hemmed in. He apparently saw no alternative except to add his signature to Acheson's.

With this in the background, Nitze had little difficulty subduing dissent from colleagues in State. He had had a problem at the outset with Kennan. In a long memorandum to Acheson, Kennan questioned the need for an additional military buildup:

> There is little justification for the impression that the "cold war," by virtue of events outside of our control, has suddenly taken some drastic turn to our disadvantage. . . .
>
> A patient and wary policy of reinforcing resistance to Soviet political pressures, wherever there was anything to reinforce, and by whatever means we had of doing thus, was dictated by the limits of the possible. It was not guaranteed to work. But it was the only thing that held out any real possibility of working. . . .
>
> Since military intimidation was another of the cold war weapons used by the Kremlin, direct action had to be taken to combat this, too. Hence our own armed establishment, the Atlantic Pact and the Arms Program. These measures threw many people off. They were not part of a policy of *military* containment; but they looked like it. They served their purpose in Europe; but they misled many people there and here into a false concept of what it was we were doing: into a tendency to view the Russian threat as just a military problem rather than as a part of a broad political offensive.[19]

Kennan added that understanding of existing policy "called for considerable subtlety and breadth of understanding. Not all the elements of our public opinion, or even of our government personnel, possessed these qualities."[20] Kennan may have had Nitze in mind, for he was to complain much later, "Paul was in one sense like a child. . . . He loved anything that could be reduced to numbers. He was mesmerized by them. . . . He had no feeling for the intangibles—values, intentions. When there was talk of intentions, as opposed to capabilities, he would say, 'How can you measure intentions? We can't be bothered to get into psychology; we have to face the Russians as competitors, militarily.' "[21] But Acheson got Kennan out of the way by sending him on a long fact-finding trip to South America.

Other State Department Soviet experts shared some of Kennan's misgivings. Chip Bohlen wrote Nitze:

> It is open to question whether or not, as stated, the fundamental design of the Kremlin is the domination of the world. If by this is meant this is the chief purpose and, as it were, the *raison d'être* of the Kremlin, this carries the implication that all other considerations are subordinate to this major purpose and that great risks would be run for the sake of its achievement. It tends, therefore, to oversimplify the problem and, in my opinion, leads inevitably to the conclusion that war is inevitable. . . . I think that the thought would be more accurate if it were to the effect that the fundamental design of those who control the USSR is (a) the maintenance of their regime in the Soviet Union and (b) its extension throughout the world to the degree that is possible without serious risk to the internal regime.[22]

Bohlen also cautioned against "kicking off a full-scale rearmament program of the standard nature, with all the consequences, political and economic, which that might involve." He suggested recommending a selective program, built around high-technology armaments obviously defensive in character, such as antitank weapons and antiaircraft missiles.[23]

At an earlier point, the Soviet experts might have mounted a campaign to tone down NSC 68. The barons of the State Department, the regional assistant secretaries, might have tried either to shelve the document or to change its message, for most of them wanted money for economic aid programs, not for military forces. Presented with a document apparently already accepted by the military establishment and blessed by Lovett, these potential opponents were paralyzed. They could do little more than cavil or, like Soviet expert Llewellyn Thompson, take comfort from the absence of any specific recommendation on additional defense spending. Thompson expressed hope that detailed review would show "that no very great increase in our present rate of expenditure would be called for, but rather a better allocation of resources and a unified national policy, which would apply our resources more directly to the solution of the basic problem."[24]

The last and highest obstacle was the president himself. NSC 68 went to Truman on April 7, 1950. The president's immediate response was to direct *"that this report be handled with special security precautions in accordance with the President's desire that no publicity be given this report or its contents without his approval"* (italics in the original). Truman asked for comment by agency heads likely to share his conservatism about military spending—the secretary of the treasury, the director of the Bureau of the Budget, the chairman of the Council of Economic Advisers, and the administrator of foreign economic aid. Even after reading NSC 68, the president said publicly that he wanted military spending to go down still more.[25]

Once the president studied the document and discovered how carefully Acheson and Nitze had built their base of support, however, he probably recognized that he was trapped. Hardly had he told reporters that he hoped to continue cutting defense spending than he began to see arguments directly out of NSC 68 appearing in the press. Ernest K. Lindley of *Newsweek,* for example, echoed one of its central themes. Because of the relative pace of military modernization in the Soviet Union and the West, wrote Lindley, the years 1952 to 1954 would be "a period of maximum danger."[26]

If Truman rejected NSC 68 outright, the fact was unlikely to remain unknown. Hostile members of Congress and newspaper editors, including anti–Fair Deal Democrats, would pounce. In face of a united bureaucracy warning that the world risked enslavement, a president already under attack from the right could not afford simply to do nothing. As a matter of practical politics, the question before Truman was not whether there should be more defense spending. It was whether he could hold down the increase sufficiently to leave something for his Fair Deal and for arms aid to Europe.

This question remained open until summer. The budget for the next fiscal year was not due to take shape until September or October. Then, on June 25, Truman learned of the North Korean invasion of South Korea. During a week of almost continual meetings, the president decided on a limited war to rescue South Korea. Convinced that Stalin was testing the West and might be preparing a move against West Germany, Truman looked again at NSC 68 and, on September 30, 1950, ordered that it be taken "as a statement of policy to be followed over the next four or five years and . . . that the implementing programs . . . be put into effect as rapidly as feasible."[27]

The president had asked the budget director to prepare two estimates for fiscal 1951—one with defense on the existing track, a second incorporating the costs of NSC 68. Had Korea not intervened, this estimating would have been done, and the ensuing budgetary struggle might have left the State Department team less well situated than in April. But Korea rendered all that moot.

As an immediate result of Truman's decree, U.S. defense spending tripled. For the next four decades, it would remain two to three times higher, as a percentage of gross national product, than in any previous periods of peace. Without the Korean War, defense spending would probably not have shot so quickly to such levels. Indeed, it might never have gone so high. But given all the support that Nitze and Acheson had mustered for a document warning that the alternative to a military buildup was enslavement for the free world, Truman would nevertheless have found it difficult, perhaps impossible, not to spend substantially more money for ready military power. NSC 68 may provide an example of how to articulate a strategy. Its history certainly provides an example of how officialdom can force a president to follow policies that are against his inclinations.

NSC 68 also provides an example of how legends grow, for the document became famous long before it became public. When Dean Acheson published his memoirs nearly twenty years later, NSC 68 was still classified top secret. "NSC-68 has not been declassified and may not be quoted," Acheson wrote. He added, however, that its substance had become public, partly through his own public statements.[28] Assuring Congress that proposals for sudden increases in defense spending had not been improvised, administration witnesses spoke in 1950 of "a long-range plan which is still in effect and which is only accelerated and enlarged by the present action in Korea."[29] It was soon common knowledge that this "long-range plan" was a National Security Council paper designated as NSC 68.

After 1953, when Dwight D. Eisenhower succeeded Truman as president, military spending remained high, but the rate of increase slowed. Acheson's successor as secretary of state, John Foster Dulles, said the new administration would not prepare to meet all types of military challenges. Instead, it would trust in capacity for massive nuclear retaliation complemented by mobile forces equipped for selective action "at times and places of our own choosing." The *New York Times,* the *Washington Post,* and other news media reported insiders criticizing the Eisenhower administration for abandoning the prudent strategy laid out in NSC 68.

Among critics of "massive retaliation," NSC 68 acquired the aura of holy writ. So much was it discussed that, in 1962, political scientist Paul Y. Hammond published a forty-thousand-word monograph based on interviews with persons who had actually seen it. A decade later, in a book on Acheson as secretary of state, Yale historian Gaddis Smith characterized NSC 68 as "the most famous unread paper of its era."[30]

In February 1975, for undisclosed reasons, Henry A. Kissinger declassified NSC 68. At the time, Kissinger was both secretary of state and President Gerald Ford's assistant for national security affairs.[31] A few months later, the full text appeared in a special issue of the *Naval War College Review*. In 1977, the State Department published NSC 68 and related documents in its historical series *Foreign Relations of the United States*. In the early 1980s, in a monograph for the School of Advanced International Studies of the Johns Hopkins University, historian Steven Rearden summarized what had been said and written over the previous thirty-five years:

> There is no doubt that NSC 68 is a document of seminal importance in the post World War II evolution of basic American security policy. Some regard it as the essential blueprint of the Truman administration's cold war military buildup, while others go so far as to say it was a clarion call for the United States to assume the role of global policeman. That its impact was profound is generally agreed.[32]

In the late 1980s and early 1990s, NSC 68 had a new rush of fame. Some writers hailed it as the master plan that had brought victory in the cold war. The Reagan administration's big military budgets were likened to those of the Korean War period. The fact that Nitze had been President Reagan's principal agent for arms control negotiations helped to suggest a link with those Truman-era programs. The argument built from this link attributed the final collapse of the Soviet Union and of Russian communism to relentless pressure from mounting U.S. military power.

Without necessarily endorsing an analogy between the 1950s and the 1980s, writers and speakers cited NSC 68 as an example of a successful strategic plan. Citing the need for a post–cold war strategy, they called for a "new NSC 68." Later in this book, Robert Blackwill, a protégé of Henry Kissinger and a National Security Council aide for Presidents Jimmy Carter and George Bush, speaks of NSC 68 as containing "gem after gem of strategic insight." In a 1989 volume surveying the national interests of the United States in the 1990s, political scientist Graham Allison, former dean of Harvard's Kennedy School of Government, took NSC 68 as the point of departure for an essay entitled "National Security Strategy for the 1990s." He asked: "Will statesmen of the 1990s be equally successful?"[33]

Not everyone accepts NSC 68 as either a document of historic significance or a model for a national strategy. In the most thorough recent analysis of Truman administration diplomacy, historian Melvyn Leffler says that he sees little to distinguish NSC 68 from earlier documents defining containment.[34] The premier American historian of the American side of the cold war, John Lewis Gaddis, does see differences, but all to the advantage of the Long Telegram and NSC 20/4. Gaddis characterizes NSC 68 as a "deeply flawed document," declaring that it "provided less than adequate guidance as to how objectives and capabilities were to be combined to produce coherent strategy."[35]

With the document here before you, you can form your own verdicts not only about the quality of NSC 68 as a summary of strategy but about many other issues. Later in these pages appear questions about NSC 68 that cannot even be posed at this point because not enough foundation has been laid. To try to understand the document you will have to not only read it but go back to it again and again, much as a literary critic goes back to a novel or a poem. In a first run-through, however, you may want to consider the following:

1. Is NSC 68 a timeless example of reason-of-state reasoning, or is it a document peculiar to a democratic system, perhaps peculiar to the American system, clanging alarm bells so as to catch the attention of politicians and couching appeals in terms that tap deep-rooted emotions?

2. Should NSC 68 be judged primarily on its internal qualities—its logic, analytic coherence, and use of evidence? Or should a critique focus instead on reasons why its logic seemed so compelling in 1950, regardless of whether that logic was flawed or the evidential base weak?

3. Should the focus instead be on what the document did or did not accomplish, as it is in work by nearly all former officials (including Nitze himself)? Did NSC 68 provide a grand strategy for the cold war? Is Robert Blackwill right in suggesting that the main propositions of NSC 68 guided U.S. policy all the way through to the Reagan and Bush administrations? Or is there more force in Robert R. Bowie's argument later in this book? Bowie, Nitze's successor and chief policy planner for the Republican administration of Dwight Eisenhower, asserts that NSC 68 proposed a fundamentally wrong strategy—not containment but forcible overthrow of Communist power. Bowie says that Eisenhower adopted a different, more patient, more moderate strategy and that it was this strategy that eventually won the cold war.

4. Is NSC 68 a model for strategy for the next phase of history, as Graham Allison contends? Or, as several commentaries here suggest, should the story of NSC 68 be read as a cautionary tale warning of the costs and dangers of conveniently oversimplifying definitions of peril, interest, and national purpose?

NOTES

[1] The term "national security adviser" crept into use in the 1970s. The proper title is assistant to the president for national security affairs. The post originally was supposed to be merely that

of a staff officer coordinating staff work in cabinet departments. Henry Kissinger so clearly dominated the process, however, that the news media came increasingly to refer to him as the president's "adviser." Zbigniew Brzezinski adopted the title, using it even in his memoirs: *Power and Principle: Memoirs of the National Security Advisor* (New York: Farrar, Straus & Giroux, 1983). On the general history of the NSC, see John Prados, *Keepers of the Keys: A History of the National Security Council from Truman to Bush* (New York: William Morrow, 1991).

[2]George H. Gallup, *The Gallup Poll: Public Opinion, 1935–1971,* 3 vols. (New York: Random House, 1972), 1,721.

[3]Harry Truman to Dean Acheson, 31 Jan. 1950, *Foreign Relations of the United States, 1950* (Washington, D.C.: Government Printing Office, 1977), 141–42. Issued by the Department of State and published in Washington by the Government Printing Office, these volumes have been appearing since the 1860s. Since World War II, the series has attempted to document policymaking and diplomacy, including important NSC and Defense materials as well as materials from State Department files. In recent times, volumes for a particular year have appeared twenty-five to thirty-five years after the dates of the documents they contain. Hereafter cited as *FRUS* with the year the document was written and the volume and page number of the series.

[4]Paul H. Nitze, *From Hiroshima to Glasnost: At the Center of Decision, A Memoir* (New York: Grove Weidenfeld, 1989), xviii.

[5]George Kennan to James F. Byrnes, 22 Feb. 1946, *FRUS, 1946,* 6:705–6.

[6]"X," "The Sources of Soviet Conduct," *Foreign Affairs* 25 (July 1947): 575–76, 581–82.

[7]*FRUS, 1948,* 1:663–69.

[8]Nitze, *From Hiroshima to Glasnost,* 86.

[9]Dean Acheson, "The President and the Secretary of State," in *The Secretary of State,* ed. Don K. Price (Englewood Cliffs, N.J.: Prentice-Hall, 1960), 37.

[10]Hiss has continued steadily to deny any guilt, most recently in *Reflections of a Life* (London: Unwin Hyman, 1988). The most scholarly study of the case, Allen Weinstein's *Perjury: The Hiss-Chambers Case* (New York: Alfred A. Knopf, 1978), sifts the evidence and concludes otherwise. Questions about Weinstein's methodology are posed, however, in John Wiener, "The Alger Hiss Case, the Archives, and Allen Weinstein," *Perspectives, the American Historical Association Newsletter* 30, no. 2 (Feb. 1992): 10–12. In November 1992, archivists in Moscow announced that they had been unable to find any documentary evidence that Hiss had work for any Soviet intelligence agency.

[11]See the excerpt from Acheson's memoirs on page 97 in this book.

[12]Dean G. Acheson, *Present at the Creation: My Years in the State Department* (New York: W. W. Norton, 1969), 374–75. Nitze's views are expressed in the excerpt on page 104 in this book. The most recent summaries are in his memoir, *From Hiroshima to Glasnost,* 93–100, and in letters of 4 Mar. and 1 Apr. 1992 to Ernest R. May, commenting on a draft of this essay. The draft has been revised to take account of his comments but not, alas, to change the interpretation enough to bring it into full accord with his.

[13]Paul H. Nitze to Ernest R. May, 1 Apr. 1992.

[14]Robert Donovan, *Tumultuous Years: The Presidency of Harry S. Truman, 1949–1953* (New York: W. W. Norton, 1982), 61.

[15]Strobe Talbott, *The Master of the Game: Paul Nitze and the Nuclear Peace* (New York: Alfred A. Knopf, 1988), 23, 12.

[16]Paul Y. Hammond, "NSC 68: Prologue to Rearmament," in *Strategy, Politics, and Defense Budgets,* ed. Warner R. Schilling, Paul Y. Hammond, and Glenn H. Snyder (New York: Columbia University Press, 1962), 295–98; Walter S. Poole, *The History of the Joint Chiefs of Staff: The Joint Chiefs of Staff and National Policy,* vol. 4, *1950–1952* (Wilmington, Del.: Michael Glazier, 1980), 6–9; Doris M. Condit, *History of the Office of the Secretary of Defense,* vol. 2, *The Test of War, 1950–1953* (Washington, D.C.: Historical Office, Office of the Secretary of Defense, 1988), 6–8, 20–21.

[17]Records of meetings, 27 Feb., 2 Mar., 10 Mar., 16 Mar., 20 Mar. 1950, *FRUS, 1950,* 1:168–82, 190–201.

[18] Acheson, *Present at the Creation,* 373.

[19] George Kennan to Dean Acheson, 17 Feb. 1950, *FRUS, 1950,* 1:160, 163, 164.

[20] *FRUS, 1950,* 1:163.

[21] Talbott, *Master of the Game,* 57.

[22] Charles Bohlen to Paul Nitze, 5 Apr. 1950, *FRUS, 1950,* 1:222.

[23] *FRUS, 1950,* 1:224–25.

[24] Llewellyn Thompson to Dean Acheson, 3 Apr. 1950, *FRUS, 1950,* 1:213–14.

[25] *Public Papers of Harry S. Truman, 1950* (Washington, D.C.: Government Printing Office, 1965), 4 May 1950, no. 105.

[26] Ernest K. Lindley, "Washington Tides," *Newsweek,* 15 May 1950, 27.

[27] *FRUS, 1950,* 1:400.

[28] Acheson, *Present at the Creation,* 374.

[29] The chairman of the Joint Chiefs of Staff, General of the Army Omar Bradley, quoted in Hammond, "NSC 68," 350.

[30] Hammond, "NSC 68"; Gaddis Smith, *Dean Acheson* (New York: Cooper Square Publishers, 1972), 161.

[31] In February of the preceding year, Nitze had been proposed by Secretary of Defense James Schlesinger for the post of assistant secretary of defense for international security affairs. (Nitze had held this same post for a time in the Kennedy administration.) The nomination was withdrawn in March. According to the *New York Times* (22 Mar. 1974), the reason was that certain conservative Republican senators believed Nitze to have been, under Kennedy, a proponent of unilateral disarmament, and Nixon, needing those senators' votes if he was to have any chance of escaping conviction for Watergate crimes, insisted on placating them. It is possible that the move to declassify NSC 68 began as part of an effort to rescue the Nitze nomination. It would not be surprising for the actual declassification to have taken a year. Indeed, in the State Department's declassification processes, one year from start to finish is the equivalent of warp speed. But this is pure surmise. No one questioned about the declassification remembers any of its details.

[32] Steven Rearden, *The Evolution of American Strategic Doctrine: Paul H. Nitze and the Soviet Challenge* (Boulder, Col.: Westview Press for the Foreign Policy Institute of the School of Advanced International Studies of the Johns Hopkins University, 1984), 7.

[33] Graham Allison, "National Security Strategy for the 1990s," in *America's Global Interests: A New Agenda,* ed. Edward K. Hamilton (New York: W. W. Norton, 1989), 240.

[34] *A Preponderance of Power: National Security, the Truman Administration, and the Cold War* (Stanford: Stanford University Press, 1991), 355ff.

[35] These quotations come from the Gaddis essay on page 141 in this book.

PART ONE

The Document

NSC 68: United States Objectives and Programs for National Security (April 14, 1950)

A Report to the President
Pursuant to the President's Directive
of January 31, 1950

TOP SECRET   [Washington,] April 7, 1950

Contents

Terms of Reference
Analysis

TERMS OF REFERENCE

The following report is submitted in response to the President's directive of January 31 which reads:

> That the President direct the Secretary of State and the Secretary of Defense to undertake a reexamination of our objectives in peace and war and of the effect of these objectives on our strategic plans, in the light of the probable fission bomb capability and possible thermonuclear bomb capability of the Soviet Union.

The document which recommended that such a directive be issued reads in part:

> It must be considered whether a decision to proceed with a program directed toward determining feasibility prejudges the more fundamental decisions (a) as to whether, in the event that a test of a thermonuclear weapon proves successful, such weapons should be stockpiled, or (b) if stockpiled, the conditions under which they might be used in war. If a test of a thermonuclear weapon proves successful, the pressures to produce and stockpile such weapons to be held for the same purposes for which fission bombs are then being held will be greatly increased. The question of use policy can be adequately assessed only as a part of a general

reexamination of this country's strategic plans and its objectives in peace and war. Such reexamination would need to consider national policy not only with respect to possible thermonuclear weapons, but also with respect to fission weapons—viewed in the light of the probable fission bomb capability and the possible thermonuclear bomb capability of the Soviet Union. The moral, psychological, and political questions involved in this problem would need to be taken into account and be given due weight. The outcome of this reexamination would have a crucial bearing on the further question as to whether there should be a revision in the nature of the agreements, including the international control of atomic energy, which we have been seeking to reach with the U.S.S.R.

ANALYSIS

I. Background of the Present Crisis

Within the past thirty-five years the world has experienced two global wars of tremendous violence. It has witnessed two revolutions—the Russian and the Chinese—of extreme scope and intensity. It has also seen the collapse of five empires—the Ottoman, the Austro-Hungarian, German, Italian, and Japanese—and the drastic decline of two major imperial systems, the British and the French. During the span of one generation, the international distribution of power has been fundamentally altered. For several centuries it had proved impossible for any one nation to gain such preponderant strength that a coalition of other nations could not in time face it with greater strength. The international scene was marked by recurring periods of violence and war, but a system of sovereign and independent states was maintained, over which no state was able to achieve hegemony.

Two complex sets of factors have now basically altered this historical distribution of power. First, the defeat of Germany and Japan and the decline of the British and French Empires have interacted with the development of the United States and the Soviet Union in such a way that power has increasingly gravitated to these two centers. Second, the Soviet Union, unlike previous aspirants to hegemony, is animated by a new fanatic faith, antithetical to our own, and seeks to impose its absolute authority over the rest of the world. Conflict has, therefore, become endemic and is waged, on the part of the Soviet Union, by violent or non-violent methods in accordance with the dictates of expediency. With the development of increasingly terrifying weapons of mass destruction, every individual faces the ever-present possibility of annihilation should the conflict enter the phase of total war.

On the one hand, the people of the world yearn for relief from the anxiety arising from the risk of atomic war. On the other hand, any substantial further extension of the area under the domination of the Kremlin would raise the possibility that no coalition adequate to confront the Kremlin with greater strength could be assembled. It is in this context that this Republic and its citizens in the ascendancy of their strength stand in their deepest peril.

The issues that face us are momentous, involving the fulfillment or destruction not only of this Republic but of civilization itself. They are issues which will not await our deliberations. With conscience and resolution this Government and the people it represents must now take new and fateful decisions.

II. Fundamental Purpose of the United States

The fundamental purpose of the United States is laid down in the Preamble to the Constitution: ". . . to form a more perfect Union, establish Justice, insure domestic Tranquility, provide for the common defence, promote the general Welfare, and secure the Blessings of Liberty to ourselves and our Posterity." In essence, the fundamental purpose is to assure the integrity and vitality of our free society, which is founded upon the dignity and worth of the individual.

Three realities emerge as a consequence of this purpose: Our determination to maintain the essential elements of individual freedom, as set forth in the Constitution and Bill of Rights; our determination to create conditions under which our free and democratic system can live and prosper; and our determination to fight if necessary to defend our way of life, for which as in the Declaration of Independence, "with a firm reliance on the protection of Divine Providence, we mutually pledge to each other our lives, our Fortunes, and our sacred Honor."

III. Fundamental Design of the Kremlin

The fundamental design of those who control the Soviet Union and the international communist movement is to retain and solidify their absolute power, first in the Soviet Union and second in the areas now under their control. In the minds of the Soviet leaders, however, achievement of this design requires the dynamic extension of their authority and the ultimate elimination of any effective opposition to their authority.

The design, therefore, calls for the complete subversion or forcible destruction of the machinery of government and structure of society in the countries of the non-Soviet world and their replacement by an apparatus and structure subservient to and controlled from the Kremlin. To that end Soviet efforts are now directed toward the domination of the Eurasian land mass. The United States, as the principal center of power in the non-Soviet world and the bulwark of opposition to Soviet expansion, is the principal enemy whose integrity and vitality must be subverted or destroyed by one means or another if the Kremlin is to achieve its fundamental design.

IV. The Underlying Conflict in the Realm of Ideas and Values between the U.S. Purpose and the Kremlin Design

A. NATURE OF CONFLICT

The Kremlin regards the United States as the only major threat to the achievement of its fundamental design. There is a basic conflict between the idea of freedom under a government of laws, and the idea of slavery under the grim oligarchy of the Kremlin, which has come to a crisis with the polarization of power described in Section I, and the exclusive possession of atomic weapons by the two protagonists. The idea of freedom, moreover, is peculiarly and intolerably subversive of the idea of slavery. But the converse is not true. The implacable purpose of the slave state to eliminate the challenge of freedom has placed the two great powers at opposite poles. It is this fact which gives the present polarization of power the quality of crisis.

The free society values the individual as an end in himself, requiring of him only that measure of self-discipline and self-restraint which make the rights of each individual compatible with the rights of every other individual. The freedom of the individual has as its counterpart, therefore, the negative responsibility of the individual not to exercise his freedom in ways inconsistent with the freedom of other individuals and the positive responsibility to make constructive use of his freedom in the building of a just society.

From this idea of freedom with responsibility derives the marvelous diversity, the deep tolerance, the lawfulness of the free society. This is the explanation of the strength of free men. It constitutes the integrity and the vitality of a free and democratic system. The free society attempts to create and maintain an environment in which every individual has the opportunity to realize his creative powers. It also explains why the free society tolerates those within it who would use their freedom to destroy it. By the same token, in relations between nations, the prime reliance of the free society is on the strength and appeal of its idea, and it feels no compulsion sooner or later to bring all societies into conformity with it.

For the free society does not fear, it welcomes, diversity. It derives its strength from its hospitality even to antipathetic ideas. It is a market for free trade in ideas, secure in its faith that free men will take the best wares, and grow to a fuller and better realization of their powers in exercising their choice.

The idea of freedom is the most contagious idea in history, more contagious than the idea of submission to authority. For the breadth of freedom cannot be tolerated in a society which has come under the domination of an individual or group of individuals with a will to absolute power. Where the despot holds absolute power—the absolute power of the absolutely powerful will—all other wills must be subjugated in an act of willing submission, a degradation willed by the individual upon himself under the compulsion of a perverted faith. It is the first article of this faith that he finds and can only find the meaning of his existence in serving the ends of the system. The system becomes God, and submission to the will of God becomes submission to the will of the system. It is not enough to yield outwardly to the system— even Gandhian non-violence is not acceptable—for the spirit of resistance and the devotion to a higher authority might then remain, and the individual would not be wholly submissive.

The same compulsion which demands total power over all men within the Soviet state without a single exception, demands total power over all Communist Parties and all states under Soviet domination. Thus Stalin has said that the theory and tactics of Leninism as expounded by the Bolshevik party are mandatory for the proletarian parties of all countries. A true internationalist is defined as one who unhesitatingly upholds the position of the Soviet Union and in the satellite states true patriotism is love of the Soviet Union. By the same token the "peace policy" of the Soviet Union, described at a Party Congress as "a more advantageous form of fighting capitalism," is a device to divide and immobilize the non-Communist world, and the peace the Soviet Union seeks is the peace of total conformity to Soviet policy.

The antipathy of slavery to freedom explains the iron curtain, the isolation, the autarchy of the society whose end is absolute power. The existence and persistence of the idea of freedom is a permanent and continuous threat to the foundation of the slave society; and it therefore regards as intolerable the long continued existence of freedom in the world. What is new, what makes the continuing crisis, is the polarization of power which now inescapably confronts the slave society with the free.

The assault on free institutions is world-wide now, and in the context of the present polarization of power a defeat of free institutions anywhere is a defeat everywhere. The shock we sustained in the destruction of Czechoslovakia was not in the measure of Czechoslovakia's material importance to us. In a material sense, her capabilities were already at Soviet disposal. But when the integrity of Czechoslovak institutions was destroyed, it was in the intangible scale of values that we registered a loss more damaging than the material loss we had already suffered.

Thus unwillingly our free society finds itself mortally challenged by the Soviet system. No other value system is so wholly irreconcilable with ours, so implacable in its purpose to destroy ours, so capable of turning to its own uses the most dangerous and divisive trends in our own society, no other so skillfully and powerfully evokes the elements of irrationality in human nature everywhere, and no other has the support of a great and growing center of military power.

B. OBJECTIVES

The objectives of a free society are determined by its fundamental values and by the necessity for maintaining the material environment in which they flourish. Logically and in fact, therefore, the Kremlin's challenge to the United States is directed not only to our values but to our physical capacity to protect their environment. It is a challenge which encompasses both peace and war and our objectives in peace and war must take account of it.

1. Thus we must make ourselves strong, both in the way in which we affirm our values in the conduct of our national life, and in the development of our military and economic strength.

2. We must lead in building a successfully functioning political and economic system in the free world. It is only by practical affirmation, abroad as well as at home, of our essential values, that we can preserve our own integrity, in which lies the real frustration of the Kremlin design.

3. But beyond thus affirming our values our policy and actions must be such as to foster a fundamental change in the nature of the Soviet system, a change toward which the frustration of the design is the first and perhaps the most important step. Clearly it will not only be less costly but more effective if this change occurs to a maximum extent as a result of internal forces in Soviet society.

In a shrinking world, which now faces the threat of atomic warfare, it is not an adequate objective merely to seek to check the Kremlin design, for the absence of order among nations is becoming less and less tolerable. This fact imposes on us, in our own interests, the responsibility of world leadership.

It demands that we make the attempt, and accept the risks inherent in it, to bring about order and justice by means consistent with the principles of freedom and democracy. We should limit our requirement of the Soviet Union to its participation with other nations on the basis of equality and respect for the rights of others. Subject to this requirement, we must with our allies and the former subject peoples seek to create a world society based on the principle of consent. Its framework cannot be inflexible. It will consist of many national communities of great and varying abilities and resources, and hence of war potential. The seeds of conflicts will inevitably exist or will come into being. To acknowledge this is only to acknowledge the impossibility of a final solution. Not to acknowledge it can be fatally dangerous in a world in which there are no final solutions.

All these objectives of a free society are equally valid and necessary in peace and war. But every consideration of devotion to our fundamental values and to our national security demands that we seek to achieve them by the strategy of the cold war. It is only by developing the moral and material strength of the free world that the Soviet regime will become convinced of the falsity of its assumptions and that the pre-conditions for workable agreements can be created. By practically demonstrating the integrity and vitality of our system the free world widens the area of possible agreement and thus can hope gradually to bring about a Soviet acknowledgement of realities which in sum will eventually constitute a frustration of the Soviet design. Short of this, however, it might be possible to create a situation which will induce the Soviet Union to accommodate itself, with or without the conscious abandonment of its design, to coexistence on tolerable terms with the non-Soviet world. Such a development would be a triumph for the idea of freedom and democracy. It must be an immediate objective of United States policy.

There is no reason, in the event of war, for us to alter our overall objectives. They do not include unconditional surrender, the subjugation of the Russian peoples or a Russia shorn of its economic potential. Such a course would irrevocably unite the Russian people behind the regime which enslaves them. Rather these objectives contemplate Soviet acceptance of the specific and limited conditions requisite to an international environment in which free institutions can flourish, and in which the Russian peoples will have a new chance to work out their own destiny. If we can make the Russian people our allies in the enterprise we will obviously have made our task easier and victory more certain.

The objectives outlined in NSC 20/4 (November 23, 1948) . . . are fully consistent with the objectives stated in this paper, and they remain valid.

The growing intensity of the conflict which has been imposed upon us, however, requires the changes of emphasis and the additions that are apparent. Coupled with the probable fission bomb capability and possible thermonuclear bomb capability of the Soviet Union, the intensifying struggle requires us to face the fact that we can expect no lasting abatement of the crisis unless and until a change occurs in the nature of the Soviet system.

C. MEANS

The free society is limited in its choice of means to achieve its ends.

Compulsion is the negation of freedom, except when it is used to enforce the rights common to all. The resort to force, internally or externally, is therefore a last resort for a free society. The act is permissible only when one individual or groups of individuals within it threaten the basic rights of other individuals or when another society seeks to impose its will upon it. The free society cherishes and protects as fundamental the rights of the minority against the will of a majority, because these rights are the inalienable rights of each and every individual.

The resort to force, to compulsion, to the imposition of its will is therefore a difficult and dangerous act for a free society, which is warranted only in the face of even greater dangers. The necessity of the act must be clear and compelling; the act must commend itself to the overwhelming majority as an inescapable exception to the basic idea of freedom; or the regenerative capacity of free men after the act has been performed will be endangered.

The Kremlin is able to select whatever means are expedient in seeking to carry out its fundamental design. Thus it can make the best of several possible worlds, conducting the struggle on those levels where it considers it profitable and enjoying the benefits of a pseudo-peace on those levels where it is not ready for a contest. At the ideological or psychological level, in the struggle for men's minds, the conflict is worldwide. At the political and economic level, within states and in the relations between states, the struggle for power is being intensified. And at the military level, the Kremlin has thus far been careful not to commit a technical breach of the peace, although using its vast forces to intimidate its neighbors, and to support an aggressive foreign policy, and not hesitating through its agents to resort to arms in favorable circumstances. The attempt to carry out its fundamental design is being pressed, therefore, with all means which are believed expedient in the present situation, and the Kremlin has inextricably engaged us in the conflict between its design and our purpose.

We have no such freedom of choice, and least of all in the use of force.

Resort to war is not only a last resort for a free society, but it is also an act which cannot definitively end the fundamental conflict in the realm of ideas. The idea of slavery can only be overcome by the timely and persistent demonstration of the superiority of the idea of freedom. Military victory alone would only partially and perhaps only temporarily affect the fundamental conflict, for although the ability of the Kremlin to threaten our security might be for a time destroyed, the resurgence of totalitarian forces and the re-establishment of the Soviet system or its equivalent would not be long delayed unless great progress were made in the fundamental conflict.

Practical and ideological considerations therefore both impel us to the conclusion that we have no choice but to demonstrate the superiority of the idea of freedom by its constructive application, and to attempt to change the world situation by means short of war in such a way as to frustrate the Kremlin design and hasten the decay of the Soviet system.

For us the role of military power is to serve the national purpose by deterring an attack upon us while we seek by other means to create an environment in which our free society can flourish, and by fighting, if necessary, to defend the integrity and vitality of our free society and to defeat any aggressor. The Kremlin uses Soviet military power to back up and serve the Kremlin design. It does not hesitate to use military force aggressively if that course is expedient in the achievement of its design. The differences between our fundamental purpose and the Kremlin design, therefore, are reflected in our respective attitudes toward and use of military force.

Our free society, confronted by a threat to its basic values, naturally will take such action, including the use of military force, as may be required to protect those values. The integrity of our system will not be jeopardized by any measures, covert or overt, violent or non-violent, which serve the purposes of frustrating the Kremlin design, nor does the necessity for conducting ourselves so as to affirm our values in actions as well as words forbid such measures, provided only they are appropriately calculated to that end and are not so excessive or misdirected as to make us enemies of the people instead of the evil men who have enslaved them.

But if war comes, what is the role of force? Unless we so use it that the Russian people can perceive that our effort is directed against the regime and its power for aggression, and not against their own interests, we will unite the regime and the people in the kind of last ditch fight in which no underlying problems are solved, new ones are created, and where our basic principles are obscured and compromised. If we do not in the application of force demonstrate the nature of our objectives we will, in fact, have compromised from the outset our fundamental purpose. In the words of the *Federalist* (No. 28) "The means to be employed must be proportioned to the extent of the mischief." The mischief may be a global war or it may be a Soviet campaign for limited objectives. In either case we should take no avoidable initiative which would cause it to become a war of annihilation, and if we have the forces to defeat a Soviet drive for limited objectives it may well be to our interest not to let it become a global war. Our aim in applying force must be to compel the acceptance of terms consistent with our objectives, and our capabilities for the application of force should, therefore, within the limits of what we can sustain over the long pull, be congruent to the range of tasks which we may encounter.

V. Soviet Intentions and Capabilities

A. POLITICAL AND PSYCHOLOGICAL

The Kremlin's design for world domination begins at home. The first concern of a despotic oligarchy is that the local base of its power and authority be secure. The massive fact of the iron curtain isolating the Soviet peoples from the outside world, the repeated political purges within the USSR and the institutionalized crimes of the MVD [the Soviet Ministry of Internal Affairs] are evidence that the Kremlin does not feel secure at home and that "the entire coercive force of the socialist state" is more than ever one of seeking to impose its absolute authority over "the economy, manner of life, and consciousness of people" (Vyshinski, *The Law of the Soviet State*, p. 74). Similar evidence in the satellite states of Eastern Europe leads to the conclusion that this same policy, in less advanced phases, is being applied to the Kremlin's colonial areas.

Being a totalitarian dictatorship, the Kremlin's objectives in these policies is the total subjective submission of the peoples now under its control. The concentration camp is the prototype of the society which these policies are designed to achieve, a society in which the personality of the individual is so broken and perverted that he participates affirmatively in his own degradation.

The Kremlin's policy toward areas not under its control is the elimination of resistance to its will and the extension of its influence and control. It is driven to follow this policy because it cannot, for the reasons set forth in Chapter IV, tolerate the existence of free societies; to the Kremlin the most mild and inoffensive free society is an affront, a challenge and a subversive influence. Given the nature of the Kremlin, and the evidence at hand, it seems clear that the ends toward which this policy is directed are the same as those where its control has already been established.

The means employed by the Kremlin in pursuit of this policy are limited only by considerations of expediency. Doctrine is not a limiting factor; rather it dictates the employment of violence, subversion, and deceit, and rejects moral considerations. In any event, the Kremlin's conviction of its own infallibility has made its devotion to theory so subjective that past or present pronouncements as to doctrine offer no reliable guide to future actions. The only apparent restraints on resort to war are, therefore, calculations of practicality.

With particular reference to the United States, the Kremlin's strategic and tactical policy is affected by its estimate that we are not only the greatest immediate obstacle which stands between it and world domination, we are also the only power which could release forces in the free and Soviet worlds which could destroy it. The Kremlin's policy toward us is consequently animated by a peculiarly virulent blend of hatred and fear. Its strategy has been one of attempting to undermine the complex of forces, in this country and in the rest of the free world, on which our power is based. In this it has both adhered to doctrine and followed the sound principle of seeking maximum results with minimum risks and commitments. The present application of this strategy is a new form of expression for traditional Russian caution. However, there is no justification in Soviet theory or practice for predicting that, should the Kremlin become convinced that it could cause our downfall by one conclusive blow, it would not seek that solution.

In considering the capabilities of the Soviet world, it is of prime importance to remember that, in contrast to ours, they are being drawn upon close to the maximum possible extent. Also in contrast to us, the Soviet world can do more with less—it has a lower standard of living, its economy requires less to keep it functioning, and its military machine operates effectively with less elaborate equipment and organization.

The capabilities of the Soviet world are being exploited to the full because the Kremlin is inescapably militant. It is inescapably militant because it possesses and is possessed by a world-wide revolutionary movement, because it is the inheritor of Russian imperialism, and because it is a totalitarian dictatorship. Persistent crisis, conflict, and expansion are the essence of the Kremlin's militancy. This dynamism serves to intensify all Soviet capabilities.

Two enormous organizations, the Communist Party and the secret police, are an outstanding source of strength to the Kremlin. In the Party, it has an apparatus designed to impose at home an ideological uniformity among its people and to act abroad as an instrument of propaganda, subversion and espionage. In its police apparatus, it has a domestic repressive instrument guaranteeing under present circumstances the continued security of the

Kremlin. The demonstrated capabilities of these two basic organizations, operating openly or in disguise, in mass or through single agents, is unparalleled in history. The party, the police and the conspicuous might of the Soviet military machine together tend to create an overall impression of irresistible Soviet power among many peoples of the free world.

The ideological pretensions of the Kremlin are another great source of strength. Its identification of the Soviet system with communism, its peace campaigns and its championing of colonial peoples may be viewed with apathy, if not cynicism, by the oppressed totalitariat of the Soviet world, but in the free world these ideas find favorable responses in vulnerable segments of society. They have found a particularly receptive audience in Asia, especially as the Asiatics have been impressed by what has been plausibly portrayed to them as the rapid advance of the USSR from a backward society to a position of great world power. Thus, in its pretensions to being (a) the source of a new universal faith and (b) the model "scientific" society, the Kremlin cynically identifies itself with the genuine aspirations of large numbers of people, and places itself at the head of an international crusade with all of the benefits which derive therefrom.

Finally, there is a category of capabilities, strictly speaking neither institutional nor ideological, which should be taken into consideration. The extraordinary flexibility of Soviet tactics is certainly a strength. It derives from the utterly amoral and opportunistic conduct of Soviet policy. Combining this quality with the elements of secrecy, the Kremlin possesses a formidable capacity to act with the widest tactical latitude, with stealth, and with speed.

The greatest vulnerability of the Kremlin lies in the basic nature of its relations with the Soviet people.

That relationship is characterized by universal suspicion, fear, and denunciation. It is a relationship in which the Kremlin relies, not only for its power but its very survival, on intricately devised mechanisms of coercion. The Soviet monolith is held together by the iron curtain around it and the iron bars within it, not by any force of natural cohesion. These artificial mechanisms of unity have never been intelligently challenged by a strong outside force. The full measure of their vulnerability is therefore not yet evident.

The Kremlin's relations with its satellites and their peoples is likewise a vulnerability. Nationalism still remains the most potent emotional-political force. The well-known ills of colonialism are compounded, however, by the excessive demands of the Kremlin that its satellites accept not only the imperial authority of Moscow but that they believe in and proclaim the

ideological primacy and infallibility of the Kremlin. These excessive requirements can be made good only through extreme coercion. The result is that
if a satellite feels able to effect its independence of the Kremlin, as Tito was
able to do, it is likely to break away.

In short, Soviet ideas and practices run counter to the best and potentially
the strongest instincts of men, and deny their most fundamental aspirations.
Against an adversary which effectively affirmed the constructive and hope-
ful instincts of men and was capable of fulfilling their fundamental aspirations, the Soviet system might prove to be fatally weak.

The problem of succession to Stalin is also a Kremlin vulnerability. In a
system where supreme power is acquired and held through violence and
intimidation, the transfer of that power may well produce a period of instability.

In a very real sense, the Kremlin is a victim of its own dynamism. This
dynamism can become a weakness if it is frustrated, if in its forward
thrusts it encounters a superior force which halts the expansion and exerts
a superior counterpressure. Yet the Kremlin cannot relax the condition of
crisis and mobilization, for to do so would be to lose its dynamism,
whereas the seeds of decay within the Soviet system would begin to flourish and fructify.

The Kremlin is, of course, aware of these weaknesses. It must know that
in the present world situation they are of secondary significance. So long as
the Kremlin retains the initiative, so long as it can keep on the offensive
unchallenged by clearly superior counter-force—spiritual as well as material—its vulnerabilities are largely inoperative and even concealed by its
successes. The Kremlin has not yet been given real reason to fear and be
diverted by the rot within its system.

B. ECONOMIC

The Kremlin has no economic intentions unrelated to its overall policies.
Economics in the Soviet world is not an end in itself. The Kremlin's policy,
in so far as it has to do with economics, is to utilize economic processes to
contribute to the overall strength, particularly the war-making capacity of
the Soviet system. The material welfare of the totalitariat is severely subordinated to the interest of the system.

As for capabilities, even granting optimistic Soviet reports of production,
the total economic strength of the U.S.S.R. compares with that of the U.S. as
roughly one to four. This is reflected not only in gross national product
(1949: USSR $65 billion; U.S. $250 billion), but in production of key commodi-
ties in 1949:

	U.S.	USSR	USSR AND EUROPEAN ORBIT COMBINED
Ingot steel (million met. tons)	80.4	21.5	28.0
Primary aluminum (thousands met. tons)	617.6	130–135	140–145
Electric power (billion kwh)	410	72	112
Crude oil (million met. tons)	276.5	33.0	38.9

Assuming the maintenance of present policies, while a large U.S. advantage is likely to remain, the Soviet Union will be steadily reducing the discrepancy between its overall economic strength and that of the U.S. by continuing to devote proportionately more to capital investment than the U.S.

But a full-scale effort by the U.S. would be capable of precipitately altering this trend. The USSR today is on a near maximum production basis. No matter what efforts Moscow might make, only a relatively slight change in the rate of increase in overall production could be brought about. In the U.S., on the other hand, a very rapid absolute expansion could be realized. The fact remains, however, that so long as the Soviet Union is virtually mobilized, and the United States has scarcely begun to summon up its forces, the greater capabilities of the U.S. are to that extent inoperative in the struggle for power. Moreover, as the Soviet attainment of an atomic capability has demonstrated, the totalitarian state, at least in time of peace, can focus its efforts on any given project far more readily than the democratic state.

In other fields—general technological competence, skilled labor resources, productivity of labor force, etc.—the gap between the USSR and the U.S. roughly corresponds to the gap in production. In the field of scientific research, however, the margin of United States superiority is unclear, especially if the Kremlin can utilize European talents.

C. MILITARY

The Soviet Union is developing the military capacity to support its design for world domination. The Soviet Union actually possesses armed forces far in excess of those necessary to defend its national territory. These armed forces are probably not yet considered by the Soviet Union to be sufficient to initiate a war which would involve the United States. This excessive strength, coupled now with an atomic capability, provides the Soviet Union with great coercive power for use in time of peace in furtherance of its objectives and serves as a deterrent to the victims of its aggression from taking any action in opposition to its tactics which would risk war.

Should a major war occur in 1950 the Soviet Union and its satellites are considered by the Joint Chiefs of Staff to be in a sufficiently advanced state of preparation immediately to undertake and carry out the following campaigns.

a. To overrun Western Europe, with the possible exception of the Iberian and Scandinavian Peninsulas; to drive toward the oil-bearing areas of the Near and Middle East; and to consolidate Communist gains in the Far East;

b. To launch air attacks against the British Isles and air and sea attacks against the lines of communications of the Western Powers in the Atlantic and the Pacific;

c. To attack selected targets with atomic weapons, now including the likelihood of such attacks against targets in Alaska, Canada, and the United States. Alternatively, this capability, coupled with other actions open to the Soviet Union, might deny the United Kingdom as an effective base of operations for allied forces. It also should be possible for the Soviet Union to prevent any allied "Normandy" type amphibious operations intended to force a reentry into the continent of Europe.

After the Soviet Union completed its initial campaigns and consolidated its positions in the Western European area, it could simultaneously conduct:

a. Full-scale air and limited sea operations against the British Isles;

b. Invasions of the Iberian and Scandinavian Peninsulas;

c. Further operations in the Near and Middle East, continued air operations against the North American continent, and air and sea operations against Atlantic and Pacific lines of communication; and

d. Diversionary attacks in other areas.

During the course of the offensive operations listed in the second and third paragraphs above, the Soviet Union will have an air defense capability with respect to the vital areas of its own and its satellites' territories which can oppose but cannot prevent allied air operations against these areas.

It is not known whether the Soviet Union possesses war reserves and arsenal capabilities sufficient to supply its satellite armies or even its own forces throughout a long war. It might not be in the interest of the Soviet Union to equip fully its satellite armies, since the possibility of defections would exist.

It is not possible at this time to assess accurately the finite disadvantages to the Soviet Union which may accrue through the implementation of the Economic Cooperation Act of 1948, as amended, and the Mutual Defense Assistance Act of 1949. It should be expected that, as this implementation progresses, the internal security situation of the recipient nations should improve concurrently. In addition, a strong United States military position, plus increases in the armaments of the nations of Western Europe, should strengthen the determination of the recipient nations to counter Soviet moves and in event of war could be considered as likely to delay operations and increase the time required for the Soviet Union to overrun Western Europe. In all probability, although United States backing will stiffen their determination, the armaments increase under the present aid programs will not be of any major consequence prior to 1952. Unless the military strength of the Western European nations is increased on a much larger scale than under current programs and at an accelerated rate, it is more than likely that those nations will not be able to oppose even by 1960 the Soviet armed forces in war with any degree of effectiveness. Considering the Soviet Union military capability, the long-range allied military objective in Western Europe must envisage an increased military strength in that area sufficient possibly to deter the Soviet Union from a major war or, in any event, to delay materially the overrunning of Western Europe and, if feasible, to hold a bridgehead on the continent against Soviet Union offensives.

We do not know accurately what the Soviet atomic capability is but the Central Intelligence Agency intelligence estimates, concurred in by State, Army, Navy, Air Force, and Atomic Energy Commission, assign to the Soviet Union a production capability giving it a fission bomb stockpile within the following ranges:

By mid-1950	10–20
By mid-1951	25–45
By mid-1952	45–90
By mid-1953	70–135
By mid-1954	200

This estimate is admittedly based on incomplete coverage of Soviet activities and represents the production capabilities of known or deducible Soviet plants. If others exist, as is possible, this estimate could lead us into a feeling of superiority in our atomic stockpile that might be dangerously misleading, particularly with regard to the timing of a possible Soviet offensive. On the other hand, if the Soviet Union experiences operating difficulties, this estimate would be reduced. There is some evidence that the Soviet Union is acquiring certain materials essential to research on and development of thermonuclear weapons.

The Soviet Union now has aircraft able to deliver the atomic bomb. Our Intelligence estimates assign to the Soviet Union an atomic bomber capability already in excess of that needed to deliver available bombs. We have at present no evaluated estimate regarding the Soviet accuracy of delivery on target. It is believed that the Soviets cannot deliver their bombs on target with a degree of accuracy comparable to ours, but a planning estimate might well place it at 40–60 percent of bombs sortied. For planning purposes, therefore, the date the Soviets possess an atomic stockpile of 200 bombs would be a critical date for the United States, for the delivery of 100 atomic bombs on targets in the United States would seriously damage this country.

At the time the Soviet Union has a substantial atomic stockpile and if it is assumed that it will strike a strong surprise blow and if it is assumed further that its atomic attacks will be met with no more effective defense opposition than the United States and its allies have programmed, results of those attacks could include:

a. Laying waste to the British Isles and thus depriving the Western Powers of their use as a base;

b. Destruction of the vital centers and of the communications of Western Europe, thus precluding effective defense by the Western Powers; and

c. Delivering devastating attacks on certain vital centers of the United States and Canada.

The possession by the Soviet Union of a thermonuclear capability in addition to this substantial atomic stockpile would result in tremendously increased damage.

During this decade, the defensive capabilities of the Soviet Union will probably be strengthened, particularly by the development and use of modern aircraft, aircraft warning and communications devices, and defensive guided missiles.

VI. U.S. Intentions and Capabilities— Actual and Potential

A. POLITICAL AND PSYCHOLOGICAL

Our overall policy at the present time may be described as one designed to foster a world environment in which the American system can survive and flourish. It therefore rejects the concept of isolation and affirms the necessity of our positive participation in the world community.

This broad intention embraces two subsidiary policies. One is a policy which we would probably pursue even if there were no Soviet threat. It is a policy of attempting to develop a healthy international community. The other is the policy of "containing" the Soviet system. These two policies are closely interrelated and interact on one another. Nevertheless, the distinction between them is basically valid and contributes to a clearer understanding of what we are trying to do.

The policy of striving to develop a healthy international community is the long-term constructive effort which we are engaged in. It was this policy which gave rise to our vigorous sponsorship of the United Nations. It is of course the principal reason for our long continuing endeavors to create and now develop the Inter-American system. It, as much as containment, underlay our efforts to rehabilitate Western Europe. Most of our international economic activities can likewise be explained in terms of this policy.

In a world of polarized power, the policies designed to develop a healthy international community are more than ever necessary to our own strength.

As for the policy of "containment," it is one which seeks by all means short of war to (1) block further expansion of Soviet power, (2) expose the falsities of Soviet pretensions, (3) induce a retraction of the Kremlin's control and influence, and (4) in general, so foster the seeds of destruction within the Soviet system that the Kremlin is brought at least to the point of modifying its behavior to conform to generally accepted international standards.

It was and continues to be cardinal in this policy that we possess superior overall power in ourselves or in dependable combination with other like-minded nations. One of the most important ingredients of power is military strength. In the concept of "containment," the maintenance of a strong military posture is deemed to be essential for two reasons: (1) as an ultimate guarantee of our national security and (2) as an indispensable backdrop to the conduct of the policy of "containment." Without superior aggregate military strength, in being and readily mobilizable, a policy of "containment"—which is in effect a policy of calculated and gradual coercion—is no more than a policy of bluff.

At the same time, it is essential to the successful conduct of a policy of "containment" that we always leave open the possibility of negotiation with the USSR. A diplomatic freeze—and we are in one now—tends to defeat the very purposes of "containment" because it raises tensions at the same time that it makes Soviet retractions and adjustments in the direction of moderated behavior more difficult. It also tends to inhibit our initiative and deprives us of opportunities for maintaining a moral ascendency in our struggle with the Soviet system.

In "containment" it is desirable to exert pressure in a fashion which will avoid so far as possible directly challenging Soviet prestige, to keep open the possibility for the USSR to retreat before pressure with a minimum loss of face and to secure political advantage from the failure of the Kremlin to yield or take advantage of the openings we leave it.

We have failed to implement adequately these two fundamental aspects of "containment." In the face of obviously mounting Soviet military strength ours has declined relatively. Partly as a byproduct of this, but also for other reasons, we now find ourselves at a diplomatic impasse with the Soviet Union, with the Kremlin growing bolder, with both of us holding on grimly to what we have, and with ourselves facing difficult decisions.

In examining our capabilities it is relevant to ask at the outset—capabilities for what? The answer cannot be stated solely in the negative terms of resisting the Kremlin design. It includes also our capabilities to attain the fundamental purpose of the United States, and to foster a world environment in which our free society can survive and flourish.

Potentially we have these capabilities. We know we have them in the economic and military fields. Potentially we also have them in the political and psychological fields. The vast majority of Americans are confident that the system of values which animates our society—the principles of freedom, tolerance, the importance of the individual, and the supremacy of reason over will—are valid and more vital than the ideology which is the fuel of Soviet dynamism. Translated into terms relevant to the lives of other peoples—our system of values can become perhaps a powerful appeal to millions who now seek or find in authoritarianism a refuge from anxieties, bafflement, and insecurity.

Essentially, our democracy also possesses a unique degree of unity. Our society is fundamentally more cohesive than the Soviet system, the solidarity of which is artificially created through force, fear, and favor. This means that expressions of national consensus in our society are soundly and solidly based. It means that the possibility of revolution in this country is fundamentally less than that in the Soviet system.

These capabilities within us constitute a great potential force in our international relations. The potential within us of bearing witness to the values by which we live holds promise for a dynamic manifestation to the rest of the world of the vitality of our system. The essential tolerance of our world outlook, our generous and constructive impulses, and the absence of covetousness in our international relations are assets of potentially enormous influence.

These then are our potential capabilities. Between them and our capabilities currently being utilized is a wide gap of unactualized power. In sharp contrast is the situation of the Soviet world. Its capabilities are inferior to those of our allies and to our own. But they are mobilized close to the maximum possible extent.

The full power which resides within the American people will be evoked only through the traditional democratic process: This process requires, firstly, that sufficient information regarding the basic political, economic, and military elements of the present situation be made publicly available so that an intelligent popular opinion may be formed. Having achieved a comprehension of the issues now confronting this Republic, it will then be possible for the American people and the American Government to arrive at a consensus. Out of this common view will develop a determination of the national will and a solid resolute expression of that will. The initiative in this process lies with the Government.

The democratic way is harder than the authoritarian way because, in seeking to protect and fulfill the individual, it demands of him understanding, judgment, and positive participation in the increasingly complex and exacting problems of the modern world. It demands that he exercise discrimination: that while pursuing through free inquiry the search for truth he knows when he should commit an act of faith; that he distinguish between the necessity for tolerance and the necessity for just suppression. A free society is vulnerable in that it is easy for people to lapse into excesses—the excesses of a permanently open mind wishfully waiting for evidence that evil design may become noble purpose, the excess of faith becoming prejudice, the excess of tolerance degenerating into indulgence of conspiracy and the excess of resorting to suppression when more moderate measures are not only more appropriate but more effective.

In coping with dictatorial governments acting in secrecy and with speed, we are also vulnerable in that the democratic process necessarily operates in the open and at a deliberate tempo. Weaknesses in our situation are readily apparent and subject to immediate exploitation. This Government therefore cannot afford in the face of the totalitarian challenge to operate on a narrow margin of strength. A democracy can compensate for its natural vulnerability only if it maintains clearly superior overall power in its most inclusive sense.

The very virtues of our system likewise handicap us in certain respects in our relations with our allies. While it is a general source of strength to us that our relations with our allies are conducted on a basis of persuasion and consent rather than compulsion and capitulation, it is also evident that dissent among us can become a vulnerability. Sometimes the dissent has its principal roots abroad in situations about which we can do nothing. Sometimes it arises largely out of certain weaknesses within ourselves, about which we can do something—our native impetuosity and a tendency to expect too much from people widely divergent from us.

The full capabilities of the rest of the free world are a potential increment to our own capabilities. It may even be said that the capabilities of the Soviet world, specifically the capabilities of the masses who have nothing to lose but their Soviet chains, are a potential which can be enlisted on our side.

Like our own capabilities, those of the rest of the free world exceed the capabilities of the Soviet system. Like our own they are far from being effectively mobilized and employed in the struggle against the Kremlin design. This is so because the rest of the free world lacks a sense of unity, confidence, and common purpose. This is true in even the most homogeneous and advanced segment of the free world—Western Europe.

As we ourselves demonstrate power, confidence, and a sense of moral and political direction, so those same qualities will be evoked in Western Europe. In such a situation, we may also anticipate a general improvement in the political tone in Latin America, Asia, and Africa and the real beginnings of awakening among the Soviet totalitariat.

In the absence of affirmative decision on our part, the rest of the free world is almost certain to become demoralized. Our friends will become more than a liability to us; they can eventually become a positive increment to Soviet power.

In sum, the capabilities of our allies are, in an important sense, a function of our own. An affirmative decision to summon up the potential within ourselves would evoke the potential strength within others and add it to our own.

B. ECONOMIC

1. Capabilities.   In contrast to the war economy of the Soviet world (cf. Ch. V-B), the American economy (and the economy of the free world as a whole) is at present directed to the provision of rising standards of living. The military budget of the United States represents 6 to 7 percent of its gross national product (as against 13.8 percent for the Soviet Union). Our North Atlantic Treaty [NAT] allies devoted 4.8 percent of their national product to military purposes in 1949.

This difference in emphasis between the two economies means that the readiness of the free world to support a war effort is tending to decline relative to that of the Soviet Union. There is little direct investment in production facilities for military end-products and in dispersal. There are relatively few men receiving military training and a relatively low rate of production of weapons. However, given time to convert to a war effort, the capabilities of the United States economy and also of the Western European economy would be tremendous. In the light of Soviet military capabilities, a question which may be of decisive importance in the event of war is the question whether there will be time to mobilize our superior human and material resources for a war effort (cf. Chs. VIII and IX).

The capability of the American economy to support a build-up of economic and military strength at home and to assist a build-up abroad is limited not, as in the case of the Soviet Union, so much by the ability to produce as by the decision on the proper allocation of resources to this and other purposes. Even Western Europe could afford to assign a substantially larger proportion of its resources to defense, if the necessary foundation in public understanding and will could be laid, and if the assistance needed to meet its dollar deficit were provided.

A few statistics will help to clarify this point [Table 1].

The Soviet Union is now allocating nearly 40 percent of its gross available resources to military purposes and investment, much of which is in war-supporting industries. It is estimated that even in an emergency the Soviet Union could not increase this proportion to much more than 50 percent, or by one-fourth. The United States, on the other hand, is allocating only about 20 percent of its resources to defense and investment (or 22 percent including foreign assistance), and little of its investment outlays are directed to war-supporting industries. In an emergency the United States could allocate more than 50 percent of its resources to military purposes and foreign assistance, or five to six times as much as at present.

The same point can be brought out by statistics on the use of important products. The Soviet Union is using 14 percent of its ingot steel, 47 percent of its primary aluminum, and 18.5 percent of its crude oil for military purposes, while the corresponding percentages for the United States are 1.7, 8.6, and 5.6. Despite the tremendously larger production of these goods in the

Table 1. Percentage of Gross Available Resources Allocated to Investment, National Defense, and Consumption in East and West, 1949 (in percent of total)

COUNTRY	GROSS INVESTMENT	DEFENSE	CONSUMPTION
USSR	25.4	13.8	60.8
Soviet Orbit	22.0[a]	4.0[b]	74.0[a]
U.S.	13.6	6.5	79.9
European NAT countries	20.4	4.8	74.8

[a]Crude estimate. [Footnote in the source text.]
[b]Includes Soviet Zone of Germany; otherwise 5 percent. [Footnote in the source text.]

United States than the Soviet Union, the latter is actually using, for military purposes, nearly twice as much steel as the United States and 8 to 26 percent more aluminum.

Perhaps the most impressive indication of the economic superiority of the free world over the Soviet world which can be made on the basis of available data is provided in comparisons (based mainly on the *Economic Survey of Europe, 1948*) [Table 2].

It should be noted that these comparisons understate the relative position of the NAT countries for several reasons: (1) Canada is excluded because comparable data were not available; (2) the data for the USSR are the 1950 targets (as stated in the fourth five-year plan) rather than actual rates of production and are believed to exceed in many cases the production actually achieved; (3) the data for the European NAT countries are actual data for 1948, and production has generally increased since that time.

Furthermore, the United States could achieve a substantial absolute increase in output and could thereby increase the allocation of resources to a build-up of the economic and military strength of itself and its allies without suffering a decline in its real standard of living. Industrial production declined by 10 percent between the first quarter of 1948 and the last quarter of 1949, and by approximately one-fourth between 1944 and 1949. In March 1950 there were approximately 4,750,000 unemployed, as compared to 1,070,000 in 1943 and 670,000 in 1944. The gross national product declined slowly in 1949 from the peak reached in 1948 ($262 billion in 1948 to an annual rate of $256 billion in the last six months of 1949), and in terms of constant prices declined by about 20 percent between 1944 and 1948.

With a high level of economic activity, the United States could soon attain a gross national product of $300 billion per year, as was pointed out in the President's Economic Report (January 1950). Progress in this direction would permit, and might itself be aided by, a buildup of the economic and military strength of the United States and the free world; furthermore, if a dynamic expansion of the economy were achieved, the necessary build-up could be accomplished without a decrease in the national standard of living because the required resources could be obtained by siphoning off a part of the annual increment in the gross national product. These are facts of fundamental importance in considering the courses of action open to the United States (cf. Ch. IX).

2. Intentions. Foreign economic policy is a major instrument in the conduct of United States foreign relations. It is an instrument which can powerfully influence the world environment in ways favorable to the security and welfare of this country. It is also an instrument which, if unwisely formu-

Table 2. Comparative Statistics on Economic Capabilities of East and West

	U.S. 1948–49	EUROPEAN NAT COUNTRIES 1948–49	TOTAL	USSR (1950 PLAN)	SATELLITES 1948–49	TOTAL
Population (millions)	149	173	322	198[a]	75	273
Employment in non-agricultural establishments (millions)	45	–	–	31[a]	–	–
Gross national production (billion dollars)	250	84	334	65[a]	21	86
National income per capita (current dollars)	1700	480	1040	330	280	315
Production data[b]:						
Coal (million tons)	582	306	888	250	88	338
Electric power (billion kwh)	356	124	480	82	15	97
Crude petroleum (million tons)	277	1	278	35	5	40
Pig iron (million tons)	55	24	79	19.5	3.2	22.7
Steel (million tons)	80	32	112	25	6	31
Cement (million tons)	35	21	56	10.5	2.1	12.6
Motor vehicles (thousands)	5273	580	5853	500	25	525

[a] 1949 data. [Footnote in the source text.]
[b] For the European NAT countries and for the satellites, the data include output by major producers. [Footnote in the source text.]

lated and employed, can do actual harm to our national interests. It is an instrument uniquely suited to our capabilities, provided we have the tenacity of purpose and the understanding requisite to a realization of its potentials. Finally, it is an instrument peculiarly appropriate to the cold war.

The preceding analysis has indicated that an essential element in a program to frustrate the Kremlin design is the development of a successfully functioning system among the free nations. It is clear that economic conditions are among the fundamental determinants of the will and the strength to resist subversion and aggression.

United States foreign economic policy has been designed to assist in the building of such a system and such conditions in the free world. The principal features of this policy can be summarized as follows:

1. assistance to Western Europe in recovery and the creation of a viable economy (the European Recovery Program);

2. assistance to other countries because of their special needs arising out of the war or the cold war and our special interests in or responsibility for meeting them (grant assistance to Japan, the Philippines, and Korea, loans and credits by the Export-Import Bank, the International Monetary Fund, and the International Bank to Indonesia, Yugoslavia, Iran, etc.);

3. assistance in the development of underdeveloped areas (the Point IV program and loans and credits to various countries, overlapping to some extent with those mentioned under 2);

4. military assistance to the North Atlantic Treaty countries, Greece, Turkey, etc.;

5. restriction of East-West trade in items of military importance to the East;

6. purchase and stockpiling of strategic materials; and

7. efforts to reestablish an international economy based on multilateral trade, declining trade barriers, and convertible currencies (the GATT-ITO program, the Reciprocal Trade Agreements program, the IMF-IBRD program, and the program now being developed to solve the problem of the United States balance of payments).

In both their short and long term aspects, these policies and programs are directed to the strengthening of the free world and therefore to the frustration of the Kremlin design. Despite certain inadequacies and inconsistencies, which are now being studied in connection with the problem of the United States balance of payments, the United States has generally pursued a foreign economic policy which has powerfully supported its overall objectives. The question must nevertheless be asked whether current and currently projected programs will adequately support this policy in the future, in terms both of need and urgency.

The last year has been indecisive in the economic field. The Soviet Union has made considerable progress in integrating the satellite economies of Eastern Europe into the Soviet economy, but still faces very large problems, especially with China. The free nations have important accomplishments to record, but also have tremendous problems still ahead. On balance, neither side can claim any great advantage in this field over its relative position a year ago. The important question therefore becomes: what are the trends?

Several conclusions seem to emerge. First, the Soviet Union is widening the gap between its preparedness for war and the unpreparedness of the free world for war. It is devoting a far greater *proportion* of its resources to military purposes than are the free nations and, in significant components of military power, a greater *absolute* quantity of resources. Second, the Communist success in China, taken with the politico-economic situation in the rest of South and South-East Asia, provides a springboard for a further incursion in this troubled area. Although Communist China faces serious economic problems which may impose some strains on the Soviet economy, it is probable that the social and economic problems faced by the free nations in this area present more than offsetting opportunities for Communist expansion. Third, the Soviet Union holds positions in Europe which, if it maneuvers skillfully, could be used to do great damage to the Western European economy and to the maintenance of the Western orientation of certain countries, particularly Germany and Austria. Fourth, despite (and in part because of) the Titoist[1] defection, the Soviet Union has accelerated its efforts to integrate satellite economy with its own and to increase the degree of autarchy within the areas under its control.

Fifth, meanwhile, Western Europe, with American (and Canadian) assistance, has achieved a record level of production. However, it faces the prospect of a rapid tapering off of American assistance without the possibility of achieving, by its own efforts, a satisfactory equilibrium with the dollar area. It has also made very little progress toward "economic integration," which would in the long run tend to improve its productivity and to provide an economic environment conducive to political stability. In particular, the movement toward economic integration does not appear to be rapid enough to provide Western Germany with adequate economic opportunities in the West. The United Kingdom still faces economic problems which may require a moderate but politically difficult decline in the British standard of living or more American assistance than is contemplated. At the same time, a strengthening of the British position is needed if the stability of the Commonwealth is not to be impaired and if it is to be a focus of resistance to Communist expansion in South and South-East Asia. Improvement of the British position is also vital in building up the defensive capabilities of Western Europe.

Sixth, throughout Asia the stability of the present moderate governments, which are more in sympathy with our purposes than any probable successor regimes would be, is doubtful. The problem is only in part an economic one. Assistance in economic development is important as a means of holding out to the peoples of Asia some prospect of improvement in standards of living under their present governments. But probably more important are a strengthening of central institutions, an improvement in administration, and generally a development of an economic and social structure within which the peoples of Asia can make more effective use of their great human and material resources.

Seventh, and perhaps most important, there are indications of a let-down of United States efforts under the pressure of the domestic budgetary situation, disillusion resulting from excessively optimistic expectations about the duration and results of our assistance programs, and doubts about the wisdom of continuing to strengthen the free nations as against preparedness measures in light of the intensity of the cold war.

Eighth, there are grounds for predicting that the United States and other free nations will within a period of a few years at most experience a decline in economic activity of serious proportions unless more positive governmental programs are developed than are now available.

In short, as we look into the future, the programs now planned will not meet the requirements of the free nations. The difficulty does not lie so much in the inadequacy or misdirection of policy as in the inadequacy of planned programs, in terms of timing or impact, to achieve our objectives. The risks inherent in this situation are set forth in the following chapter and a course of action designed to reinvigorate our efforts in order to reverse the present trends and to achieve our fundamental purpose is outlined in Chapter IX.

C. MILITARY

The United States now possesses the greatest military potential of any single nation in the world. The military weaknesses of the United States vis-à-vis the Soviet Union, however, include its numerical inferiority in forces in being and in total manpower. Coupled with the inferiority of forces in being, the United States also lacks tenable positions from which to employ its forces in event of war and munitions power in being and readily available.

It is true that the United States armed forces are now stronger than ever before in other times of apparent peace; it is also true that there exists a sharp disparity between our actual military strength and our commitments. The relationship of our strength to our present commitments, however, is not alone the governing factor. The world situation, as well as commitments, should govern; hence, our military strength more properly should be related to the world situation confronting us. When our military strength is related to the world situation and balanced against the likely exigencies of such a situation, it is clear that our military strength is becoming dangerously inadequate.

If war should begin in 1950, the United States and its allies will have the military capability of conducting defensive operations to provide a reasonable measure of protection to the Western Hemisphere, bases in the Western Pacific, and essential military lines of communication; and an inadequate measure of protection to vital military bases in the United Kingdom and in the Near and Middle East. We will have the capability of conducting powerful offensive air operations against vital elements of the Soviet war-making capacity.

The scale of the operations listed in the preceding paragraph is limited by the effective forces and material in being of the United States and its allies vis-à-vis the Soviet Union. Consistent with the aggressive threat facing us and in consonance with overall strategic plans, the United States must provide to its allies on a continuing basis as large amounts of military assistance as possible without serious detriment to the United States operational requirements.

If the potential military capabilities of the United States and its allies were rapidly and effectively developed, sufficient forces could be produced probably to deter war, or if the Soviet Union chooses war, to withstand the initial Soviet attacks, to stabilize supporting attacks, and to retaliate in turn with even greater impact on the Soviet capabilities. From the military point of view alone, however, this would require not only the generation of the necessary military forces but also the development and stockpiling of improved weapons of all types.

Under existing peacetime conditions, a period of from two to three years is required to produce a material increase in military power. Such increased power could be provided in a somewhat shorter period in a declared period of emergency or in wartime through a full-out national effort. Any increase in military power in peacetime, however, should be related both to its probable military role in war, to the implementation of immediate and long-term United States foreign policy vis-à-vis the Soviet Union, and to the realities of the existing situation. If such a course of increasing our military power is adopted now, the United States would have the capability of eliminating the disparity between its military strength and the exigencies of the situation we face; eventually of gaining the initiative in the "cold" war and of materially delaying if not stopping the Soviet offensives in war itself.

VII. Present Risks

A. GENERAL

It is apparent from the preceding sections that the integrity and vitality of our system is in greater jeopardy than ever before in our history. Even if there were no Soviet Union we would face the great problem of the free society, accentuated many fold in this industrial age, of reconciling order, security, the need for participation, with the requirement of freedom. We would face the fact that in a shrinking world the absence of order among nations is becoming less and less tolerable. The Kremlin design seeks to impose order among nations by means which would destroy our free and democratic system. The Kremlin's possession of atomic weapons puts new power behind its design, and increases the jeopardy to our system. It adds new strains to the uneasy equilibrium-without-order which exists in the world and raises new doubts in men's minds whether the world will long tolerate this tension without moving toward some kind of order, on somebody's terms.

The risks we face are of a new order of magnitude, commensurate with the total struggle in which we are engaged. For a free society there is never total victory, since freedom and democracy are never wholly attained, are always in the process of being attained. But defeat at the hands of the totalitarian is total defeat. These risks crowd in on us, in a shrinking world of polarized power, so as to give us no choice, ultimately, between meeting them effectively or being overcome by them.

B. SPECIFIC

It is quite clear from Soviet theory and practice that the Kremlin seeks to bring the free world under its dominion by the methods of the cold war. The preferred technique is to subvert by infiltration and intimidation. Every institution of our society is an instrument which it is sought to stultify and turn against our purposes. Those that touch most closely our material and moral strength are obviously the prime targets, labor unions, civic enterprises, schools, churches, and all media for influencing opinion. The effort is not so much to make them serve obvious Soviet ends as to prevent them from serving our ends, and thus to make them sources of confusion in our economy, our culture, and our body politic. The doubts and diversities that in terms of our values are part of the merit of a free system, the weaknesses and the problems that are peculiar to it, the rights and privileges that free men enjoy, and the disorganization and destruction left in the wake of the last attack on our freedoms, all are but opportunities for the Kremlin to do its evil work. Every advantage is taken of the fact that our means of prevention and retaliation are limited by those principles and scruples which are precisely the ones that give our freedom and democracy its meaning for us. None of our scruples deter those whose only code is "morality is that which serves the revolution."

Since everything that gives us or others respect for our institutions is a suitable object for attack, it also fits the Kremlin's design that where, with impunity, we can be insulted and made to suffer indignity the opportunity shall not be missed, particularly in any context which can be used to cast dishonor on our country, our system, our motives, or our methods. Thus the means by which we sought to restore our own economic health in the '30's, and now seek to restore that of the free world, come equally under attack. The military aid by which we sought to help the free world was frantically denounced by the Communists in the early days of the last war, and of course our present efforts to develop adequate military strength for ourselves and our allies are equally denounced.

At the same time the Soviet Union is seeking to create overwhelming military force, in order to back up infiltration with intimidation. In the only terms in which it understands strength, it is seeking to demonstrate to the free world that force and the will to use it are on the side of the Kremlin, that those who lack it are decadent and doomed. In local incidents it threatens and encroaches both for the sake of local gains and to increase anxiety and defeatism in all the free world.

The possession of atomic weapons at each of the opposite poles of power, and the inability (for different reasons) of either side to place any trust in the other, puts a premium on a surprise attack against us. It equally puts a premium on a more violent and ruthless prosecution of its design by cold war, especially if the Kremlin is sufficiently objective to realize the improbability of our prosecuting a preventive war. It also puts a premium on piecemeal aggression against others, counting on our unwillingness to engage in atomic war unless we are directly attacked. We run all these risks and the added risk of being confused and immobilized by our inability to weigh and choose, and pursue a firm course based on a rational assessment of each.

The risk that we may thereby be prevented or too long delayed in taking all needful measures to maintain the integrity and vitality of our system is great. The risk that our allies will lose their determination is greater. And the risk that in this manner a descending spiral of too little and too late, of doubt and recrimination, may present us with ever narrower and more desperate alternatives, is the greatest risk of all. For example, it is clear that our present weakness would prevent us from offering effective resistance at any of several vital pressure points. The only deterrent we can present to the

Kremlin is the evidence we give that we may make any of the critical points which we cannot hold the occasion for a global war of annihilation.

The risk of having no better choice than to capitulate or precipitate a global war at any of a number of pressure points is bad enough in itself, but it is multiplied by the weakness it imparts to our position in the cold war. Instead of appearing strong and resolute we are continually at the verge of appearing and being alternately irresolute and desperate; yet it is the cold war which we must win, because both the Kremlin design, and our fundamental purpose give it the first priority.

The frustration of the Kremlin design, however, cannot be accomplished by us alone, as will appear from the analysis in Chapter IX, B. Strength at the center, in the United States, is only the first of two essential elements. The second is that our allies and potential allies do not as a result of a sense of frustration or of Soviet intimidation drift into a course of neutrality eventually leading to Soviet domination. If this were to happen in Germany the effect upon Western Europe and eventually upon us might be catastrophic.

But there are risks in making ourselves strong. A large measure of sacrifice and discipline will be demanded of the American people. They will be asked to give up some of the benefits which they have come to associate with their freedoms. Nothing could be more important than that they fully understand the reasons for this. The risks of a superficial understanding or of an inadequate appreciation of the issues are obvious and might lead to the adoption of measures which in themselves would jeopardize the integrity of our system. At any point in the process of demonstrating our will to make good our fundamental purpose, the Kremlin may decide to precipitate a general war, or in testing us, may go too far. These are risks we will invite by making ourselves strong, but they are lesser risks than those we seek to avoid. Our fundamental purpose is more likely to be defeated from lack of the will to maintain it, than from any mistakes we may make or assault we may undergo because of asserting that will. No people in history have preserved their freedom who thought that by not being strong enough to protect themselves they might prove inoffensive to their enemies.

VIII. Atomic Armaments

A. MILITARY EVALUATION OF U.S.
AND USSR ATOMIC CAPABILITIES

1. The United States now has an atomic capability, including both numbers and deliverability, estimated to be adequate, if effectively utilized, to

deliver a serious blow against the war-making capacity of the USSR. It is doubted whether such a blow, even if it resulted in the complete destruction of the contemplated target systems, would cause the USSR to sue for terms or prevent Soviet forces from occupying Western Europe against such ground resistance as could presently be mobilized. A very serious initial blow could, however, so reduce the capabilities of the USSR to supply and equip its military organization and its civilian population as to give the United States the prospect of developing a general military superiority in a war of long duration.

2. As the atomic capability of the USSR increases, it will have an increased ability to hit at our atomic bases and installations and thus seriously hamper the ability of the United States to carry out an attack such as that outlined above. It is quite possible that in the near future the USSR will have a sufficient number of atomic bombs and a sufficient deliverability to raise a question whether Britain with its present inadequate air defense could be relied upon as an advance base from which a major portion of the U.S. attack could be launched.

It is estimated that, within the next four years, the USSR will attain the capability of seriously damaging vital centers of the United States, provided it strikes a surprise blow and provided further that the blow is opposed by no more effective opposition than we now have programmed. Such a blow could so seriously damage the United States as to greatly reduce its superiority in economic potential.

Effective opposition to this Soviet capability will require among other measures greatly increased air warning systems, air defenses, and vigorous development and implementation of a civilian defense program which has been thoroughly integrated with the military defense systems.

In time the atomic capability of the USSR can be expected to grow to a point where, given surprise and no more effective opposition than we now have programmed, the possibility of a decisive initial attack cannot be excluded.

3. In the initial phases of an atomic war, the advantages of initiative and surprise would be very great. A police state living behind an iron curtain has an enormous advantage in maintaining the necessary security and centralization of decision required to capitalize on this advantage.

4. For the moment our atomic retaliatory capability is probably adequate to deter the Kremlin from a deliberate direct military attack against ourselves or other free peoples. However, when it calculates that it has a sufficient atomic capability to make a surprise attack on us, nullifying our atomic superiority and creating a military situation decisively in its favor, the Kremlin might be tempted to strike swiftly and with stealth. The exis-

tence of two large atomic capabilities in such a relationship might well act, therefore, not as a deterrent, but as an incitement to war.

5. A further increase in the number and power of our atomic weapons is necessary in order to assure the effectiveness of any U.S. retaliatory blow, but would not of itself seem to change the basic logic of the above points. Greatly increased general air, ground, and sea strength, and increased air defense and civilian defense programs would also be necessary to provide reasonable assurance that the free world could survive an initial surprise atomic attack of the weight which it is estimated the USSR will be capable of delivering by 1954 and still permit the free world to go on to the eventual attainment of its objectives. Furthermore, such a build-up of strength could safeguard and increase our retaliatory power, and thus might put off for some time the date when the Soviet Union could calculate that a surprise blow would be advantageous. This would provide additional time for the effects of our policies to produce a modification of the Soviet system.

6. If the USSR develops a thermonuclear weapon ahead of the U.S., the risks of greatly increased Soviet pressure against all the free world, or an attack against the U.S., will be greatly increased.

7. If the U.S. develops a thermonuclear weapon ahead of the USSR, the U.S. should for the time being be able to bring increased pressure on the USSR.

B. STOCKPILING AND USE OF ATOMIC WEAPONS

1. From the foregoing analysis it appears that it would be to the long-term advantage of the United States if atomic weapons were to be effectively eliminated from national peacetime armaments; the additional objectives which must be secured if there is to be a reasonable prospect of such effective elimination of atomic weapons are discussed in Chapter IX. In the absence of such elimination and the securing of these objectives, it would appear that we have no alternative but to increase our atomic capability as rapidly as other considerations make appropriate. In either case, it appears to be imperative to increase as rapidly as possible our general air, ground, and sea strength and that of our allies to a point where we are militarily not so heavily dependent on atomic weapons.

2. As is indicated in Chapter IV, it is important that the United States employ military force only if the necessity for its use is clear and compelling and commends itself to the overwhelming majority of our people. The United States cannot therefore engage in war except as a reaction to aggression of so clear and compelling a nature as to bring the overwhelming majority of our people to accept the use of military force. In the event war comes, our use of force must be to compel the acceptance of our objectives and must be congruent to the range of tasks which we may encounter.

In the event of a general war with the USSR, it must be anticipated that atomic weapons will be used by each side in the manner it deems best suited to accomplish its objectives. In view of our vulnerability to Soviet atomic attack, it has been argued that we might wish to hold our atomic weapons only for retaliation against prior use by the USSR. To be able to do so and still have hope of achieving our objectives, the non-atomic military capabilities of ourselves and our allies would have to be fully developed and the political weaknesses of the Soviet Union fully exploited. In the event of war, however, we could not be sure that we could move toward the attainment of these objectives without the USSR's resorting sooner or later to the use of its atomic weapons. Only if we had overwhelming atomic superiority and obtained command of the air might the USSR be deterred from employing its atomic weapons as we progressed toward the attainment of our objectives.

In the event the USSR develops by 1954 the atomic capability which we now anticipate, it is hardly conceivable that, if war comes, the Soviet leaders would refrain from the use of atomic weapons unless they felt fully confident of attaining their objectives by other means.

In the event we use atomic weapons either in retaliation for their prior use by the USSR or because there is no alternative method by which we can attain our objectives, it is imperative that the strategic and tactical targets against which they are used be appropriate and the manner in which they are used be consistent with those objectives.

It appears to follow from the above that we should produce and stockpile thermonuclear weapons in the event they prove feasible and would add significantly to our net capability. Not enough is yet known of their potentialities to warrant a judgment at this time regarding their use in war to attain our objectives.

3. It has been suggested that we announce that we will not use atomic weapons except in retaliation against the prior use of such weapons by an aggressor. It has been argued that such a declaration would decrease the danger of an atomic attack against the United States and its allies.

In our present situation of relative unpreparedness in conventional weapons, such a declaration would be interpreted by the USSR as an admission of great weakness and by our allies as a clear indication that we intended to abandon them. Furthermore, it is doubtful whether such a declaration would be taken sufficiently seriously by the Kremlin to constitute an important factor in determining whether or not to attack the United States. It is to be anticipated that the Kremlin would weigh the facts of our capability far more heavily than a declaration of what we proposed to do with that capability.

Unless we are prepared to abandon our objectives, we cannot make such a declaration in good faith until we are confident that we will be in a position to attain our objectives without war, or, in the event of war, without recourse to the use of atomic weapons for strategic or tactical purposes.

C. INTERNATIONAL CONTROL OF ATOMIC ENERGY

1. A discussion of certain of the basic considerations involved in securing effective international control is necessary to make clear why the additional objectives discussed in Chapter IX must be secured.

2. No system of international control could prevent the production and use of atomic weapons in the event of a prolonged war. Even the most effective system of international control could, of itself, only provide (a) assurance that atomic weapons had been eliminated from national peacetime armaments and (b) immediate notice of a violation. In essence, an effective international control system would be expected to assure a certain amount of time after notice of violation before atomic weapons could be used in war.

3. The time period between notice of violation and possible use of atomic weapons in war which a control system could be expected to assure depends upon a number of factors.

The dismantling of existing stockpiles of bombs and the destruction of casings and firing mechanisms could by themselves give little assurance of securing time. Casings and firing mechanisms are presumably easy to produce, even surreptitiously, and the assembly of weapons does not take much time.

If existing stocks of fissionable materials were in some way eliminated and the future production of fissionable materials effectively controlled, war could not start with a surprise atomic attack.

In order to assure an appreciable time lag between notice of violation and the time when atomic weapons might be available in quantity, it would be necessary to destroy all plants capable of making large amounts of fissionable material. Such action would, however, require a moratorium on those possible peacetime uses which call for large quantities of fissionable materials.

Effective control over the production and stockpiling of raw materials might further extend the time period which effective international control would assure. Now that the Russians have learned the technique of producing atomic weapons, the time between violation of an international control agreement and production of atomic weapons will be shorter than was estimated in 1946, except possibly in the field of thermonuclear or other new types of weapons.

4. The certainty of notice of violation also depends upon a number of factors. In the absence of good faith, it is to be doubted whether any system

can be designed which will give certainty of notice of violation. International ownership of raw materials and fissionable materials and international ownership and operation of dangerous facilities, coupled with inspection based on continuous unlimited freedom of access to all parts of the Soviet Union (as well as to all parts of the territory of other signatories to the control agreement) appear to be necessary to give the requisite degree of assurance against secret violations. As the Soviet stockpile of fissionable materials grows, the amount which the USSR might secretly withhold and not declare to the inspection agency grows. In this sense, the earlier an agreement is consummated the greater the security it would offer. The possibility of successful secret production operations also increases with developments which may reduce the size and power consumption of individual reactors. The development of a thermonuclear bomb would increase many fold the damage a given amount of fissionable material could do and would, therefore, vastly increase the danger that a decisive advantage could be gained through secret operations.

5. The relative sacrifices which would be involved in international control need also to be considered. If it were possible to negotiate an effective system of international control the United States would presumably sacrifice a much larger stockpile of atomic weapons and a much larger production capacity than would the USSR. The opening up of national territory to international inspection involved in an adequate control and inspection system would have a far greater impact on the USSR than on the United States. If the control system involves the destruction of all large reactors and thus a moratorium on certain possible peacetime uses, the USSR can be expected to argue that it, because of greater need for new sources of energy, would be making a greater sacrifice in this regard than the United States.

6. The United States and the peoples of the world as a whole desire a respite from the dangers of atomic warfare. The chief difficulty lies in the danger that the respite would be short and that we might not have adequate notice of its pending termination. For such an arrangement to be in the interest of the United States, it is essential that the agreement be entered into in good faith by both sides and the probability against its violation high.

7. The most substantial contribution to security of an effective international control system would, of course, be the opening up of the Soviet Union, as required under the UN plan. Such opening up is not, however, compatible with the maintenance of the Soviet system in its present rigor. This is a major reason for the Soviet refusal to accept the UN plan.

The studies which began with the Acheson-Lilienthal committee and culminated in the present UN plan made it clear that inspection of atomic facilities would not alone give the assurance of control; but that ownership and operation by an international authority of the world's atomic energy activities from the mine to the last use of fissionable materials was also essential. The delegation of sovereignty which this implies is necessary for effective control and, therefore, is as necessary for the United States and the rest of the free world as it is presently unacceptable to the Soviet Union.

It is also clear that a control authority not susceptible directly or indirectly to Soviet domination is equally essential. As the Soviet Union would regard any country not under its domination as under the potential if not the actual domination of the United States, it is clear that what the United States and the non-Soviet world must insist on, the Soviet Union at present rejects.

The principal immediate benefit of international control would be to make a surprise atomic attack impossible, assuming the elimination of large reactors and the effective disposal of stockpiles of fissionable materials. But it is almost certain that the Soviet Union would not agree to the elimination of large reactors, unless the impracticability of producing atomic power for peaceful purposes had been demonstrated beyond a doubt. By the same token, it would not now agree to elimination of its stockpile of fissionable materials.

Finally, the absence of good faith on the part of the USSR must be assumed until there is concrete evidence that there has been a decisive change in Soviet policies. It is to be doubted whether such a change can take place without a change in the nature of the Soviet system itself.

The above considerations make it clear that at least a major change in the relative power positions of the United States and the Soviet Union would have to take place before an effective system of international control could be negotiated. The Soviet Union would have had to have moved a substantial distance down the path of accommodation and compromise before such an arrangement would be conceivable. This conclusion is supported by the Third Report of the United Nations Atomic Energy Commission to the Security Council, May 17, 1948, in which it is stated that ". . . the majority of the Commission has been unable to secure . . . their acceptance of the nature and extent of participation in the world community required of all nations in this field. . . . As a result, the Commission has been forced to recognize that agreement on effective measures for the control of atomic energy is itself dependent on cooperation in broader fields of policy."

In short, it is impossible to hope than an effective plan for international control can be negotiated unless and until the Kremlin design has been frustrated to a point at which a genuine and drastic change in Soviet policies has taken place.

IX. Possible Courses of Action

Introduction. Four possible courses of action by the United States in the present situation can be distinguished. They are:

a. Continuation of current policies, with current and currently projected programs for carrying out these policies;

b. Isolation;

c. War; and

d. A more rapid building up of the political, economic, and military strength of the free world than provided under a, with the purpose of reaching, if possible, a tolerable state of order among nations without war and of preparing to defend ourselves in the event that the free world is attacked.

The role of negotiation. Negotiation must be considered in relation to these courses of action. A negotiator always attempts to achieve an agreement which is somewhat better than the realities of his fundamental position would justify and which is, in any case, not worse than his fundamental position requires. This is as true in relations among sovereign states as in relations between individuals. The Soviet Union possesses several advantages over the free world in negotiations on any issue:

a. It can and does enforce secrecy on all significant facts about conditions within the Soviet Union, so that it can be expected to know more about the realities of the free world's position than the free world knows about its position;

b. It does not have to be responsive in any important sense to public opinion;

c. It does not have to consult and agree with any other countries on the terms it will offer and accept; and

d. It can influence public opinion in other countries while insulating the peoples under its control.

These are important advantages. Together with the unfavorable trend of our power position, they militate, as is shown in Section A below, against successful negotiation of a general settlement at this time. For although the United States probably now possesses, principally in atomic weapons, a force adequate to deliver a powerful blow upon the Soviet Union and to open the road to victory in a long war, it is not sufficient by itself to advance the position of the United States in the cold war.

The problem is to create such political and economic conditions in the free world, backed by force sufficient to inhibit Soviet attack, that the Kremlin will accommodate itself to these conditions, gradually withdraw, and eventually change its policies drastically. It has been shown in Chapter VIII that truly effective control of atomic energy would require such an opening up of the Soviet Union and such evidence in other ways of its good faith and its intent to co-exist in peace as to reflect or at least initiate a change in the Soviet system.

Clearly under present circumstances we will not be able to negotiate a settlement which calls for a change in the Soviet system. What, then, is the role of negotiation?

In the first place, the public in the United States and in other free countries will require, as a condition to firm policies and adequate programs directed to the frustration of the Kremlin design, that the free world be continuously prepared to negotiate agreements with the Soviet Union on equitable terms. It is still argued by many people here and abroad that equitable agreements with the Soviet Union are possible, and this view will gain force if the Soviet Union begins to show signs of accommodation, even on unimportant issues.

The free countries must always, therefore, be prepared to negotiate and must be ready to take the initiative at times in seeking negotiation. They must develop a negotiating position which defines the issues and the terms on which they would be prepared—and at what stages—to accept agreements with the Soviet Union. The terms must be fair in the view of popular opinion in the free world. This means that they must be consistent with a positive program for peace—in harmony with the United Nations' Charter and providing, at a minimum, for the effective control of all armaments by the United Nations or a successor organization. The terms must not require more of the Soviet Union than such behavior and such participation in a world organization. The fact that such conduct by the Soviet Union is impossible without such a radical change in Soviet policies as to constitute a change in the Soviet system would then emerge as a result of the Kremlin's unwillingness to accept such terms or of its bad faith in observing them.

A sound negotiating position is, therefore, an essential element in the ideological conflict. For some time after a decision to build up strength, any offer of, or attempt at, negotiation of a general settlement along the lines of the Berkeley speech by the Secretary of State could be only a tactic.[2] Nevertheless, concurrently with a decision and a start on building up the strength of the free world, it may be desirable to pursue this tactic both to gain public support for the program and to minimize the immediate risks of war. It is urgently necessary for the United States to determine its negotiating position and to obtain agreement with its major allies on the purposes and terms of negotiation.

In the second place, assuming that the United States in cooperation with other free countries decides and acts to increase the strength of the free world and assuming that the Kremlin chooses the path of accommodation, it will from time to time be necessary and desirable to negotiate on various specific issues with the Kremlin as the area of possible agreement widens.

The Kremlin will have three major objectives in negotiations with the United States. The first is to eliminate the atomic capabilities of the United States; the second is to prevent the effective mobilization of the superior potential of the free world in human and material resources; and the third is to secure a withdrawal of United States forces from, and commitments to, Europe and Japan. Depending on its evaluation of its own strengths and weaknesses as against the West's (particularly the ability and will of the West to sustain its efforts), it will or will not be prepared to make important concessions to achieve these major objectives. It is unlikely that the Kremlin's evaluation is such that it would now be prepared to make significant concessions.

The objectives of the United States and other free countries in negotiations with the Soviet Union (apart from the ideological objectives discussed above) are to record, in a formal fashion which will facilitate the consolidation and further advance of our position, the process of Soviet accommodation to the new political, psychological, and economic conditions in the world which will result from adoption of the fourth course of action and which will be supported by the increasing military strength developed as an integral part of that course of action. In short, our objectives are to record, where desirable, the gradual withdrawal of the Soviet Union and to facilitate that process by making negotiation, if possible, always more expedient than resort to force.

It must be presumed that for some time the Kremlin will accept agreements only if it is convinced that by acting in bad faith whenever and wherever there is an opportunity to do so with impunity, it can derive greater advantage from the agreements than the free world. For this reason, we must take care that any agreements are enforceable or that they are not susceptible of violation without detection and the possibility of effective countermeasures.

This further suggests that we will have to consider carefully the order in which agreements can be concluded. Agreement on the control of atomic energy would result in a relatively greater disarmament of the United States than of the Soviet Union, even assuming considerable progress in building up the strength of the free world in conventional forces and weapons. It might be accepted by the Soviet Union as part of a deliberate design to move against Western Europe and other areas of strategic importance with conventional forces and weapons. In this event, the United States would find itself at war, having previously disarmed itself in its most important weapon, and would be engaged in a race to redevelop atomic weapons.

This seems to indicate that for the time being the United States and other free countries would have to insist on concurrent agreement on the control of nonatomic forces and weapons and perhaps on the other elements of a general settlement, notably peace treaties with Germany, Austria, and Japan and the withdrawal of Soviet influence from the satellites. If, contrary to our expectations, the Soviet Union should accept agreements promising effective control of atomic energy and conventional armaments, without any other changes in Soviet policies, we would have to consider very carefully whether we could accept such agreements. It is unlikely that this problem will arise.

To the extent that the United States and the rest of the free world succeed in so building up their strength in conventional forces and weapons that a Soviet attack with similar forces could be thwarted or held, we will gain increased flexibility and can seek agreements on the various issues in any order, as they become negotiable.

In the third place, negotiation will play a part in the building up of the strength of the free world, apart from the ideological strength discussed above. This is most evident in the problems of Germany, Austria, and Japan. In the process of building up strength, it may be desirable for the free nations, without the Soviet Union, to conclude separate arrangements with Japan, Western Germany, and Austria which would enlist the energies and resources of these countries in support of the free world. This will be difficult unless it has been demonstrated by attempted negotiation with the Soviet Union that the Soviet Union is not prepared to accept treaties of peace which would leave these countries free, under adequate safeguards, to participate in the United Nations and in regional or broader associations of states consistent with the United Nations' Charter and providing security and adequate opportunities for the peaceful development of their political and economic life.

This demonstrates the importance, from the point of view of negotiation as well as for its relationship to the building up of the strength of the free world (see Section D below), of the problem of closer association—on a regional or a broader basis—among the free countries.

In conclusion, negotiation is not a possible separate course of action but rather a means of gaining support for a program of building strength, of recording, where necessary and desirable, progress in the cold war, and of facilitating further progress while helping to minimize the risks of war. Ultimately, it is our objective to negotiate a settlement with the Soviet Union (or a successor state or states) on which the world can place reliance as an enforceable instrument of peace. But it is important to emphasize that such a settlement can only record the progress which the free world will have made in creating a political and economic system in the world so successful that the frustration of the Kremlin's design for world domination will be complete. The analysis in the following sections indicates that the building of such a system requires expanded and accelerated programs for the carrying out of current policies.

A. THE FIRST COURSE—CONTINUATION OF CURRENT POLICIES,
WITH CURRENT AND CURRENTLY PROJECTED PROGRAMS
FOR CARRYING OUT THESE POLICIES

1. Military aspects. On the basis of current programs, the United States has a large potential military capability but an actual capability which, though improving, is declining relative to the USSR, particularly in light of its probable fission bomb capability and possible thermonuclear bomb capability. The same holds true for the free world as a whole relative to the Soviet world as a whole. If war breaks out in 1950 or in the next few years, the United States and its allies, apart from a powerful atomic blow, will be compelled to conduct delaying actions, while building up their strength for a general offensive. A frank evaluation of the requirements, to defend the United States and its vital interests and to support a vigorous initiative in the cold war, on the one hand, and of present capabilities, on the other, indicates that there is a sharp and growing disparity between them.

A review of Soviet policy shows that the military capabilities, actual and potential, of the United States and the rest of the free world, together with the apparent determination of the free world to resist further Soviet expansion, have not induced the Kremlin to relax its pressures generally or to give up the initiative in the cold war. On the contrary, the Soviet Union has consistently pursued a bold foreign policy, modified only when its probing revealed a determination and an ability of the free world to resist encroachment upon it. The relative military capabilities of the free world are declining, with the result that its determination to resist may also decline and that the security of the United States and the free world as a whole will be jeopardized.

From the military point of view, the actual and potential capabilities of the United States, given a continuation of current and projected programs, will become less and less effective as a war deterrent. Improvement of the state of readiness will become more and more important not only to inhibit the launching of war by the Soviet Union but also to support a national policy designed to reverse the present ominous trends in international relations. A building up of the military capabilities of the United States and the free world is a pre-condition to the achievement of the objectives outlined in this report and to the protection of the United States against disaster.

Fortunately, the United States military establishment has been developed into a unified and effective force as a result of the policies laid down by the Congress and the vigorous carrying out of these policies by the Administration in the fields of both organization and economy. It is, therefore, a base upon which increased strength can be rapidly built with maximum efficiency and economy.

2. Political aspects.   The Soviet Union is pursuing the initiative in the conflict with the free world. Its atomic capabilities, together with its successes in the Far East, have led to an increasing confidence on its part and to an increasing nervousness in Western Europe and the rest of the free world. We cannot be sure, of course, how vigorously the Soviet Union will pursue its initiative, nor can we be sure of the strength or weakness of the other free countries in reacting to it. There are, however, ominous signs of further deterioration in the Far East. There are also some indications that a decline in morale and confidence in Western Europe may be expected. In particular, the situation in Germany is unsettled. Should the belief or suspicion spread that the free nations are not now able to prevent the Soviet Union from taking, if it chooses, the military actions outlined in Chapter V, the determination of the free countries to resist probably would lessen and there would be an increasing temptation for them to seek a position of neutrality.

Politically, recognition of the military implications of a continuation of present trends will mean that the United States and especially other free countries will tend to shift to the defensive, or to follow a dangerous policy of bluff, because the maintenance of a firm initiative in the cold war is closely related to aggregate strength in being and readily available.

This is largely a problem of the incongruity of the current actual capabilities of the free world and the threat to it, for the free world has an economic and military potential far superior to the potential of the Soviet Union and its satellites. The shadow of Soviet force falls darkly on Western Europe and Asia and supports a policy of encroachment. The free world lacks adequate means—in the form of forces in being—to thwart such expansion locally. The United States will therefore be confronted more frequently with the dilemma of reacting totally to a limited extension of Soviet control or of not reacting at all (except with ineffectual protests and half measures). Continuation of present trends is likely to lead, therefore, to a gradual withdrawal under the direct or indirect pressure of the Soviet Union, until we discover one day that we have sacrificed positions of vital interest. In other words, the United States would have chosen, by lack of the necessary decisions and actions, to fall back to isolation in the Western Hemisphere. This course would at best result in only a relatively brief truce and would be ended either by our capitulation or by a defensive war—on unfavorable terms from unfavorable positions—against a Soviet Empire compromising all or most of Eurasia. (See Section B.)

3. Economic and social aspects. As was pointed out in Chapter VI, the present foreign economic policies and programs of the United States will not produce a solution to the problem of international economic equilibrium, notably the problem of the dollar gap, and will not create an economic base conducive to political stability in many important free countries.

The European Recovery Program has been successful in assisting the restoration and expansion of production in Western Europe and has been a major factor in checking the dry rot of Communism in Western Europe. However, little progress has been made toward the resumption by Western Europe of a position of influence in world affairs commensurate with its potential strength. Progress in this direction will require integrated political, economic, and military policies and programs, which are supported by the United States and the Western European countries and which will probably require a deeper participation by the United States than has been contemplated.

The Point IV Program and other assistance programs will not adequately supplement, as now projected, the efforts of other important countries to develop effective institutions, to improve the administration of their affairs, and to achieve a sufficient measure of economic development. The moderate regimes now in power in many countries, like India, Indonesia, Pakistan, and the Philippines, will probably be unable to restore or retain their popular support and authority unless they are assisted in bringing about a more rapid improvement of the economic and social structure than present programs will make possible.

The Executive Branch is now undertaking a study of the problem of the United States balance of payments and of the measures which might be taken by the United States to assist in establishing international economic equilibrium. This is a very important project and work on it should have a high priority. However, unless such an economic program is matched and supplemented by an equally far-sighted and vigorous political and military program, we will not be successful in checking and rolling back the Kremlin's drive.

4. Negotiation. In short, by continuing along its present course the free world will not succeed in making effective use of its vastly superior political, economic, and military potential to build a tolerable state of order among nations. On the contrary, the political, economic, and military situation of the free world is already unsatisfactory and will become less favorable unless we act to reverse present trends.

This situation is one which militates against successful negotiations with the Kremlin—for the terms of agreements on important pending issues would reflect present realities and would therefore be unacceptable, if not disastrous, to the United States and the rest of the free world. Unless a decision had been made and action undertaken to build up the strength, in the broadest sense, of the United States and the free world, an attempt to negotiate a general settlement on terms acceptable to us would be ineffective and probably long drawn out, and might thereby seriously delay the necessary measures to build up our strength.

This is true despite the fact that the United States now has the capability of delivering a powerful blow against the Soviet Union in the event of war, for one of the present realities is that the United States is not prepared to threaten the use of our present atomic superiority to coerce the Soviet Union into acceptable agreements. In light of present trends, the Soviet Union will not withdraw and the only conceivable basis for a general settlement would be spheres of influence and of no influence—a "settlement" which the Kremlin could readily exploit to its great advantage. The idea that Germany or Japan or other important areas can exist as islands of neutrality in a divided world is unreal, given the Kremlin design for world domination.

B. THE SECOND COURSE—ISOLATION

Continuation of present trends, it has been shown above, will lead progressively to the withdrawal of the United States from most of its present commitments in Europe and Asia and to our isolation in the Western Hemisphere and its approaches. This would result not from a conscious decision but from a failure to take the actions necessary to bring our capabilities into line with our commitments and thus to a withdrawal under pressure. This pressure might come from our present Allies, who will tend to seek other "solutions" unless they have confidence in our determination to accelerate our efforts to build a successfully functioning political and economic system in the free world.

There are some who advocate a deliberate decision to isolate ourselves. Superficially, this has some attractiveness as a course of action, for it appears to bring our commitments and capabilities into harmony by reducing the former and by concentrating our present, or perhaps even reduced, military expenditures on the defense of the United States.

This argument overlooks the relativity of capabilities. With the United States in an isolated position, we would have to face the probability that the

Soviet Union would quickly dominate most of Eurasia, probably without meeting armed resistance. It would thus acquire a potential far superior to our own, and would promptly proceed to develop this potential with the purpose of eliminating our power, which would, even in isolation, remain as a challenge to it and as an obstacle to the imposition of its kind of order in the world. There is no way to make ourselves inoffensive to the Kremlin except by complete submission to its will. Therefore isolation would in the end condemn us to capitulate or to fight alone and on the defensive, with drastically limited offensive and retaliatory capabilities in comparison with the Soviet Union. (These are the only possibilities, unless we are prepared to risk the future on the hazard that the Soviet Empire, because of over-extension or other reasons, will spontaneously destroy itself from within.)

The argument also overlooks the imponderable, but nevertheless drastic, effects on our belief in ourselves and in our way of life of a deliberate decision to isolate ourselves. As the Soviet Union came to dominate free countries, it is clear that many Americans would feel a deep sense of responsibility and guilt for having abandoned their former friends and allies. As the Soviet Union mobilized the resources of Eurasia, increased its relative military capabilities, and heightened its threat to our security, some would be tempted to accept "peace" on its terms, while many would seek to defend the United States by creating a regimented system which would permit the assignment of a tremendous part of our resources to defense. Under such a state of affairs our national morale would be corrupted and the integrity and vitality of our system subverted.

Under this course of action, there would be no negotiation, unless on the Kremlin's terms, for we would have given up everything of importance.

It is possible that at some point in the course of isolation, many Americans would come to favor a surprise attack on the Soviet Union and the area under its control, in a desperate attempt to alter decisively the balance of power by an overwhelming blow with modern weapons of mass destruction. It appears unlikely that the Soviet Union would wait for such an attack before launching one of its own. But even if it did and even if our attack were successful, it is clear that the United States would face appalling tasks in establishing a tolerable state of order among nations after such a war and after Soviet occupation of all or most of Eurasia for some years. These tasks appear so enormous and success so unlikely that reason dictates an attempt to achieve our objectives by other means.

C. THE THIRD COURSE—WAR

Some Americans favor a deliberate decision to go to war against the Soviet Union in the near future. It goes without saying that the idea of "preventive" war—in the sense of a military attack not provoked by a military attack upon us or our allies—is generally unacceptable to Americans. Its supporters argue that since the Soviet Union is in fact at war with the free world now and that since the failure of the Soviet Union to use all-out military force is explainable on grounds of expediency, we are at war and should conduct ourselves accordingly. Some further argue that the free world is probably unable, except under the crisis of war, to mobilize and direct its resources to the checking and rolling back of the Kremlin's drive for world dominion. This is a powerful argument in the light of history, but the considerations against war are so compelling that the free world must demonstrate that this argument is wrong. The case for war is premised on the assumption that the United States could launch and sustain an attack of sufficient impact to gain a decisive advantage for the free world in a long war and perhaps to win an early decision.

The ability of the United States to launch effective offensive operations is now limited to attack with atomic weapons. A powerful blow could be delivered upon the Soviet Union, but it is estimated that these operations alone would not force or induce the Kremlin to capitulate and that the Kremlin would still be able to use the forces under its control to dominate most or all of Eurasia. This would probably mean a long and difficult struggle during which the free institutions of Western Europe and many freedom-loving people would be destroyed and the regenerative capacity of Western Europe dealt a crippling blow.

Apart from this, however, a surprise attack upon the Soviet Union, despite the provocativeness of recent Soviet behavior, would be repugnant to many Americans. Although the American people would probably rally in support of the war effort, the shock of responsibility for a surprise attack would be morally corrosive. Many would doubt that it was a "just war" and that all reasonable possibilities for a peaceful settlement had been explored in good faith. Many more, proportionately, would hold such views in other countries, particularly in Western Europe and particularly after Soviet occupation, if only because the Soviet Union would liquidate articulate opponents. It would, therefore, be difficult after such a war to create a satisfactory international order among nations. Victory in such a war would have brought us little if at all closer to victory in the fundamental ideological conflict.

These considerations are no less weighty because they are imponderable, and they rule out an attack unless it is demonstrably in the nature of a counter-attack to a blow which is on its way or about to be delivered. (The military advantages of landing the first blow become increasingly important with modern weapons, and this is a fact which requires us to be on the alert in order to strike with our full weight as soon as we are attacked, and, if possible, before the Soviet blow is actually delivered.) If the argument of Chapter IV is accepted, it follows that there is no "easy" solution and that the only sure victory lies in the frustration of the Kremlin design by the steady development of the moral and material strength of the free world and its projection into the Soviet world in such a way as to bring about an internal change in the Soviet system.

D. THE REMAINING COURSE OF ACTION——A RAPID BUILD-UP
OF POLITICAL, ECONOMIC, AND MILITARY STRENGTH
IN THE FREE WORLD

A more rapid build-up of political, economic, and military strength and thereby of confidence in the free world than is now contemplated is the only course which is consistent with progress toward achieving our fundamental purpose. The frustration of the Kremlin design requires the free world to develop a successfully functioning political and economic system and a vigorous political offensive against the Soviet Union. These, in turn, require an adequate military shield under which they can develop. It is necessary to have the military power to deter, if possible, Soviet expansion, and to defeat, if necessary, aggressive Soviet or Soviet-directed actions of a limited or total character. The potential strength of the free world is great; its ability to develop these military capabilities and its will to resist Soviet expansion will be determined by the wisdom and will with which it undertakes to meet its political and economic problems.

1. Military aspects.   It has been indicated in Chapter VI that U.S. military capabilities are strategically more defensive in nature than offensive and are more potential than actual. It is evident, from an analysis of the past and of the trend of weapon development, that there is now and will be in the future no absolute defense. The history of war also indicates that a favorable decision can only be achieved through offensive action. Even a defensive strategy, if it is to be successful, calls not only for defensive forces to hold vital positions while mobilizing and preparing for the offensive, but also for offensive forces to attack the enemy and keep him off balance.

The two fundamental requirements which must be met by forces in being or readily available are support of foreign policy and protection against disaster. To meet the second requirement, the forces in being or readily available must be able, at a minimum, to perform certain basic tasks:

a. To defend the Western Hemisphere and essential allied areas in order that their war-making capabilities can be developed;

b. To provide and protect a mobilization base while the offensive forces required for victory are being built up;

c. To conduct offensive operations to destroy vital elements of the Soviet war-making capacity, and to keep the enemy off balance until the full offensive strength of the United States and its allies can be brought to bear;

d. To defend and maintain the lines of communication and base areas necessary to the execution of the above tasks; and

e. To provide such aid to allies as is essential to the execution of their role in the above tasks.

In the broadest terms, the ability to perform these tasks requires a build-up of military strength by the United States and its allies to a point at which the combined strength will be superior for at least these tasks, both initially and throughout a war, to the forces that can be brought to bear by the Soviet Union and its satellites. In specific terms, it is not essential to match item for item with the Soviet Union, but to provide an adequate defense against air attack on the United States and Canada and an adequate defense against air and surface attack on the United Kingdom and Western Europe, Alaska, the Western Pacific, Africa, and the Near and Middle East, and on the long lines of communication to these areas. Furthermore, it is mandatory that in building up our strength, we enlarge upon our technical superiority by an accelerated exploitation of the scientific potential of the United States and our allies.

Forces of this size and character are necessary not only for protection against disaster but also to support our foreign policy. In fact, it can be argued that larger forces in being and readily available are necessary to inhibit a would-be aggressor than to provide the nucleus of strength and the mobilization base on which the tremendous forces required for victory can be built. For example, in both World Wars I and II the ultimate victors had the strength, in the end, to win though they had not had the strength in being or readily available to prevent the outbreak of war. In part, at least, this was because they had not had the military strength on which to base a strong foreign policy. At any rate, it is clear that a substantial and rapid building up of strength in the free world is necessary to support a firm policy intended to check and to roll back the Kremlin's drive for world domination.

Moreover, the United States and the other free countries do not now have the forces in being and readily available to defeat local Soviet moves with local action, but must accept reverses or make these local moves the occasion for war—for which we are not prepared. This situation makes for great uneasiness among our allies, particularly in Western Europe, for whom total war means, initially, Soviet occupation. Thus, unless our combined strength is rapidly increased, our allies will tend to become increasingly reluctant to support a firm foreign policy on our part and increasingly anxious to seek other solutions, even though they are aware that appeasement means defeat. An important advantage in adopting the fourth course of action lies in its psychological impact—the revival of confidence and hope in the future. It is recognized, of course, that any announcement of the recommended course of action could be exploited by the Soviet Union in its peace campaign and would have adverse psychological effects in certain parts of the free world until the necessary increase in strength has been achieved. Therefore, in any announcement of policy and in the character of the measures adopted, emphasis should be given to the essentially defensive character and care should be taken to minimize, so far as possible, unfavorable domestic and foreign reactions.

2. Political and economic aspects.   The immediate objectives—to the achievement of which such a build-up of strength is a necessary though not a sufficient condition—are a renewed initiative in the cold war and a situation to which the Kremlin would find it expedient to accommodate itself, first by relaxing tensions and pressures and then by gradual withdrawal. The United States cannot alone provide the resources required for such a build-up of strength. The other free countries must carry their part of the burden, but their ability and determination to do it will depend on the action the United States takes to develop its own strength and on the adequacy of its foreign political and economic policies. Improvement in political and economic conditions in the free world, as has been emphasized above, is necessary as a basis for building up the will and the means to resist and for dynamically affirming the integrity and vitality of our free and democratic way of life on which our ultimate victory depends.

At the same time, we should take dynamic steps to reduce the power and influence of the Kremlin inside the Soviet Union and other areas under its control. The objective would be the establishment of friendly regimes not under Kremlin domination. Such action is essential to engage the Kremlin's attention, keep it off balance, and force an increased expenditure of Soviet resources in counteraction. In other words, it would be the current Soviet cold war technique used against the Soviet Union.

A program for rapidly building up strength and improving political and economic conditions will place heavy demands on our courage and intelligence; it will be costly; it will be dangerous. But half-measures will be more costly and more dangerous, for they will be inadequate to prevent and may actually invite war. Budgetary considerations will need to be subordinated to the stark fact that our very independence as a nation may be at stake.

A comprehensive and decisive program to win the peace and frustrate the Kremlin design should be so designed that it can be sustained for as long as necessary to achieve our national objectives. It would probably involve:

1. The development of an adequate political and economic framework for the achievement of our long-range objectives.

2. A substantial increase in expenditures for military purposes adequate to meet the requirements for the tasks listed in Section D-1.

3. A substantial increase in military assistance programs, designed to foster cooperative efforts, which will adequately and efficiently meet the requirements of our allies for the tasks referred to in Section D-1-e.

4. Some increase in economic assistance programs and recognition of the need to continue these programs until their purposes have been accomplished.

5. A concerted attack on the problem of the United States balance of payments, along the lines already approved by the President.

6. Development of programs designed to build and maintain confidence among other peoples in our strength and resolution, and to wage overt psychological warfare calculated to encourage mass defections from Soviet allegiance and to frustrate the Kremlin design in other ways.

7. Intensification of affirmative and timely measures and operations by covert means in the fields of economic warfare and political and psychological warfare with a view to fomenting and supporting unrest and revolt in selected strategic satellite countries.

8. Development of internal security and civilian defense programs.

9. Improvement and intensification of intelligence activities.

10. Reduction of Federal expenditures for purposes other than defense and foreign assistance, if necessary by the deferment of certain desirable programs.

11. Increased taxes.

Essential as prerequisites to the success of this program would be (a) consultations with Congressional leaders designed to make the program the object of non-partisan legislative support, and (b) a presentation to the public of a full explanation of the facts and implications of present international trends.

The program will be costly, but it is relevant to recall the disproportion between the potential capabilities of the Soviet and non-Soviet worlds (cf. Chapters V and VI). The Soviet Union is currently devoting about 40 percent of available resources (gross national product plus reparations, equal in 1949 to about $65 billion) to military expenditures (14 percent) and to investment

(26 percent), much of which is in war-supporting industries. In an emergency the Soviet Union could increase the allocation of resources to these purposes to about 50 percent, or by one-fourth.

The United States is currently devoting about 22 percent of its gross national product ($255 billion in 1949) to military expenditures (6 percent), foreign assistance (2 percent), and investment (14 percent), little of which is in war-supporting industries. (As was pointed out in Chapter V, the "fighting value" obtained per dollar of expenditure by the Soviet Union considerably exceeds that obtained by the United States, primarily because of the extremely low military and civilian living standards in the Soviet Union.) In an emergency the United States could devote upward of 50 percent of its gross national product to these purposes (as it did during the last war), an increase of several times present expenditures for direct and indirect military purposes and foreign assistance.

From the point of view of the economy as a whole, the program might not result in a real decrease in the standard of living, for the economic effects of the program might be to increase the gross national product by more than the amount being absorbed for additional military and foreign assistance purposes. One of the most significant lessons of our World War II experience was that the American economy, when it operates at a level approaching full efficiency, can provide enormous resources for purposes other than civilian consumption while simultaneously providing a high standard of living. After allowing for price changes, personal consumption expenditures rose by about one-fifth between 1939 and 1944, even though the economy had in the meantime increased the amount of resources going into Government use by $60–$65 billion (in 1939 prices).

This comparison between the potentials of the Soviet Union and the United States also holds true for the Soviet world and the free world and is of fundamental importance in considering the courses of action open to the United States.

The comparison gives renewed emphasis to the fact that the problems faced by the free countries in their efforts to build a successfully functioning system lie not so much in the field of economics as in the field of politics. The building of such a system may require more rapid progress toward the closer association of the free countries in harmony with the concept of the United Nations. It is clear that our long-range objectives require a strengthened United Nations, or a successor organization, to which the world can look for the maintenance of peace and order in a system based on freedom and justice. It also seems clear that a unifying ideal of this kind might awaken and arouse the latent spiritual energies of free men everywhere and obtain their enthusiastic support for a positive program for peace going far beyond the frustration of the Kremlin design and opening vistas to the future that would outweigh short-run sacrifices.

The threat to the free world involved in the development of the Soviet Union's atomic and other capabilities will rise steadily and rather rapidly. For the time being, the United States possesses a marked atomic superiority over the Soviet Union which, together with the potential capabilities of the United States and other free countries in other forces and weapons, inhibits aggressive Soviet action. This provides an opportunity for the United States, in cooperation with other free countries, to launch a build-up of strength which will support a firm policy directed to the frustration of the Kremlin design. The immediate goal of our efforts to build a successfully functioning political and economic system in the free world backed by adequate military strength is to postpone and avert the disastrous situation which, in light of the Soviet Union's probable fission bomb capability and possible thermonuclear bomb capability, might arise in 1954 on a continuation of our present programs. By acting promptly and vigorously in such a way that this date is, so to speak, pushed into the future, we would permit time for the process of accommodation, withdrawal and frustration to produce the necessary changes in the Soviet system. Time is short, however, and the risks of war attendant upon a decision to build up strength will steadily increase the longer we defer it.

CONCLUSIONS AND RECOMMENDATIONS

Conclusions

The foregoing analysis indicates that the probable fission bomb capability and possible thermonuclear bomb capability of the Soviet Union have greatly intensified the Soviet threat to the security of the United States. This threat is of the same character as that described in NSC 20/4 (approved by the President on November 24, 1948) but is more immediate than had previously been estimated. In particular, the United States now faces the contingency that within the next four or five years the Soviet Union will possess the military capability of delivering a surprise atomic attack of such weight that the United States must have substantially increased general air, ground, and sea strength, atomic capabilities, and air and civilian defenses to deter war and to provide reasonable assurance, in the event of war, that it could survive the initial blow and go on to the eventual attainment of its objectives. In return, this contingency requires the intensification of our efforts in the fields of intelligence and research and development.

Allowing for the immediacy of the danger, the following statement of Soviet threats, contained in NSC 20/4, remains valid:

14. The gravest threat to the security of the United States within the foreseeable future stems from the hostile designs and formidable power of the USSR, and from the nature of the Soviet system.

15. The political, economic, and psychological warfare which the USSR is now waging has dangerous potentialities for weakening the relative world position of the United States and disrupting its traditional institutions by means short of war, unless sufficient resistance is encountered in the policies of this and other non-communist countries.

16. The risk of war with the USSR is sufficient to warrant, in common prudence, timely and adequate preparation by the United States.

a. Even though present estimates indicate that the Soviet leaders probably do not intend deliberate armed action involving the United States at this time, the possibility of such deliberate resort to war cannot be ruled out.

b. Now and for the foreseeable future there is a continuing danger that war will arise either through Soviet miscalculation of the determination of the United States to use all the means at its command to safeguard its security, through Soviet misinterpretation of our intentions, or through U.S. miscalculation of Soviet reactions to measures which we might take.

17. Soviet domination of the potential power of Eurasia, whether achieved by armed aggression or by political and subversive means, would be strategically and politically unacceptable to the United States.

18. The capability of the United States either in peace or in the event of war to cope with threats to its security or to gain its objectives would be severely weakened by internal development, important among which are:

a. Serious espionage, subversion and sabotage, particularly by concerted and well-directed communist activity.

b. Prolonged or exaggerated economic instability.

c. Internal political and social disunity.

d. Inadequate or excessive armament or foreign aid expenditures.

e. An excessive or wasteful usage of our resources in time of peace.

f. Lessening of U.S. prestige and influence through vacillation or appeasement or lack of skill and imagination in the conduct of its foreign policy or by shirking world responsibilities.

g. Development of a false sense of security through a deceptive change in Soviet tactics.

Although such developments as those indicated in paragraph 18 above would severely weaken the capability of the United States and its allies to cope with the Soviet threat to their security, considerable progress has been made since 1948 in laying the foundation upon which adequate strength can now be rapidly built.

The analysis also confirms that our objectives with respect to the Soviet Union, in time of peace as well as in time of war, as stated in NSC 20/4 (para. 19), are still valid, as are the aims and measures stated therein (paras. 20 and 21). Our current security programs and strategic plans are based upon these objectives, aims, and measures:

19.

a. To reduce the power and influence of the USSR to limits which no longer constitute a threat to the peace, national independence, and stability of the world family of nations.

b. To bring about a basic change in the conduct of international relations by the government in power in Russia, to conform with the purposes and principles set forth in the UN Charter.

In pursuing these objectives, due care must be taken to avoid permanently impairing our economy and the fundamental values and institutions inherent in our way of life.

20. We should endeavor to achieve our general objectives by methods short of war through the pursuit of the following aims:

a. To encourage and promote the gradual retraction of undue Russian power and influence from the present perimeter areas around traditional Russian boundaries and the emergence of the satellite countries as entities independent of the USSR.

b. To encourage the development among the Russian peoples of attitudes which may help to modify current Soviet behavior and permit a revival of the national life of groups evidencing the ability and determination to achieve and maintain national independence.

c. To eradicate the myth by which people remote from Soviet military influence are held in a position of subservience to Moscow and to cause the world at large to see and understand the true nature of the USSR and the Soviet-directed world communist party, and to adopt a logical and realistic attitude toward them.

d. To create situations which will compel the Soviet Government to recognize the practical undesirability of acting on the basis of its present concepts and the necessity of behaving in accordance with precepts of international conduct, as set forth in the purposes and principles of the UN Charter.

21. Attainment of these aims requires that the United States:

a. Develop a level of military readiness which can be maintained as long as necessary as a deterrent to Soviet aggression, as indispensable support to our political attitude toward the USSR, as a source of encouragement to nations resisting Soviet political aggression, and as an adequate basis for immediate military commitments and for rapid mobilization should war prove unavoidable.

b. Assure the internal security of the United States against dangers of sabotage, subversion, and espionage.

c. Maximize our economic potential, including the strengthening of our peacetime economy and the establishment of essential reserves readily available in the event of war.

d. Strengthen the orientation toward the United States of the non-Soviet nations; and help such of those nations as are able and willing to make an important contribution to U.S. security, to increase their economic and political stability and their military capability.

e. Place the maximum strain on the Soviet structure of power and particularly on the relationships between Moscow and the satellite countries.

f. Keep the U.S. public fully informed and cognizant of the threats to our national security so that it will be prepared to support the measures which we must accordingly adopt.

In the light of present and prospective Soviet atomic capabilities, the action which can be taken under present programs and plans, however, becomes dangerously inadequate, in both timing and scope, to accomplish the rapid progress toward the attainment of the United States political, economic, and military objectives which is now imperative.

A continuation of present trends would result in a serious decline in the strength of the free world relative to the Soviet Union and its satellites. This unfavorable trend arises from the inadequacy of current programs and plans rather than from any error in our objectives and aims. These trends lead in the direction of isolation, not by deliberate decision but by lack of the necessary basis for a vigorous initiative in the conflict with the Soviet Union.

Our position as the center of power in the free world places a heavy responsibility upon the United States for leadership. We must organize and enlist the energies and resources of the free world in a positive program for peace which will frustrate the Kremlin design for world domination by creating a situation in the free world to which the Kremlin will be compelled to adjust. Without such a cooperative effort, led by the United States, we will have to make gradual withdrawals under pressure until we discover one day that we have sacrificed positions of vital interest.

It is imperative that this trend be reversed by a much more rapid and concerted build-up of the actual strength of both the United States and the other nations of the free world. The analysis shows that this will be costly and will involve significant domestic financial and economic adjustments.

The execution of such a build-up, however, requires that the United States have an affirmative program beyond the solely defensive one of countering the threat posed by the Soviet Union. This program must light the path to peace and order among nations in a system based on freedom and justice, as contemplated in the Charter of the United Nations. Further, it must envisage the political and economic measures with which and the military shield behind which the free world can work to frustrate the Kremlin design by the strategy of the cold war; for every consideration of devotion to our fundamental values and to our national security demands that we achieve our objectives by the strategy of the cold war, building up our military strength in order that it may not have to be used. The only sure victory lies in the frustration of the Kremlin design by the steady development of the moral and material strength of the free world and its projection into the Soviet world in such a way as to bring about an internal change in the Soviet system. Such a positive program—harmonious with our fundamental national purpose and our objectives—is necessary if we are to regain and retain the initiative and to win and hold the necessary popular support and cooperation in the United States and the rest of the free world.

This program should include a plan for negotiation with the Soviet Union, developed and agreed with our allies and which is consonant with our objectives. The United States and its allies, particularly the United Kingdom and France, should always be ready to negotiate with the Soviet Union on terms consistent with our objectives. The present world situation, however, is one which militates against successful negotiations with the Kremlin—for the terms of agreements on important pending issues would reflect present realities and would therefore be unacceptable, if not disastrous, to the United States and the rest of the free world. After a decision and a start on building up the strength of the free world has been made, it might then be desirable for the United States to take an initiative in seeking negotiations in the hope that it might facilitate the process of accommodation by the Kremlin to the new situation. Failing that, the unwillingness of the Kremlin to accept equitable terms or its bad faith in observing them would assist in consolidating popular opinion in the free world in support of the measures necessary to sustain the build-up.

In summary, we must, by means of a rapid and sustained build-up of the political, economic, and military strength of the free world, and by means of an affirmative program intended to wrest the initiative from the Soviet

Union, confront it with convincing evidence of the determination and ability of the free world to frustrate the Kremlin design of a world dominated by its will. Such evidence is the only means short of war which eventually may force the Kremlin to abandon its present course of action and to negotiate acceptable agreements on issues of major importance.

The whole success of the proposed program hangs ultimately on recognition by this Government, the American people, and all free peoples, that the cold war is in fact a real war in which the survival of the free world is at stake. Essential prerequisites to success are consultations with Congressional leaders designed to make the program the object of non-partisan legislative support, and a presentation to the public of a full explanation of the facts and implications of the present international situation. The prosecution of the program will require of us all the ingenuity, sacrifice, and unity demanded by the vital importance of the issue and the tenacity to persevere until our national objectives have been attained.

Recommendations

That the President:

a. Approve the foregoing Conclusions.

b. Direct the National Security Council, under the continuing direction of the President, and with the participation of other Departments and Agencies as appropriate, to coordinate and insure the implementation of the Conclusions herein on an urgent and continuing basis for as long as necessary to achieve our objectives. For this purpose, representatives of the member Departments and Agencies, the Joint Chiefs of Staff or their deputies, and other Departments and Agencies as required should be constituted as a revised and strengthened staff organization under the National Security Council to develop coordinated programs for consideration by the National Security Council.

NOTES

[1] Marshal Tito, the Communist leader of Yugoslavia, broke away from the Soviet bloc in 1948.

[2] The Secretary of State listed seven areas in which the Soviet Union could modify its behavior in such a way as to permit co-existence in reasonable security. These were:

1. Treaties of peace with Austria, Germany, Japan and relaxation of pressures in the Far East;

2. Withdrawal of Soviet forces and influence from satellite area;

3. Cooperation in the United Nations;

4. Control of atomic energy and of conventional armaments;

5. Abandonment of indirect aggression;

6. Proper treatment of official representatives of the U.S.;

7. Increased access to the Soviet Union of persons and ideas from other countries. [Footnote in the source text. For the text of the address delivered by Secretary Acheson at the University of California, Berkeley, on March 16, 1950, concerning United States–Soviet relations, see Department of State *Bulletin,* March 27, 1950, pp. 473–478.]

PART TWO

Commentaries

1

Biases, Official and Scholarly

Some art galleries are designed around ramps. The Guggenheim in New York and the Hirshhorn in Washington are two. The visitor circles upward, viewing a painting first from below left, then front on, then from above right, and last from a distance, looking down. Sometimes, as a result, a viewer gets a better understanding of a work than by seeing it just in one plane. The commentaries included here are intended to give you something akin to this experience as you try to understand NSC 68.

Chapters 2 and 3 contain commentaries from Truman administration officials George Kennan, Dean Acheson, and Paul Nitze as well as officials from later administrations. Through these retrospective comments, you can see the document with the eyes of persons primarily interested in what happens—in the *consequences* of policy choices. Because of differences not only in angles of vision but in policy preferences, these former officials give differing readings of what NSC 68 intended and accomplished.

The commentaries in Chapter 4 come from specialists on U.S. foreign policy. Their common objective is *explanation* of the origins of NSC 68 and its immediate impact. These scholars deal with the identical document yet their opinions differ so widely that a reader could reasonably react as President Kennedy did once to a briefing on Vietnam. The briefers were a general and a diplomat, both just back from Saigon. After hearing first one, then the other, Kennedy asked, "Were you two gentlemen in the same country?"[1]

That students of U.S. foreign policy arrive at differing interpretations of NSC 68 is partly evidence of the power of premises, for each essay—like any exercise in historical reconstruction—has an underpinning of basic assumptions about why humans and societies behave as they do. These assumptions are rarely stated. They have to be inferred. But if you take the time, you will notice wide divergences in scholars' premises about, for example, paramount human drives, with some scholars seeing will to power foremost, others greed, and still others beliefs or ideas.

Chapters 5 and 6 present commentaries from scholars who are not specialists in U.S. foreign policy and who place the document in differing contexts. One sets it in the history of American domestic politics, another looks at it as a text in American intellectual history. A third approaches it as a cultural historian, focusing on the language of the document. Another scholar asks what should be said about NSC 68 as a document not just in American history but in modern world history. Yet another comments from the vantage point of a political scientist, concerned with how the document speaks to issues in the theory of international relations. These commentaries indicate what widely varying *significance* the document can be given, depending on the context in which it is viewed.

Finally, Chapter 7 contains commentaries from scholars located in other lands—Great Britain, Germany, Norway, Russia, and China. These commentaries illustrate differences due to *perspective*. Choices by the U.S. government affect many people other than Americans. Consequences seem different if viewed from the receiving end. In an affected person's national history, an American policy document may have significance quite different from that in America's own history or politics. (Russia, we are told, felt the strongest effect from NSC 68 not when it was adopted in Washington in 1950 but a quarter-century later, in 1977, when it was declassified and published. Russian leaders used it as a brief for their own heavy spending on defense!)

Walking the ramp up to, past, and beyond NSC 68, you should keep in mind these four different approaches. It is one thing to ask about a document's intentions and consequences. It is another to ask about underlying motivations or causes. It is yet another to ask how it fits into some broader landscape. And all three questions invite different answers if the vantage point is foreign.

To think not about differences among these four groups of commentators but about differences *within* each group, you can do worse than to start with the street question "Where is this person coming from?" What, in other words, are the person's biases, political or personal?

The question concerning political or policy bias has two levels. The bias can relate to a *current policy concern* or it can relate to a *past policy concern*.

In the next two chapters, commentaries by former officials provide illustrations. As you read the recollections of Kennan and Acheson, remember that they were written at the height of the Vietnam War. When reading those of Nitze, remember that they were written almost a decade later, at a time when Nitze was leading a public campaign against the defense policies of President Jimmy Carter.

After-the-fact accounts by Kennan, Acheson, and Nitze also refight contests of 1950. Each does so in some degree to his own advantage. In retrospect, Kennan criticizes NSC 68 more sharply than he did at the time. He says that *his* containment ideas, enunciated in the "long telegram," the "X" articles, and NSC 20/4, had the goal of *"creating* strength in the West rather than *destroying* strength in Russia." NSC 68, he charges, shifted focus to a "chimera"—a Russian " 'grand design' . . . for the early destruction of American power and for world conquest."

Acheson is politely scornful of criticisms such as Kennan's. While Acheson does not argue that there actually was an imminent military threat, he provides an explanation of why it was useful to have a document warning of such a threat. It was needed to "bludgeon the mass mind of 'top government.' "

Nitze by contrast defends the specific content of NSC 68. He concedes that intelligence estimates overstated Red Army readiness. He says, however, that they were the best estimates available at the time and that, in any case, the error was insignificant. Subsequent history, he asserts, shows NSC 68's diagnosis to have been right. Western military power would not have been a match for the Soviet Union's without the buildup that NSC 68 advocated. Nitze also disputes Acheson's description of the document's purpose. NSC 68 was not designed for exhortation, Nitze says; it was effective because of the "substance of its analysis."[2]

These recollections are intended both to illuminate and to persuade. Each writer obviously hopes that the student of history will come away seeing truth as he or she sees it—and recognizing that the writer is the hero of the tale.

Current and past policy concerns figure also in retrospective comments by former officials not involved in creating NSC 68. Those in Chapter 3 come from Robert R. Bowie, who was Nitze's successor in the State Department; Carl Kaysen, onetime deputy national security assistant to President Kennedy; Robert Blackwill, National Security Council aide for Presidents Carter and Bush; and—with a special vantage point—Georgi Kornienko, longtime American expert in the Soviet Foreign Ministry. Written specifically for this volume, all the essays show, in some degree, concern about policy issues of the early 1990s. All are also affected by concerns from the past—Bowie's from the 1950s, Kaysen's from the 1960s, Blackwill's from the late phases of the cold war; and Kornienko's—by analyzing Washington for Soviet leaders—from Stalin's time to Gorbachev's.

To say this is not to impeach the testimony or commentaries from these former officials. Each is a person not only of broad experience but of formidable mind. Research libraries contain millions of pages written by former officeholders. In only a tiny percentage will one find words chosen with an exactitude and conscientiousness comparable to that of Kennan, Acheson, Nitze, Bowie, Kaysen, Blackwill, and Kornienko. The fact that what they write shows marks of policy concerns, present and past, is merely proof that such concern is nearly always evident when men or women accustomed to action turn to reconstructing history. As you use such reconstructions, just keep in mind that they are subject to that built-in bias.

You also need to remain alert for what the French call "professional deformation." Kennan was a diplomat for more than twenty years. After retiring from the foreign service, he became a distinguished historian. Acheson, before and after his stint in government, was an eminent Washington lawyer. Nitze, as noted earlier, had been an investment banker. Bowie was a law professor, then a professor of government. Kaysen was a professor of economics and later of political economy. Blackwill, like Kennan, had a career as a professional diplomat. So did Kornienko. A close reader of their essays may find differences that are best explained as resulting from styles of reasoning associated with their differing crafts.

In the later chapters, which contain essays by scholars, you will also find evidence of policy biases. At least faintly, almost every essay shows concern about current issues. For four out of five of the American contributors, you can probably infer preferences based on differences between the Democratic and Republican parties or even on differences within those parties. Some essays have strong overtones of past policy debates, particularly about Vietnam and arms control. Partly because of the stronger focus on explanation or significance as opposed to consequences, however, the scholars' policy biases have less apparent effect on their conclusions.

The scholars' writings do show, as much as those of former officials, the effects of professional deformation. Historians and political scientists do not reason quite alike, and historians vary in some degree according to specialty. A reader with a feel for the differences among scholarly tribes would have little difficulty inferring the discipline and specialty of most of the American scholars here, even if not aided by biographical notes.

In writings by scholars, however, the crucial biases usually stem not from politics, present or past, or from discipline per se but rather from present or past debates inside the scholars' respective fields. Just as you must know something about relevant national history to "place" the concerns of an official, so you must know something of trends within academic disciplines to place properly the concerns of a scholar.[3]

For many of the American scholars here, the key past debate has been that on the origins of the cold war. During the 1950s, most American scholars accepted the premise of containment, namely that the cold war had begun because the Soviet Union sought aggressively to expand its territorial and ideological empire. Historians and political scientists wrote and taught that the United States and the West had responded to a Soviet challenge.

This orthodox view of the 1950s also contained an element of self-congratulation. After Pearl Harbor, most Americans agreed that American foreign policy in the years between the First and the Second World Wars had been mistaken. They thought that the United States should have taken part in the League of Nations after World War I and should not have isolated itself during the 1930s.[4] Led by Chicago political scientist Hans J. Morgenthau, a number of analysts argued that these mistakes had their roots in American ideology. Historically, Americans had pursued ideals like democracy and self-determination. They had not focused on hard national interests. These self-styled realists applauded containment as a policy keyed not to idealism but to the preservation of American national security.

In the 1960s, revisionists attacked both realism and the orthodox view of the origin of the cold war. They denied that American foreign policy had ever been idealistic. From the beginning, they charged, foreign policy had served the interests of a business elite. Not only in Asia but around the world, the United States had pursued an "open door imperialism" aimed at maximizing American corporate profits. The appearance of opposing imperialism and colonialism had merely enabled Americans to avoid the costs and risks of formally administering colonies.

Revisionists charged that in formulating cold war policy, American leaders had invented or exaggerated a Soviet threat in order to pursue their historic goals. The real challenge had been that to capitalism, revisionists argued; and the purpose of American policy had been to stifle socialism and anticapitalist nationalism. The Communist coup in Prague, the Berlin blockade, and other such events, said some revisionists, had been Soviet responses to Western provocations, not the reverse.

The revisionists' theses provoked an enormous amount of scholarly work on the whole history of American foreign policy. Out of it emerged a number of new syntheses, discarding older interpretations but modifying, to say the least, the proposition that all could be explained as "open door imperialism." More often than not, the result was to emphasize the interplay among popular beliefs, diplomatic calculations, and domestic politics.[5]

The realist perspective was not completely eclipsed. Outside of academic circles, most Americans continued to see the cold war as a Western reaction to Soviet or Communist imperialism. Some scholars defended this view as essentially correct. They acknowledged that the Soviet threat might have been overdrawn, but they contended that there *had* been a threat. The important question had to do with the response of the United States to that threat. The most significant historical fact was that the United States had chosen to assume a risk of war on behalf of nations that, without U.S. protection, might have been absorbed into the Soviet empire. This *neorealism* is represented here by Samuel F. Wells, Jr., of the Woodrow Wilson International Center for Scholars.

In academic writing about the cold war, the 1970s brought postrevisionism. John Lewis Gaddis of Ohio University was in the fore. Both the West and the East, said Gaddis and other postrevisionists, had started with some hostility toward each other. Each had had goals of its own. Each had given the other some cause for alarm. The cold war had not been exclusively Western defense against a Soviet threat or vice versa. It had been a matter of mutual escalation.

This postrevisionist critique brought responses from revisionists. Some of their responses accepted elements of the postrevisionist case much as postrevisionists accepted elements of the cases put by realists, revisionists, and neorealists. A neorevisionist or post-postrevisionist line of interpretation emerged. Represented here in an essay by Lloyd Gardner of Rutgers University, this school retains characteristics of the earlier revisionism, particularly in the extent to which its adherents see American decision makers as having had wide ranges of choice and having often made the wrong choices. Some of the scholarly debate about the cold war has been, underneath, a debate about what *should* have happened. Some has also been a debate about what *could* have happened.

To onlookers such debates sometimes seem like debates between lawyers in court. They assume that though the parties disagree, one side is right. A judge or jury will eventually decide which. There is all the more reason for such an assumption because history, as a discipline, is often put under the heading "social science," and the sciences are popularly (if wrongly) supposed to produce exact and unequivocal answers.

In fact, debates among historians may have less in common with disputes in courts or laboratories than with those among critics of literature, art, or music. Differences may be primarily in preferred visions or in frames of reference or comparison. Within limits, interpretations that seem directly contradictory can all be "true."

There are limits, of course. Events occurred in a certain sequence, and contemporaneous documents indicate how and whether they were noticed. A historian cannot explain Soviet actions in 1945 as responses to U.S. containment since containment did not become U.S. policy until later. Nor can a historian explain the hardening shift from the Long Telegram to NSC 20/4 as influenced by concern about the fast-paced Soviet nuclear weapons program without adducing some evidence—so far not found—that Americans had intelligence of that Soviet program. But so many events occur, and so many documents exist, that scholars have considerable latitude for locating evidence that is consistent with their premises or prejudices.

The political scientist Joseph S. Nye, Jr., suggests that there is a spectrum along which scholarly work falls.[6] At one end, scholars' findings tend to be regulated by replicable evidence. At the other end, pure imagination has freer rein. The physical sciences are at the former end, literary and artistic criticism at the latter. Political science and history sit somewhere in between. In this metaphor, physics might be thought of as red, the study of surrealistic art violet, with history somewhere near baby blue and political science perhaps between green and yellow. The commentaries in this book are all disciplined by dealing with a document that anyone else can consult. No conscientious scholar can ascribe something to NSC 68 without being able to quote or cite supporting passages. The commentaries are also disciplined by having to take into account common knowledge of the period when the document was created. A scholar may argue, for example, the influence on NSC 68 of anti-Communist fervor among the American public. That scholar has to be cautious, however, about using the term "McCarthyism," for McCarthy's heyday came slightly later.

Within these wide limits, the scholarly commentaries here exemplify how differently individuals can perceive a particular document not because one is right and another wrong but just because of differences in perspective. Several are excerpted from material in print, partly so that readers can consider the question of the extent to which scholars, too, are influenced by current policy issues or past policy issues. And the commentators run a gamut from behavioral political science to linguistic deconstructionism, offering plenty of opportunity to gauge professional deformation.

Lest I seem to be pretending that only others have biases, I should add something about biases that may affect the basic architecture of this book as well as a word about where to locate the Introduction in cold war historiography. For that chapter is not just a chronicle of accepted facts. It puts forward an interpretation somewhat different from most of those described here or illustrated in Chapter 4.

First, a confession of personal bias: I have long known and admired Kennan, Nitze, and Bowie. I think of the latter two as friends and of Bowie as an especially close friend. We once taught in tandem, and we have collaborated in several projects. Blackwill is now a teaching colleague and also a good friend. Acquaintance thus informs but may also corrupt how I tell the story of NSC 68 and what I say about various interpretations.

As for scholarly bias, I quote my Harvard colleague Charles Maier. In an essay for the American Historical Association on contemporary American scholarship on international relations, Maier writes:

> Investigation of domestic pressures has consistently marked May's work. . . . But these pressures, for May, have not been those of the social or economic system as a whole; thus he diverges from Left historians who likewise stress the primacy of domestic politics. Rather, the formative influences remain the contingent and more fragmented exertions of specific professional groups of bureaucracies; and the explanation they help to provide does not respond to the general question "Why imperialism?" or "Why war?" but rather "Why this war or this initiative at this time?" The result is to answer testable questions, but at the cost of skirting some of the larger and imponderable ones.[7]

Chapter 1 offers an interpretation based on the premise that specific government policies are usually products more of intragovernmental politics than of either a realist's "national interest" or a prevailing ideology such as "open door imperialism." A bias toward such explanation may influence not only that first chapter but editorial notes elsewhere in the book and, indeed, the shape of the book. You, the reader, should be on guard.

Ideally, however, you will find here a rich enough mixture of firsthand testimony, expert retrospection, and specialized and nonspecialized scholarly opinion so as to be able to compose your own version of truth.

NOTES

[1] Arthur M. Schlesinger, *A Thousand Days: John F. Kennedy in the White House* (Boston: Houghton Mifflin, 1965), 993.

[2] Most of the foregoing summarizes Nitze's essay later in this book (page 104). The concluding phrase, however, is from Paul H. Nitze to Ernest R. May, 5 Mar. 1992.

[3] The notion of "placing" someone against a timeline of events or trends is developed in Richard E. Neustadt and Ernest R. May, *Thinking in Time: The Uses of History for Decision-Makers* (New York: Free Press, 1986), 157–211.

[4] See Ernest R. May, *"Lessons" of the Past: The Use and Misuse of History in American Foreign Policy* (New York: Oxford University Press, 1973), 3–18.

[5] The best general survey of historical scholarship on American foreign policy is Jerald A. Combs, *American Diplomatic History: Two Centuries of Changing Interpretations* (Berkeley: University of California Press, 1983).

[6]Joseph S. Nye, Jr., to Ernest R. May, 12 Mar. 1992.

[7]From Charles S. Maier, "Marking Time: The Historiography of International Relations," in *The Past before Us: Contemporary Historical Writing in the United States,* ed. Michael Kammen (Ithaca: Cornell University Press, 1980), 376. A recent essay on historiography describes me as a "crossover" from realism into a new internationalism, which emphasizes less U.S. national interests than interests of other populations as affected by the United States: Michael Hunt, "The Long Crisis in Diplomatic History," *Diplomatic History* 16 (Winter 1992): 133 n. 44.

2

Eyewitness Testimony

This chapter contains the recollections of three key participants in the making of NSC 68: George Kennan, Dean Acheson, and Paul Nitze. They flesh out the story told earlier. More important, they provide samples of a second type of source for historical reconstruction—after-the-fact testimony by participants or eyewitnesses.

GEORGE F. KENNAN
(Director of the State Department Policy Planning Staff, 1947–1950)

The following text was composed by Kennan at the end of the 1960s or the beginning of the 1970s, when he was in his mid-sixties. He had begun his new career as writer and scholar by publishing *American Diplomacy, 1900–1950* (Chicago: University of Chicago Press, 1951). This slender but elegant volume marked Kennan as a realist of the Morgenthau school. In it, he indicted major American policy choices of the twentieth century as fruits of imprudent moralism and legalism. In the mid-1950s Kennan also became a public critic of what he saw as too rigid application of containment. In a set of Reith lectures for the BBC published in 1958 as *Russia, the Atom and the West* (New York: Harper, 1958), Kennan advocated détente with the Soviets on the basis of a permanently neutralized Germany.

By 1967, when Kennan published the first part of an autobiography, *Memoirs, 1925–1950* (Boston: Little, Brown, 1967), he had become also an outspoken critic of the war in Vietnam. He nevertheless remained a professional diplomat, chary of disclosing differences with his former colleagues. Only close reading between the lines could find in that first volume of memoirs clues that he had not seen eye to eye with Nitze and Acheson. Part two of his autobiography, *Memoirs, 1950–1963* (Boston: Little, Brown, 1972), from which comes the following text, speaks more explicitly of differences of opinion. Still, it says nothing specific about either NSC 68 or Nitze.

Reading Kennan, you should reflect on the extent to which his words may be affected by his concern at the time with the Vietnam War and the nuclear arms race as opposed to past policy concerns of the period about which he is writing. Reflect also on the extent to which his style shows professional deformation and, if so, that of which profession: diplomat? historian? policy advocate? Afterward, identify anything in the text that is *not* to be discounted on grounds of bias. What is the contribution of Kennan's testimony to the hard core of fact that must discipline any interpretation of NSC 68 and U.S. cold war strategy?

Kennan's Commentary

In 1948, I had had the impression that American opinion, official and otherwise, recovering from the pro-Soviet euphoria of the period around the end of World War II, had been restored to a relatively even keel. True: it was hard to get the Pentagon to desist from seeing in Stalin another Hitler and fighting the last war all over again in its plans for the next one. True: we still had a vigorous right-wing faction which called for war with Russia— usually over China. But by and large, the moderate Marshall Plan approach—an approach aimed at *creating* strength in the West rather than *destroying* strength in Russia—seemed to have prevailed; and I, like those others who went by the name of "Russian experts," felt that our view of the Russian problem—a view that accepted Russian-Communist attitudes and policies as a danger at the political level, but did not see either a likelihood or a necessity of war and did not regard the military plane as the one on which our response ought to be concentrated—seemed to have found general acceptance.

Two years later, all this was rapidly changing. A number of disturbing

From George F. Kennan, *Memoirs, 1950–1963* (Boston: Little, Brown, 1972), 90–92.

trends were now detectable, as a result of which I found myself increasingly concerned over the course of American opinion and policy precisely in the area where I was thought to have, and fancied myself to have, the greatest influence. . . .

. . . I could not forget that even prior to the Korean War our military—and to some extent our political—planners had adopted for military planning purposes, against my anguished objections, the year 1952 as the probable "peak" of danger which our preparations should be designed to meet. They did not themselves intend to start a war at that time, but they assumed there would be a real danger of the Russians doing so as soon as their current program of military preparations was completed—and for this, 1952, apparently, seemed to them the most likely date. They could not free themselves from the image of Hitler and his timetables. They viewed the Soviet leaders as absorbed with the pursuit of something called a "grand design"—a design for the early destruction of American power and for world conquest. In vain I pleaded with people to recognize that this was a chimera: that the Russians were not like that; that they were weaker than we supposed; that they had many internal problems of their own; that they had no "grand design" and did not intend, in particular, to pursue their competition with us by means of a general war. What we were confronted with from the Soviet side was, I insisted, a long-term effort of rivalry and pressure by means short of general war. We should make our plans for steady, consistent effort over a long period of time, and not for any imaginary "peak" of danger. It was, in fact, dangerous for us to think in terms of such a "peak"; for military plans had a way of giving reality to the very contingencies against which they purported to prepare. ∎

DEAN ACHESON
(Secretary of State, 1949–1953)

Dean Acheson remained secretary of state throughout Truman's presidency. As McCarthyism flourished, he became more and more a central target for the Republican right. Alluding to the dean of Canterbury in the Anglican Church, who was conspicuously pro-Soviet and was called the "Red Dean," Republicans called Acheson the American "Red Dean." When Truman left office, Acheson went back to his law firm for good. He subsequently made speeches and wrote essays and books in hope of aiding Democrats or the Democratic party.

By the 1960s, Acheson's position in his party was rather what it had been during Franklin Roosevelt's early New Deal, when he was best known for having resigned as under secretary of the treasury because of disapproval of FDR's tinkering with the gold standard. Serving as an informal adviser to both Presidents Kennedy and Johnson, Acheson usually figured among the "hawks." He counseled a tougher line than Kennedy took with regard both to Berlin in 1961 and to the Soviet missiles in Cuba in 1962, and in the late 1960s he was one of the last of Johnson's "wise men" to conclude that Vietnam was a lost cause. The following text was written at about the time of that change of mind.

As with the selection from Kennan, you should read this text with the debate over the Vietnam War in mind. With an inner ear, how many axes from the late 1960s do you hear grinding, and how many from 1950? Comparing Kennan and Acheson, to what extent, if any, do you see differences attributable to the former's being a diplomat, the latter's being a lawyer? How many differences might be attributable to Kennan's government experience having been wholly that of a career official within the executive branch while Acheson's was that of an appointed "in-and-outer" directly answerable to, and at the beck and call of, an elected president and elected members of Congress? What, if any, of Acheson's testimony must a scholar take as fact?

Acheson's Commentary

From the outset, . . . I became aware, without full comprehension, that our colleagues [George] Kennan and [Soviet expert Charles E.] Bohlen approached the problem of policy definition with a very different attitude and from a different angle from the rest of us. At the time, impatient with obscure argument, I had to push through it to do what the President had asked of me. Now, understanding better what they were driving at and why, it seems to me rather more important and interesting than its application to the particular issues involved. Their viewpoint . . . may be summarized, with some damage, in two points:

1. The attempt to compress into a manageable paper, "cleared" by superiors, the vast and infinitely complex considerations upon which such decisions as those involved here should rest, would so distort the issues presented as to affect the decisions.

From Dean Acheson, *Present at the Creation: My Years in the State Department* (New York: Norton, 1969), 347–48, 374–76.

2. The creation of such a document not only affects the immediate decision but also introduces into policy making a new rigidity that limits flexible response to unexpected developments and thus affects future decisions as well. . . .

. . . At the time I recognized and highly appreciated the personal and esoteric skill of our Foreign Service officers, but believed that insofar as their wisdom was "noncommunicable," its value, though great in operations abroad, was limited in Washington. There major foreign policies must be made by the man charged with that responsibility in the Constitution, the President. He rarely came to his task trained in foreign affairs, nor did his personal entourage. What he needed was communicable wisdom, not mere conclusions, however soundly based in experience or intuition. . . . I saw my duty as gathering all the wisdom available and communicating it amid considerable competition. . . .

NSC 68 lacked, as submitted, any section discussing costs. This was not an oversight. To have attempted one would have made impossible all those concurrences and prevented any recommendation to the President. It would have raised at once the extent and tempo of the program deemed necessary to carry out the conclusions and recommendations. Each department, each service, and each individual would have become a special pleader or an assistant President weighing all the needs of the nation and the political problems presented by each need. Our function was to get the international situation analyzed, the problems it presented stated, and recommendations made. . . .

. . . Discussing the paper some years later with a group of veterans of this campaign [to have NSC 68 approved before submitting it to Truman], one who had entered it toward its end remarked that when he first read NSC 68 he thought that it was "the most ponderous expression of elementary ideas" he had ever come across. Allowing for the natural exaggeration and tartness of a bon mot, this was so. . . . The purpose of NSC 68 was to so bludgeon the mass mind of "top government" that not only could the President make a decision but that the decision could be carried out. Even so, it is doubtful whether anything like what happened in the next few years could have been done had not the Russians been stupid enough to have instigated the attack against South Korea and opened the "hate America" campaign.

NSC 68, a formidable document, presents more than a clinic in political science's latest, most fashionable, and most boring study, the "decision-making process," for it carries us beyond decisions to what should be their fruits, action. . . .

NSC 68 has not been declassified and may not be quoted, but its contents have been widely discussed in print. Many of my own public statements were properly based upon the fundamental conclusions stated in this leading embodiment of Government policy.

The paper began with a statement of the conflicting aims and purposes of the two superpowers: the priority given by the Soviet rulers to the Kremlin design, world domination, contrasted with the American aim, an environment in which free societies could exist and flourish. . . .

The task of a public officer seeking to explain and gain support for a major policy is not that of the writer of a doctoral thesis. Qualification must give way to simplicity of statement, nicety and nuance to bluntness, almost brutality, in carrying home a point. . . . If we made our points clearer than truth, we did not differ from most other educators and could hardly do otherwise. . . .

Such an analysis was decried by some liberals and some Kremlinologists. The real threat, they said, lay in the weakness of the Western European social, economic, and political structure. Correct that and the Russian danger would disappear. This I did not believe. The threat to Western Europe seemed to me singularly like that which Islam had posed centuries before, with its combination of ideological zeal and fighting power. Then it had taken the same combination to meet it: Germanic power in the east and Frankish in Spain, both energized by a great outburst of military power and social organization in Europe. This time it would need the added power and energy of America, for the drama was now played on a world stage.   ■

PAUL H. NITZE

(Director of the State Department Policy Planning Staff, 1950–1953)

The final document in this chapter is Nitze's first published account of the composition of NSC 68. Partly because of Nitze's central role, partly because he remained more active in government than either Kennan or Acheson, and partly because his text appeared a decade later than theirs, more needs to be said by way of introduction.

Nitze had remained head of the State Department Policy Planning Staff until early in the Eisenhower administration. Though he had switched from the Republican to the Democratic party during the election of 1952, he had hoped to be kept on by John Foster Dulles, Eisenhower's secretary of state. Dulles told him that he would instead become assistant secretary of defense for international security affairs. Just on the point of moving memorabilia into a new office in the Pentagon, Nitze was told that right-wing senators had vetoed the appointment. They refused to confirm anyone so close to Acheson.

Nitze became a private citizen, devoting most of his time, however, to continued analysis of defense policy issues. He published penetrating articles on the nature of policy and the ethics of statecraft. Bitter toward the Republicans and especially toward Dulles, whom he had disliked when they did business on Wall Street in the 1930s, Nitze became also a more and more outspoken critic of the Eisenhower administration. He especially attacked efforts to economize on defense by emphasizing "massive retaliation." As he says in the following text, he saw the Eisenhower-Dulles policies as "a reverse of the NSC 68 line of policy," leading to "a potentially disastrous and immoral kind of nuclear strategy."

During Eisenhower's second term, surprisingly, Nitze found himself in a position to try to repeat what he had accomplished in 1950—to maneuver a reluctant president into increasing military spending. Eisenhower, under bureaucratic and public pressure to undertake a big civil defense program, created a committee of private citizens to study the matter. H. Rowan Gaither, board chairman of both the Ford Foundation and the Rand Corporation, headed the committee. Despite Nitze's open opposition to the administration, members of the committee enlisted him as a consultant. By force of mind and personality, he came to dominate the effort. He helped persuade the committee that it should give Eisenhower a much broader report than requested, one dealing not just with fallout shelters and such but with the whole range of U.S. defense requirements in an age of thermonuclear warheads and long-range missiles. He became chief drafter of the committee's report, shaping it much as he had shaped NSC 68.

Just as the Gaither Report was taking final form, the Soviets sent up their *Sputnik* satellites. By putting the first artificial earth satellites in orbit, the Soviets thus demonstrated that they had the technology to build ballistic missiles of intercontinental range. The fact that their space technology had done what American rockets could not yet do produced a panic reaction among the public. In Congress and the press, critics charged that Eisenhower had permitted development of a dangerous "missile gap."

This clamor provided perfect atmospherics for the document that Nitze had drafted. With intense West-East antagonism seemingly a settled condition of life, the new document had no need of rhetoric about slavery versus freedom. It went straight to the point that, in NSC 68, had required a long prologue. The Soviets, it said, were within a year or two of achieving menacing military superiority. In response, the United States should greatly increase spending for all categories of military forces. Unlike NSC 68, the Gaither Report mentioned a figure—$44 billion over five years, or fifteen to twenty percent per year more for defense—but the figure was notional and "a minimum." The political message was almost identical with that of NSC 68: "The next two years seem to us critical. If we fail to act at once, the risk, in our opinion will be unacceptable."[1]

The Gaither Report created for Eisenhower a situation similar to that created for Truman by NSC 68. Like Truman, Eisenhower ordered that the report be kept under wraps. Also like Truman, he quickly saw signs that it would not remain so. This time, the press leaks were loud and explicit. Chalmers Johnson of the *Washington Post* published a story with the lead "The still top-secret Gaither Report portrays a United States in the gravest danger in its history." The brothers Joseph and Stewart Alsop, columnists who were friends of Nitze's, kept up a din for release of the document. Democrats in Congress, particularly presidential aspirants John Kennedy and Lyndon Johnson, cited the Gaither Report as authoritative evidence that the Republicans had been guilty of feckless economy in national defense.[2] The Gaither Report did not, however, produce the effects of NSC 68. The *Sputnik*s did not turn Eisenhower around as the Korean War had turned Truman. Closely held high-altitude photographs of Soviet test sites, taken by U-2 spy planes, gave Eisenhower reason to believe that the Soviets were not, in fact, ahead of the United States in missile development. He had high confidence in his own military expertise (and not much in that of the Gaither committee). Quite possibly, he also had concluded in his own mind that actual thermonuclear war was unthinkable for either Americans or Russians.[3] Yielding to the general pressure, the president did increase his budget request for missile programs, but not by much. The immediate practical effect of the Gaither Report was less, probably, than would have been the immediate effect of NSC 68, absent the North Korean attack on South Korea.

The clamor died only after Kennedy succeeded Eisenhower as president, stepped up defense spending, and then discovered, via new reconnaissance satellites with much wider coverage of the Soviet Union, that the "missile gap" was actually hugely in favor of the United States.

Meanwhile, Nitze returned to government. Under the Democratic Kennedy, Nitze got the job he had been denied in 1953. He went to the Pentagon under Robert McNamara as assistant secretary of defense for international security affairs. There he had a central role in planning U.S. responses during the crisis surrounding the Soviets' erection of a wall across Berlin in 1961, and he was part of the small group that advised Kennedy during the Cuban missile crisis in 1962.

Nitze hoped to become McNamara's deputy secretary, but the chemistry with the Kennedy brothers did not work well enough. Kennedy instead exiled Nitze to the post of secretary of the Navy. Much later, three years after Johnson succeeded the murdered Kennedy, Nitze finally got his wish. Frazzled by failure in Vietnam, McNamara was about to depart, and Nitze became deputy secretary. Continuing under McNamara's successor, Clark Clifford, he played some part in beginning the turn toward withdrawal from the Vietnam War.

After the election of 1968, when Richard Nixon replaced Johnson as president, Nitze expected again to become a private citizen. This time, however, he found that a Republican administration wanted his services. As deputy secretary of defense, he had managed preparations for American-Soviet negotiations about limiting intercontinental (or strategic) nuclear weapons. Nixon and his national security adviser, Henry Kissinger, asked Nitze to help them continue the negotiations. He was thus a member of the delegation that worked out the 1972 agreement known as SALT I.

In 1974, with Watergate investigations working toward possible impeachment of Nixon, Nitze was asked to return to his old post as assistant secretary of defense for international security affairs. Once again, right-wing Senators blocked his way. Back in 1960, Nitze had given a playful talk before a group of defense analysts, challenging them to consider the pros and cons of turning the U.S. Strategic Air Command over to NATO or possibly putting all U.S. and NATO military forces under the UN. In 1964 he had helped Johnson against his Republican opponent, Barry Goldwater, by providing material to answer Goldwater's criticisms of Democratic defense policies. Some Senators of both parties believed (or pretended to believe) that Nitze had meant what he said in 1960. Goldwater, a senator from Arizona and a key member of the Armed Services Committee, encouraged this belief and not only vowed to vote against Nitze but hinted that, if Nixon persisted, he might find it hard to vote for the president's acquittal on Watergate charges. Nixon backed off, and Nitze once again found himself a private citizen.

The election of Democrat Jimmy Carter as president in 1976 did not result in Nitze's being asked to come again out of retirement. Carter entered office committed to cutting back defense spending and to negotiating with the Soviets over reductions in strategic nuclear forces much beyond those of SALT I. When he announced his choices for key appointments to the White House staff and in the State and Defense departments, Carter not only did not include Nitze; he named men whom Nitze regarded as wrong-headed.

At the very outset of the Carter administration, Nitze stepped forward to oppose appointment of Washington lawyer Paul Warnke as head of the Arms Control and Disarmament Agency. Though he did not prevent

Warnke's confirmation, Nitze took comfort from a fifty-eight to forty vote in the Senate, which seemed a clear augury of ratification difficulty for any arms limitation treaty of which Nitze was critical.

Nitze had already become a leader in the Committee on the Present Danger, organized to make a public case against Carter's projected defense policies. Throughout the remainder of the 1970s, Nitze waged an unrelenting campaign against large reductions in defense spending and particularly against a SALT II agreement slowly worked out between the Carter administration and the Brezhnev regime in Moscow.

Late in 1979, Soviet armed forces suddenly invaded Afghanistan. In Iran, the pro-American shah had already been forced out of office, and violently anti-American Muslim clergy had taken power. After an Iranian crowd stormed the U.S. embassy and made prisoners of the Americans there, American public opinion came to seem dominated by frustration at the administration's inability to rescue the hostages. The SALT II agreement went on the shelf. Carter's ratings in public opinion polls plummeted. It began to seem likely that Carter would not be reelected, possible even that he would not be renominated, and that the new president after 1980 would be someone espousing policies much like those embodied in NSC 68 and the later Gaither Report—maybe even former Governor Ronald Reagan of California.

It was in this environment that Nitze composed the essay on NSC 68 from which excerpts follow. When Reagan, in fact, succeeded Carter, Nitze became the key arms control negotiator, but that was later. What you must ask of the text here is how much it may have been influenced by Nitze's preoccupation in 1979–80 with SALT II questions and perhaps by his hope of yet again attaining a position from which he could influence U.S. policy. You need also to keep in mind Nitze's success and disappointments in the years between 1950 and 1980, asking how, even subtly, concerns of the Eisenhower or Nixon era may have affected Nitze's retrospective thinking about NSC 68.

Then there is the question of whether parts of Nitze's testimony respond directly to points in the Kennan or Acheson memoirs or in the scholarly literature. Is his testimony not only more full but different from what it would have been if he had not read Kennan or Acheson or scholars such as John Lewis Gaddis?

Just from reading the following text, would you be able to guess that the author was not a career diplomat or a lawyer or a historian or a political scientist? Does anything in form or style provide a basis for inferring Nitze's actual career? And last, as with Kennan and Acheson, what are the elements in Nitze's retrospective testimony that are to be taken as hard fact?

Nitze's Commentary

NSC 68 was very much a product of its times. Those in the U.S. security community who confronted the international tensions of fall 1949 and spring 1950 had generally known each other since early in World War II. The degree of understanding, friendship, and respect within this group was considerable. And it was understood that the stakes involved in our arguments and conflicting positions were very high indeed. The United States had won a tremendous war at great cost, even if at less real cost than suffered by any of the other participants. Although the country was returning successfully to domestic prosperity, international developments appeared exceedingly ominous. There was a feeling that the United States was losing the peace.

In 1946 and 1947 it had looked as if economic disaster in Europe and the Far East would result in political collapse. From 1947 on, this threat received our principal attention. Political and foreign economic problems were dealt with by the Marshall Plan, the International Monetary Fund and the World Bank, the interim aid arrangements and the like. . . . From 1947 to 1950 almost all our policy initiatives had been economic and political; little attention had been given to our or anyone else's military capabilities. . . .

The Brussels Pact had been created earlier by Britain, France, and the Low Countries. The British military planners had asked a team from the Pentagon to visit and discuss the Pact's capacities. I was sent over by the State Department to follow the joint effort at military planning. It was apparent that the planners faced a real problem. They estimated that the cost of the military equipment for a force strong enough to hold at the Rhine was $45 billion in 1949 dollars. That was triple the cost of the entire Marshall Plan. Could the United States institute a military aid program to help? It was my view that the maximum we could support and had any hope of getting through Congress was $1 billion a year. The Pentagon was shocked when I sent back a telegram to that effect. But Secretary Marshall was skeptical that U.S. public opinion and the Congress would long support even that level. The West's security in effect rested on the Soviet Union's need for a period of national rebuilding, and on a small U.S. stockpile of nuclear weapons.

The President was determined to hold down the defense budget at $12.5 billion. Louis Johnson had been appointed secretary of defense with precisely that instruction, and he considered carrying out that mandate to be his main chance for political advancement. What could the United States do with

From Paul H. Nitze, "The Development of NSC 68," *International Security* 4 (Spring 1980): 170–74.

$12.5 billion? This was a question we had all worked hard on, including George Kennan and I during Spring 1949. Kennan believed that two high-quality Marine divisions would be sufficient to support the military requirements of U.S. containment policies. I disagreed.

It is untrue to claim that we thought the Russians were about to attack. We took seriously Stalin's speech of February 1946 which indicated that Moscow anticipated at least three Five Year Plans before it would be in position to take account of all contingencies. However, we regarded the Kremlin's behavior as indicative of an aggressive and deliberate program to place the Soviet Union in the best position eventually to implement what Stalin had outlined in that speech. But our prime concern had remained with the economic situation in Europe. It was in such an atmosphere that the United States was faced with the flight of Chiang Kai-shek from China, and with the Russian testing of an atomic weapon. The issue was then, what do we do? I remember Secretary Acheson asking Kennan and me to spend a weekend thinking through the significance of these events. Acheson believed that American nuclear weapons were unlikely to stop the Russians if they had once embarked upon an invasion of Western Europe: in his judgment, even attacks upon the Russian homeland would not stop such an attack. Thus, the United States had to concentrate on rebuilding the conventional defense of the West. It would prove to be my view that to do that was an extremely difficult task, as had been shown by the estimates arising from the Brussels Pact. I was also persuaded that, over time, the U.S. atomic monopoly, and the strategic significance thereof, would progressively decline. We would eventually have to move away from primary reliance upon nuclear weapons. But I did not think that we could rebuild our conventional defenses, in conjunction with our allies, in time entirely to avoid a reliance upon our nuclear capability. We would therefore have to try to maintain some margin of nuclear superiority for as long as possible. So the question remained: what should the United States do to avoid complete reliance upon nuclear weapons?

The entire national security community in Washington felt that the Soviet Union posed the main threat to the United States. The debate over Soviet intentions was not significant. George Kennan, after all, had drafted NSC 20/4, the policy recommendations of which were reconfirmed by NSC 68. One of the significant issues concerned atomic strategy. . . . NSC 68 sought to move us away from primary reliance upon nuclear weapons, and toward building up conventional forces. The question was, how long would it take? History shows that we were right that it would take much more than two Marine divisions and much longer than a few years to achieve the necessary conventional buildup.

Concerning the economic costs, President Truman believed that the

United States could not afford more than a $12.5 billion defense budget, but the Policy Planning Staff felt that, if necessary, a $40 billion budget could be met—provided that the administration took the necessary concomitant steps in taxation and control over scarce materials. Indeed, Truman's economic advisers, notably Leon Keyserling of the Council of Economic Advisors, had advanced the argument in late 1949 and early 1950 that if the administration was to get over its preoccupation with balancing the budget and accept deficits for a few years, then the administration could implement the Fair Deals [sic] programs without draining the economy. Keyserling and I discussed these matters frequently; though he wanted to spend the money on other programs, he was convinced that the country could afford $40 billion for defense if necessary. But those of us who worked on NSC 68 were more conservative. We believed that increases in defense spending should be coupled with increases in taxes, rather than relying on deficit spending. . . .

With respect to Soviet military capabilities, who were U.S. analysts supposed to rely upon for their intelligence estimates? We relied upon the intelligence community; we were not in a position in the three months we had to write NSC 68 to make an independent estimate. Later, the intelligence people would state that of their estimated 175 Soviet divisions, one third were at full strength, one third were at partial strength, and the final third were cadres. But even after this became apparent the question remained: how long would it take the Soviet Union to fill in those divisions, given their very good reserves? It is still my view that they could have done so in a few weeks. How long would it have taken us to reply? We were in no position to mobilize that fast. Indeed today there are still questions about readiness and how soon more than a division or two can be deployed to Europe. . . .

There is always an inter-relationship between capabilities and intentions, tactics, and strategy. Because of the limitations of means—we had only seven active divisions at the time of the outbreak of the Korean War—our policy choices were obviously constrained. We had to tailor planning to the means available. As the means increased, we could contemplate other, more powerful reactions in other places. However, we did not foresee any time when U.S. means, combined with those of our allies, would be such as to give us an unlimited range of political/military options. For instance, it did not seem politically and economically feasible that our West European allies could support forces equal to Soviet conventional forces in the central European region. . . .

Thus, the suggestion that we were not sensitive to the means available is a misreading both of the document itself and of the attitudes of those who had anything to do with the document. In fact, exactly the opposite was the principal point of NSC 68. Those who thought we must live within a $12.5 billion budget would in fact have been responsible for our having no alternative to a doctrine of massive retaliation. That was the essence of what happened in 1953, when there was a reverse of the NSC 68 line of policy, and when President Eisenhower decided to cut $5 billion per year from the defense budget. As it turned out this could not be taken out of fat, but only out of real military capability. What followed was a potentially disastrous and immoral kind of nuclear strategy. . . .

Connected with these concerns over European vulnerabilities, Soviet political intentions and weapon development, and U.S. spending capacities was a hope that eventually, there would be a change in Soviet society. . . . We believed that change would be more likely if the containment policy could be effectively implemented over a long period of time. We did not make any predictions about when change in the Soviet Union would occur.

NOTES

[1]Like NSC 68, the Gaither Report long remained classified. It was finally published as 94 Cong., 2 sess., Joint Committee on Defense Production, *Report:* " 'Deterrence and Survival in the Nuclear Age' (The 'Gaither Report' of 1957)" (Washington, DC: Government Printing Office, 1976).

[2]See McGeorge Bundy, *Danger and Survival: Choices about the Bomb in the First Fifty Years* (New York: Random House, 1988), 334–44, and Fred Kaplan, *The Wizards of Armageddon* (New York: Simon & Schuster, 1983), 125–54.

[3]Bundy, *Danger and Survival,* 236–318, suggests as much. The point is further developed in a study of Eisenhower as president by Andrew Erdmann, prepared as a contribution to a volume on cold war statecraft and nuclear weapons to be edited by John Lewis Gaddis and Ernest R. May.

3

Later Officials' Retrospects

In this chapter appear commentaries by four former officials. Three are Americans; one is Russian. The three Americans all sat in positions somewhat similar to those of George Kennan and Paul Nitze in the period of NSC 68. One American was Nitze's immediate successor as State Department Policy Planning Staff chief. One served in the White House in the early 1960s, under John Kennedy, the third in the State Department and White House in the late 1970s and again in 1989–90. The Russian served in the Soviet government from the 1950s to the 1980s as a high-level expert on the United States.

These commentaries differ from those of Kennan, Acheson, and Nitze in Chapter 2 in that they provide no firsthand source material about NSC 68. The authors are not much better positioned than anyone else to say how NSC 68 came into being or what its authors intended. Though all four spent parts of their lives as researchers or teachers, their commentaries differ also from those of writers who have had careers only as scholars. They do testify at first hand about what was said and thought (or not said or thought) about NSC 68 in later administrations. And when they write of events outside their own knowledge, they do so with the advantage of experience. They have been on the inside. Their comments are informed by observation of how governments work. They have an advantage similar to that of a drama critic who has worked in the theater and knows what happens backstage.

This advantage can also be a disadvantage. Someone who has been in government is prey to supposing that government always works as he or she saw it working. The pure scholar may be more sensitive to changes, recognizing, for example, that the National Security Council of 1950 was very different from that of later years. What former officials write, however, deserves to be read as something different from either firsthand testimony or scholarly analysis. It is like the testimony in a court proceeding of someone called as an expert witness.

ROBERT R. BOWIE
(Director of the State Department Policy Planning Staff, 1953–1957)

Prior to 1953, when he took over the State Department Policy Planning Staff from Paul Nitze, Robert R. Bowie had been a professor at the Harvard Law School, specializing in antitrust law. He had also served as legal adviser to the chief Americans in occupied Germany, General Lucius Clay and his civilian successor, John J. McCloy. When scouting for someone to replace Nitze, John Foster Dulles, Acheson's successor as secretary of state, consulted McCloy, a fellow Wall Street lawyer. McCloy recommended Bowie so strongly that Dulles appointed him despite knowing that he was a registered Democrat.

After the end of Eisenhower's first term in 1957, Bowie returned to teaching, but as a professor of political science, not of law.[1] Bowie also founded, and was to be for fifteen years director of, a new Center for International Affairs at Harvard, which became a major locus for research on international political and strategic issues.

Bowie went to Washington again in the mid-1960s, during the Johnson administration, as counselor of the Department of State. Always a champion of the NATO alliance, he managed delicate U.S.-European relationships that Secretary of State Dean Rusk had to neglect because of his preoccupation with the war in Vietnam. After another decade in academe, Bowie joined the Carter administration as deputy director of intelligence in the Central Intelligence Agency. In the 1980s he went into active retirement as a Washington-based commentator on and frequent critic of U.S. policies toward allies and of U.S. national strategy.

Written specifically for this volume, Bowie's commentary on NSC 68 shows glints of his policy concerns at the beginning of the 1990s. Though Bowie confines himself rigorously to commenting on the 1950s, his essay implicitly challenges the contention that the Reagan military buildup "won"

the cold war. Reading it closely, you can also see signs of a general prefer-
ence for having U.S. policy reflect the views and interests of NATO rather
than those of the United States alone.

Bowie's essay is particularly interesting, however, as an example of how
past policy concerns can shape the framework of analysis. Its context is a
basic debate of the period when he headed the Policy Planning Staff. As he
relates, that period began with a review of cold war options. Dubbed the
"Solarium exercise, it would later be called, in policy terms, a "zero-budget-
ing exercise." The new president, Eisenhower, gathered a high-level group
to put as best they could the cases for alternatives to current U.S. policy. The
group included Kennan and Nitze. One alternative stressed conciliation and
negotiation. Another, rollback, had as its most extreme variation a preventive war. The exercise ended by affirming patient containment.

In Eisenhower's version of containment, high importance attached to
economy and flexibility. Eisenhower would often caution that the United
States could lose the cold war by letting military outlays sap its basic
economic strength. He and Dulles said that, while they would resist any
Soviet expansion, they would not necessarily do so at the exact point of
challenge. They would not get drawn into another Korean War. The United
States would act at times and places of its own choosing, and it would rely
on mobile military forces backed by a capacity for "massive retaliation."

Ex–Truman administration officials and other outsiders attacked Eisenhower's policy, particularly for its apparent willingness to risk nuclear
annihilation for the sake of a balanced budget. Nitze was a leader in this
attack, seeing in Eisenhower's approach, as he noted in his commentary, "a
reverse of the NSC 68 line of policy" leading to "a potentially disastrous and
immoral kind of nuclear strategy."

Bowie here comes to the defense of Eisenhower policy. Reexamining NSC
68, Bowie sees in it essentially the case for rollback. His essay dissects that
case and pinpoints its weaknesses. The essay is both an acute analysis of the
implications of NSC 68 and a rejoinder to what Nitze wrote and said in the
1950s.

Bowie's Commentary

How did the Eisenhower national security strategy relate to the concepts of
NSC 68?

When Eisenhower took office in January 1953, four conditions obtained:

a. The United States was achieving enormous capacity to produce nuclear weapons. The number of plutonium reactors was being increased from five to thirteen and of U-235 gaseous diffusion plants, from two to twelve. The hydrogen bomb, authorized in January 1950, would soon enter the stockpile. With these facilities, the weapons stockpile, which was about one thousand in mid-1953, rose steeply from then on, to nearly eighteen thousand by 1960. And with the hydrogen bomb and far higher fission yields, megatonnage multiplied nearly 150 times within about three years.[2]

b. A huge buildup in defense spending and forces had been under way since the Korean attack. The fiscal year 1951 defense budget, which Truman had capped at $13.5 billion as late as May 1950 (despite reading NSC 68), had jumped to $48.4 billion; by fiscal year 1953 (July 1, 1952 to June 30, 1953), actual spending had soared to $50.4 billion, with an unspent carryover of some $62 billion.

c. In February 1952, while Eisenhower was still supreme allied commander in Europe, NATO had adopted the Lisbon force goals, declaring that more than ninety divisions were needed for holding back the Red Army. NATO was also seeking to rearm Germany, within a European Defense Community. On January 19, 1953, its last full day in office, the Truman administration had approved NSC 141, appraising the buildup and calling for substantial new funds for continental defense and other purposes.[3]

d. The Korean War had been going on for more than two and a half years. Truce negotiations, in progress since July 1951, seemed to be getting nowhere. Casualties continued to mount.

Eisenhower defined his own national security policy during 1953, culminating in NSC 162/2, adopted in late October.[4] In doing so, he revised many ongoing and projected programs and rejected or modified some of the key premises, concepts, and prescriptions of NSC 68.

NSC 68 depicted the Soviet Union as an implacable, ruthless enemy dedicated to world domination as its top priority and to the destruction (or undermining) of the United States, its main obstacle to achieving its "design." Already dominant in conventional forces, the Soviets would be able to cripple the United States by a surprise nuclear attack when they achieved an adequate capability, estimated to be about two hundred weapons, which they were expected to have by 1954. This was seen as the year of maximum danger. Nuclear plenty on both sides would not produce stalemate but could be an "incitement to war" and to a Soviet surprise attack.

Eisenhower took a somewhat different view of the Soviet Union, nearer to that of Chip Bohlen, a Soviet expert in the State Department. The president accepted that the Soviets were deeply hostile to the non-Communist world and were dedicated to expanding their area of control and influence. But in his view, they were opportunistic and cautious in their actions; they were rational and calculating, not blind zealots. In his words, they were "not early Christian martyrs." Their highest priority was to maintain their regime and their power. Hence Soviet leaders would not risk jeopardizing the Soviet regime for the sake of expansion. Consequently, he was convinced that they would not deliberately start a direct conflict with the United States by surprise attack or otherwise if they faced the risk of retaliation and understood the disastrous consequences. They could be made to realize that they could not count on disarming the U.S. capacity for retaliating with enough force to disrupt the regime if the United States maintained an adequate strategic arsenal and took prudent steps to reduce its vulnerability.[5] Accordingly, Eisenhower rejected the notion of a year of "maximum danger" in favor of a level of defense for the long haul, which could be extended as far into the future as necessary.

NSC 68 called for a "dynamic" policy to induce the "retraction" or "rollback" of Soviet power and influence. Defensive containment to frustrate Soviet aggression or subversion was necessary, but too limited an objective for the emerging danger. That course merely counted on internal forces to cause the eventual decay or erosion of the Soviet threat. But faced with a nuclear-armed USSR, the United States would never be secure without a basic change in the Soviet purposes and system, and it could not afford to wait passively for that change to occur. It must take the initiative to induce Soviet retraction and expedite such internal change. Backed by superior military power, it should pursue a positive policy of "calculated and gradual coercion" for that purpose, including covert operations to foment and support unrest and revolt in selected strategic satellite countries.[6]

In September 1952, NSC 135/3 reaffirmed the course of NSC 68, with a caveat that its effectiveness should not be overestimated and that risks should be balanced against possible gains.[7] In a memorandum to Acheson on January 12, 1953, commenting on a draft of the follow-on paper, NSC 141, Nitze complained that actual national security programs had never been designed to produce the "situation of strength" needed to achieve the objectives of NSC 68 and NSC 135/3. Should we settle, he asked, for programs "making us a sort of hedgehog, unattractive to attack," or instead do "what is necessary to give us some chance of seeing these objectives attained"?[8]

In a famous May 1952 article in *Life* magazine,[9] John Foster Dulles, soon to be Eisenhower's secretary of state, had also criticized the "negative," "treadmill" policy toward the Soviet satellites and called for a more "dynamic" policy. "Rollback" became one theme in the 1952 Republican campaign, though Eisenhower stressed that it be pursued by peaceful means.

But Eisenhower was not comfortable with this concept. Shortly after Stalin's death in March 1953, he arranged for what was called the "Solarium exercise." High-level teams were tasked with developing the best possible cases for alternative strategies, including an active policy of rollback. As he probably intended, the exercise exposed the likely futility and high risks of such a policy and thus put the idea to rest.

NSC 162/2, the Eisenhower administration's statement of basic national security policy, did not adopt the rollback objective. It recognized that Soviet force would be able to maintain control in Eastern Europe in the absence of war but that it could not destroy the desire for freedom. By blocking Soviet expansion, containment was intended to foster conditions under which internal ferment and unrest would ultimately compel change in the Soviet Union and Eastern Europe. The West should seek to nurture or bolster such feelings but must avoid inciting any premature revolt. Forces for eventual change included

> such factors as the slackening of revolutionary zeal, the growth of vested managerial and bureaucratic interests, and popular pressures for consumption goods. Such changes, combined with the growing strength of the free world and the failure to break its cohesion, and the possible aggravation of weaknesses within the Soviet bloc through U.S. or allied action or otherwise, might induce a willingness to negotiate. The Soviet leadership might find it desirable and even essential to reach agreements acceptable to the United States and its allies, without necessarily abandoning its basic hostility to the non-Soviet world.[10]

The issue arose again in late 1954, when the National Security Council once more reviewed basic national security policy. The Joint Chiefs of Staff strongly criticized NSC 162/2 as embodying a "policy of reaction" to the Soviet Union and urged that it be replaced by a "policy of unmistakably positive quality." In discussion, Secretary of State Dulles opposed the Joint Chiefs. Conceding that in the 1952 campaign he had called for a "more dynamic U.S. policy," he said "experience had indicated that it was not easy to go very much beyond" containment. The official record summarized the views of Dulles:

> In certain quarters it is suggested . . . that while we continue to have atomic superiority over the enemy, we should apply strong and forceful measures to change the basic character of the Soviet system. . . . This would call, in effect, for an effort to overthrow the Communist regimes in China and in the European satellites and to detach these countries from the USSR. In his opinion, . . . the effort to implement such a course of action would involve the United States in general war. If it did not, however, and

we did succeed in detaching Communist China and the satellites from their alliance with the Soviet Union, this in itself would not actually touch the heart of the problem: Soviet atomic plenty. Even if we split the Soviet bloc, in other words, we would still have to face the terrible problem and threat of an unimpaired nuclear capability in the USSR itself. . . . Moreover, while these more aggressive policies, if successful, might result in the disintegration of the Soviet bloc, they would almost certainly cause the disintegration of the free world bloc, of which we were the leaders, for our allies in the free world would never go along with such courses of action as these. In sum, Secretary Dulles said that he must conclude that this kind of aggressive policy was not in the best interests of the United States.[11]

NSC 68 had set the goal of a massive and rapid buildup of U.S. and allied military forces to achieve overall military superiority. These forces had several purposes: to balance the very large Soviet and satellite conventional forces in Europe; to reduce reliance on nuclear weapons; and to serve as backup for the drive to roll back Soviet control and power.

By January 1953, the program review of the Truman administration (NSC 141) recognized that the buildup fell far short of these aims, despite a quadrupling in defense spending and substantial military assistance to allies. The Europeans were already backing away from the Lisbon goals. A projected twelve German divisions were clearly some years off. U.S. strategic nuclear forces would have to provide the backbone for NATO deterrence and defense for many years to come.

Eisenhower modified the force goals as well as the strategy prescribed by NSC 68 and its sequels. He decided to rely primarily on the threat of massive nuclear retaliation for deterrence of major Soviet aggression. NATO conventional forces would supplement the nuclear deterrent and reassure the Europeans. This decision resulted from many factors, among them the following:

First, Eisenhower was convinced that any major war between the United States and the Soviet Union would inevitably and rapidly escalate into a catastrophic nuclear war, however it began. The threat of prompt nuclear response would ensure that Soviet leaders recognized this reality. If they did, they would not be tempted to start any conflict in Europe, conventional or otherwise. And the capacity to retaliate despite a first strike would be assured by continental defense and later by the submarine-based Polaris missiles and the triad—sea-based and land-based missiles complemented by manned bombers.

Second, Eisenhower's experience as NATO supreme commander had convinced him that the Europeans would not, for political and economic reasons, build up and maintain conventional forces adequate to deter a

Soviet attack. With the eventual German divisions, NATO forces could supplement deterrence, especially if equipped with tactical nuclear weapons; but they could not serve as the primary deterrent.

Third, Eisenhower was convinced that security for the long haul depended greatly on the health of the U.S. economy. He apparently believed that a defense budget below $40 billion could be maintained without undue strain on the vitality of the economy; but he did his utmost to avoid spending beyond that level.

"Massive retaliation" was not an all-purpose doctrine. But the Eisenhower strategy differed from that of NSC 68 for dealing with local or regional conflict. Eisenhower was determined not to become embroiled on the ground again as the United States had in Korea, but massive use of nuclear weapons was clearly not a suitable alternative. He resolved instead to assist vulnerable nations on the periphery to maintain indigenous forces and to support them with mobile U.S. air and naval forces, which could respond against aggression at times and places of American choosing, not limited to the point of aggression. And tactical nuclear weapons would be available for use, when politically and militarily appropriate. As Dulles stressed in April 1953, that policy implied flexible but measured or proportionate response, not massive retaliation.[12]

Whereas NSC 68 had virtually written off negotiation except for public relations purposes (until basic change occurred in the Soviet system), Eisenhower was eager to keep open the chances for settling specific issues or controlling armaments. After Stalin's death in March 1953, he made an eloquent speech urging the new Soviet leaders to join in curbing the wasteful arms race and in resolving issues such as the future of Austria, while recognizing that the cold war would end only when the Soviets liberated Eastern Europe and abandoned expansionism. Throughout his two terms as president, Eisenhower pursued negotiations, especially seeking ways of reducing the nuclear peril. Failure to achieve concrete results was one of his keenest disappointments.[13]

To conclude: There was, of course, much continuity from Truman to Eisenhower. In setting his own strategy Eisenhower, however, made major changes from the premises, objectives, and policies elaborated in NSC 68. He also reshaped Truman's programs to conform to his strategy mainly by scaling down the projected Army and Navy buildup. Because the programmed forces were well short of those required for the "dynamic" objectives of NSC 68, the program changes, while substantial, were less radical.

The course Eisenhower set assured security while avoiding major conflict in a turbulent decade when both sides were learning to live with nuclear plenty. To a large extent, his strategy established the guidelines for the long haul leading to the ultimate ending of the cold war.   ▮

CARL KAYSEN

(Deputy Assistant to the President for National Security Affairs, 1961–1963)

Born in 1920 in Philadelphia, Carl Kaysen graduated from the University of Pennsylvania in 1940. During World War II, he served with the Office of Strategic Services (the forerunner of the Central Intelligence Agency) and then as an intelligence officer with the Army Air Corps (the forerunner of the U.S. Air Force). He was involved in selecting bombing targets in Germany and in evaluating bomb damage—work that had some similarity to Nitze's in the U.S. Strategic Bombing Survey and that laid the foundation for some aspects of later theorizing about nuclear war.

After World War II, Kaysen received a Ph.D. in economics at Harvard University. He remained at Harvard as, eventually, a professor of economics. Some of his work overlapped Bowie's in that it dealt with the economic consequences of antitrust law. Some of it continued to touch military issues. He was an occasional consultant for the Weapons System Evaluation Group, which prepared operational and strategic analyses for the Joint Chiefs of Staff.

Following John Kennedy's election as president in 1960, Kaysen went to Washington as deputy to his former Harvard dean, McGeorge Bundy, Kennedy's equivalent of the later national security adviser. Though Bundy stayed on after Kennedy's assassination, Kaysen did not. He returned to academic life and succeeded Robert Oppenheimer as director of Princeton's Institute for Advanced Study. After a decade in that post, he came back to Cambridge as professor of political economy at MIT and as director of MIT's Program in Science, Technology, and Public Policy.

In Kaysen's essay here, as in Bowie's, you can see traces of current or comparatively current policy concerns. Kaysen was on the opposite side from Nitze in many debates about defense policy. He favored arms control agreements that Nitze fought, and he criticized programs that Nitze championed. Kaysen is more explicit than Bowie in expressing doubt about the proposition that the NSC 68 strategy "won" the cold war.[1]

As in Bowie's essay, however, it is a set of past policy concerns that supplies the framework. Kaysen does not focus on containment versus rollback. In his time in Washington these were not interesting options. Kennedy never considered any general policy other than the conduct of a "long twilight war." To Kaysen, the pertinent question about NSC 68 is whether *any* such document can be useful. Kennedy and his aides came into office thinking not. They dismantled much of the National Security Council's staff and stopped commissioning or showing much interest in treatises on the scale of NSC 68. These actions drew criticism later, especially as students of the presidency began to award kudos to Eisenhower's management system.[2]

Kaysen's Commentary

Ronald Reagan, calling the Soviet Union "the evil empire" in March 1983 was, probably unconsciously, repeating the thought if not the words of Paul Nitze more than thirty years earlier. The apocalyptic tone of the first dozen pages of NSC 68 sounds more like the prose of John Bunyan than that of a committee of Washington bureaucrats drafting a top secret document. The escalating struggle between the United States and the Soviet Union was at bottom moral: a contest between Freedom and Slavery, Good and Evil. The Soviets aimed at world dominion, preferably without open war, but, if necessary, by direct military force. They were building up the military power, including a nuclear and possibly thermonuclear capability to conquer Western Europe and areas adjacent to them in the Middle East, neutralize Great Britain, and cripple the United States by atomic attack.

Ten years later John Kennedy's presidential campaign rhetoric echoed Nitze's tones and themes: the Soviet lead in military power—particularly missile strength—and economic growth threatened the United States and the whole world; a drastic response was in order. Further—though much fainter—echoes were heard in Kennedy's inaugural address and in his message to Congress in May 1961 outlining a supplemental budget request, including additional spending for military assistance, defense, and space. But as the administration went on, discussions of foreign policy in general and Soviet-American relations specifically changed in character. They became softer, more focused on concrete issues, and they balanced assertions of strength and steadfastness with recognition of the need for and possibility of coexistence, though this was by no means a steady process.

Whatever its lingering resonances in the public rhetoric of 1961–63, NSC

68 itself lay peacefully buried in the classified archives. As a senior member of the NSC staff and a participant in the (few) formal council deliberations and (endless) informal meetings, I never once heard NSC 68 mentioned or cited in a written document, although its chief author [Nitze] held an important post in the national security bureaucracy—as assistant secretary of defense for international security affairs.

This absence may testify to nothing more than the present-mindedness of governmental Washington, even in an administration studded with ex-academics. In my judgment, however, it does reflect something more, and more significant—namely, a distaste for broad doctrinal pronouncements inside the government on matters of foreign policy and national security in the Kennedy administration, especially on the part of the president himself. He and his senior advisers emphasized concrete decisions, both reflecting and limited to the specific circumstances that occasioned them, rather than broad doctrinal pronouncements. At the outset of his term, the president asked his national security adviser to review the NSC and interdepartmental machinery built up under his predecessor to provide regular surveys, appraisals, and policy papers on the entire international spectrum of issues and problems. The review resulted in the abolition of the whole process.

Later, officers of the State Department asked the president to endorse and issue in his name an overarching classified policy paper under the title Basic National Security Policy (BNSP). Such a paper had been issued annually in the previous administration as a policy guideline for the executive branch, covering the major problems of foreign and military policy. These papers were certainly akin to, if not lineal descendants of, NSC 68. Kennedy decided not to continue to issue them. He believed that the papers either would be too general and abstract to be useful or would be inappropriate as guides to specific decisions in circumstances largely unforeseen and inevitably different from what had been anticipated. Never doubting the need for and utility of broad public statements of policy, though these also frequently reflected the concrete occasions that called them forth, Kennedy remained skeptical of the utility of attempts to reduce the variety of possible U.S. responses to future international contingencies to an authoritative text that could guide executive decision making.

Looking back over more than forty years, rather than only ten, what does NSC 68 tell us today? The cold war is over. Certainly, the former Soviet Union, either itself or in its claimed if not always accepted role as the leader and embodiment of international communism, has lost. The United States and all the world have won, in the sense that we and all other nations are much better off in two very important ways. First, the possibility that the political and ideological confrontation that has divided the world at least since NSC 68 might lead to a devastating war involving the explosion of thousands or even tens of thousands of nuclear warheads with incalculable consequences is gone. Perhaps the probability of such a war has always been very low—whatever that statement means. It has now vanished. Second, the sway over a large fraction of the world's people of a barbarous, repressive, cruel political system, justified by a powerful ideology with universalistic claims, has ended. A utopia of peace, plenty, and justice has not arrived, but no one can doubt that the whole world is better off for the end of communism in what was the Soviet Union and its subordinate client states in Eastern Europe.

Was NSC 68 the blueprint for the policies that produced these successes? Many are making this claim, if not quite in these terms, not least the representatives of the dominant conservative part of the U.S. political spectrum. In the nature of the case, it is hard either to prove or to disprove them, but great skepticism is in order, on at least two grounds.

First, the significance of any policy blueprint in guiding the actual doings of nations is questionable, and especially so for the United States. It was not the rhetoric and analysis of NSC 68, but the Korean War and our immediate interpretation of what it signified that turned the policy of first deploring and then resisting the Soviet advance and seeking to restore the balance of power in Europe into the all-out militarized confrontation with the Soviet Union and "international communism" that dominated world politics for the last four decades. Current scholarship casts great doubt on the validity of our 1950 interpretation. It seems that the Soviet role in the outbreak of the Korean War was at most permissive. Until the former Soviet archives are opened, we cannot be sure that Khrushchev's memoirs—which in essence have Stalin saying to North Korea's Kim Il-sung, "Attack South Korea if you wish, but you are on your own"—accurately represent what happened. Further, Bruce Cumings's recent work raises the possibility that the timing of the North Korean attack was fortuitous, the result of unexpected success in one of the many border skirmishes that both Koreas had initiated at one time or another in the years preceding the war.[3] To be sure, NSC 68 represents just the mind-set that generated the immediate interpretation of the war as an aggressive Soviet move, but it is the prevalence of the mind-set, and not the document, that is important.

The deeper question is whether the militarized confrontation, with its buildup of incomprehensibly massive nuclear arsenals on both sides and its strong tendency to transform all of international politics into a zero-sum game, was necessary to the collapse of the Soviet empire. If not necessary, was it sufficient, or mostly irrelevant? Even the first judgment should await evidence from the Soviet side. But the evidence, if it comes, is unlikely to be at all conclusive, and we will probably be left with another unresolvable historical crux, in which analysts will find what they look for.

As a distillation of what became the dominant American attitude toward the Soviet Union for the whole period of the cold war, NSC 68 is exemplary. No more than any other abstract document was it a cause of policy.

ROBERT D. BLACKWILL
(Assistant to the President for European and Soviet Affairs, 1989–1990)

Born and reared in Kansas, Robert D. Blackwill served as a Peace Corps volunteer in the mid-1960s and then joined the foreign service. Noticing Blackwill's extraordinary energy and intelligence, Henry Kissinger, then secretary of state, pulled him out for special duties. Jimmy Carter's national security adviser, Zbigniew Brzezinski, made use of Blackwill as a National Security Council staffer. From 1983 to 1985 Blackwill made his first transition toward an academic career, taking leave from the Department of State to serve as a faculty member and an associate dean at Harvard University's John F. Kennedy School of Government, a professional school providing training for public service.

Blackwill returned to diplomacy during the Reagan administration as the U.S. ambassador conducting negotiations to limit nonnuclear military forces in Europe. From the beginning of the Bush administration in 1987 until mid-1990, Blackwill was President Bush's assistant for European and Soviet affairs, playing a key role in managing U.S. policy toward German reunification. He then retired from the foreign service and returned to Harvard, where he teaches and writes on issues in U.S. foreign policy and trains future and current public officials from around the world. (As one token of the end of the cold war, Blackwill in 1991 became faculty chair for a program that brings Russian generals and admirals to Harvard for education on civil-military relations in democracies.

Blackwill's essay contrasts with Bowie's and Kaysen's in two respects. First, Blackwill is more inclined to see NSC 68 as a model for how policy ought to be defined. Bowie and Kaysen argue implicitly that it is a bad model—too Manichean, too simplistic, too little concerned either with non-military aspects of national security or with international cooperation. Blackwill thinks it not a bad thing to make sharp value judgments and to strive for "a position of strength."

Second, Blackwill is concerned almost exclusively with the present and the future. He says nothing about containment versus rollback. That issue is not of his time. Neither is the issue of whether the government should prepare long papers on basic policy. Blackwill looks back in wonderment that officials ever had time even to *read* such documents, let alone to write them. To the extent that past policy concerns figure at all in his essay, they are concerns from a past that is so recent as to be almost current. His essay is a crystalline example of history as it is internalized by thoughtful policymakers. Almost none of it has to do with the past in its own right. What matters are the lessons.

Blackwill's Commentary

Reading again NSC 68 has been to some degree an eerie experience. Many of the ideas in this remarkable document have sent their echoes loudly and persistently into U.S. administrations through the decades.

That few, if any, of the presidents who have served after Truman and Eisenhower ever examined the study, or even knew of its existence, is both unsurprising and unimportant. Unsurprising because presidents seldom read such lengthy policy papers, including those produced in their own administrations. To imagine Kennedy, Carter, or Bush thumbing through the pages of Nitze's old paper is to misunderstand the time pressures that accompany most postwar presidential decision making. Unimportant because what really counts is not whether presidents had read or knew about NSC 68, but instead if the ideas contained in the document were specifically familiar to the occupants of the Oval Office and, more important, if those ideas have held up over the years. The answer to both these tests is an emphatic yes.

There are, to be sure, concepts in the study that have not worn well with age. The constant repetition of the notion of a "Kremlin design," a strategic blueprint toward world domination with subtle and flexible tactical implementation, appears in retrospect to have given Stalin and certainly his successors far too much credit. Indeed, following the Soviet occupation of Eastern Europe, politburo policy over the decades appears much more opportunistic than strategic, more episodic probing than the execution of a master plan. From the 1958–62 Berlin confrontations through the Cuban missile crisis, the periodic bloody crushings of rebellions in Eastern Europe, Vietnam and 1973 Middle East war, the invasion of Afghanistan, and the 1983 INF deployment struggle in West Germany, Soviet policymakers seemed in fact less able than their American counterparts, who were fortified by the central long-term concepts of NSC 68 itself, to adopt a coherent strategy and stick to it.

A second curiosity in the study from the present perspective is the emphasis on the Soviet Union's "new fanatical faith" and its goal to head "an international crusade." The danger of the red tentacles of the Soviet octopus energetically spreading Communist ideology across the globe seemed by the late 1960s a bygone threat of ideas from an increasingly secular adversary. By 1970, Soviet influence beyond its borders had little to do with the export of ideological zeal. Rather, military force, arms sales, covert action, and political threats and intimidation were the instruments of Moscow's attempts to bend the international environment in ways that served Soviet interests. And at home, mass cynicism born of a deeply corrupt system was hardly an enduring foundation for the spread of Marx's utopia.

A few such anomalies aside, Nitze's conclusions in 1950 had startling relevance and application until Mikhail Gorbachev's "new thinking" was well along at the end of the 1980s. The central theme in NSC 68 that U.S. and Western policy must seek to prevent the hegemonic gathering of power on the continent by any single European nation—that is to say, the Soviet Union—was the mainstay of NATO communiqués and presidential statements for forty years. Indeed, even in 1991 at the May Copenhagen NATO ministerial meeting, the alliance still used the concept of deterring attempts at hegemony in Europe, although by this time in Gorbachev's reform effort NATO was too polite to mention the Soviet Union by name.

But Nitze's preoccupation with deterring Soviet power was not at the expense of seeking negotiated improvements in the East-West relationship. NSC 68 calls for constant vigilance on the part of the United States for opportunities based on reasonable Soviet behavior to make qualitative improvements in East-West relations. As NSC 68 puts it, "A diplomatic freeze . . . tends to defeat the very purposes of 'containment' because it raises tensions at the same time that it makes Soviet retractions and adjustments in the direction of moderated behavior more difficult." Nevertheless, Nitze thoughtfully recognized that the United States was unlikely to successfully negotiate with the hard men in the Kremlin unless Washington did so from a position of strength. This insight, which escaped some of Nitze's successors in government, was sadly demonstrated during the dark days of America's retreat from Vietnam and throughout the Watergate constitutional crisis and its melancholy geopolitical aftermath in the Ford administration and, conversely, in the positive impact on Soviet external policies of Ronald Reagan's military buildup and George Bush's historic diplomatic accomplishment, the unification of Germany with full sovereignty and within the Atlantic alliance.

As much of the actual language of the document makes obvious, one finds in NSC 68 gem after gem of strategic insight that American presidents often knew in their bones but did not always put in their policies:

— The tolerance and generosity of the American people and the quality of American democratic institutions were enormous assets in the cold war, but ones that could be exploited by the other side.
— Absence of good faith on the part of the Soviet Union must be assumed.
— There were risks in making America strong; these, however, were less than those inherent in allowing the United States to become weak.
— The military potential of the United States and its allies would far surpass the capacities of the Soviet Union, if that potential were ever realized.
— The United States alone could not provide the resources to contain the Soviet Union; a coalition strategy was a clear requirement as the allies bore their fair share of the burden.
— There would in the future be no absolute defense, given the trends in weapons development.
— There existed a sharp disparity between actual U.S. military strength and its international commitments.
— No system of international control could prevent the production and use of nuclear weapons in the event of a prolonged war.
— A policy of isolation would be disastrous to American interests in the world.
— We must avoid an excessive or wasteful usage of our resources in time of peace; maximizing the peacetime economy was a must.
— American leadership was the key to the West's successful defense of its interests against Soviet probes and worse.

Most prescient perhaps of all of NSC 68's strategic advice is its emphasis on the requirement "to foster fundamental change in the nature of the Soviet system," following the phase in which Moscow's geopolitical offensive had been blunted. Even more striking is the study's recognition that it would be "more effective if this change occurs to a maximum extent as a result of internal forces in Soviet society" and that "we can expect no lasting abatement of the crisis unless and until a change occurs in the nature of the Soviet system."

This long-term objective with regard to the internal makeup of the Soviet Union found its origin in George Kennan's earlier Long Telegram from Embassy Moscow and his "X" article in *Foreign Affairs* and reached its zenith in the Reagan administration. Many U.S. policymakers along the way from 1950, including Richard Nixon, believed such a goal was overly ambitious, even misty-eyed optimism. Jimmy Carter could never quite decide what his approach to Moscow was, until the invasion of Afghanistan sent the U.S.-Soviet relationship into sharp decline. Some of America's political elite during and after the Vietnam period became confused about the clear superiority of Western values over Soviet ones, especially when these individuals were out of office for years and indeed decades at a stretch. Few were as clear-sighted and determined as Ronald Reagan to bring an end to the "evil empire." But when the August 1991 revolution shattered the Communist system's hold on that vast conglomerate east of the Bug River and the West won the cold war, the strategic soundness of NSC 68 and the wisdom of the former governor of California who came to the White House as well as that of his successor in the Oval Office were amply confirmed.

GEORGI M. KORNIENKO

(American Expert, Foreign Ministry of the USSR, 1949–1990)

A veteran observer of the United States, Georgi M. Kornienko was born in the Ukraine in 1925 and graduated during World War II from the Moscow Law Institute. He apprenticed for the Soviet diplomatic service by working as an English-language translator, and he remembers being involved in preparing for Stalin a translation of Kennan's "X" article. The final version, he says, pandered to Stalin's paranoia by rendering containment not as *sderzhivanie*, which would have been accurate, but as *udushenie*—strangulation.[1]

Admitted to the Soviet diplomatic service in 1949, Kornienko was assigned to a small committee with a function somewhat like that of the contemporaneous Board of National Estimates in the U.S. Central Intelligence Agency. He has no recollection of any reports on NSC 68 in the period of its composition and approval. At the time, Harold ("Kim") Philby headed the British secret service liaison with the CIA, and Donald Maclean headed the American desk in the British foreign office. Both were Soviet spies. That Kornienko knew nothing of NSC 68 may indicate that Philby and Maclean did not pick up news of it. Alternatively, Kornienko may have been too junior to be told or may have been in the wrong part of the Soviet intelligence apparatus.

In any event, Kornienko's commentary is entirely retrospective, giving his reactions to reading the full text of NSC 68 in the 1970s and rereading it in the early 1990s. In the intervening years, Kornienko had become one of the prime Soviet experts on the United States. From 1960 to 1965—from the end of the Eisenhower administration to the beginning of Johnson's full term—Kornienko was in the Soviet embassy in Washington. From 1965 to 1978, he was in the American department of the Soviet foreign ministry, most of the time as the department's chief. From 1977 to 1986 he was first deputy foreign minister. Under Gorbachev, he moved in 1986 to an even more important post as first deputy head of the International Department of the Central Committee of the Communist party. Now he is in retirement in Moscow as a research fellow at the Institute for the Study of the U.S.A. and Canada.

Kornienko's Commentary[2]

Having first become acquainted with the entire text of NSC 68 at the end of the 1970s and then rereading it in 1991, I have consistently noted—leaving aside the question as to whether I agree or disagree with its substance—the high quality of this document: its seriousness, thoroughness, clarity, and persuasiveness (in any case for those who did not themselves possess a deep knowledge of the issues considered in NSC 68 and had no personal opinions about them). And I must note with regret that we had no comparable foreign policy document in the postwar period.

To be sure, on account of the changes that have occurred and that are going on in the Soviet Union, the surviving authors of NSC 68, above all Paul Nitze, and like-minded people consider that the analysis and recommendations contained in the document were completely borne out by reality.

I, however, do not believe this. From my perspective the authors' fundamental premises, theoretical and factual, were incorrect. And hence so is the essence of their recommendations, which laid the groundwork for a more confrontational Soviet-American relationship in the postwar period than was objectively necessary. Aside from the fact that because of it, both of our countries, along with the rest of the world, more than once approached the line across which the irretrievable would have happened, I personally think that the far-reaching changes in the USSR would also have started much earlier in a different, more favorable international climate.

The fundamental conceptual flaw of NSC 68, to my mind, consists in the fact that its authors—consciously or not—equated the Soviet government's declared confidence in the victory of communism around the world with an imaginary aspiration of the Soviet Union as a state "to establish its absolute power over the rest of the world." The thesis that the Soviet Union was striving for world domination is often repeated in the text as something perfectly self-evident without the slightest attempts to base it either theoretically or factually.

In truth, from the time of Lenin two policy approaches were characteristic of the Soviet leadership: the "Comintern" (ideological) and "Narkomindel" (state-governmental). Although at times they were hard to differentiate, in practice they never did merge entirely. In any case, it was simply preposterous to speak in 1950 of the existence of a Soviet plan—in terms of a practical course of action—to establish domination over the world or as a start just over the European continent. The American leaders knew very well, for example, that the coming to power of Communists in China was not at all equivalent to the establishment of Soviet hegemony over that country.

The preceding does not constitute a denial by me of the fact that the Soviet Union had a tendency—as, indeed, have other great powers, including not least the United States—to strive for expansion of its sphere of influence. And it is only natural that where it had the opportunity, the USSR influenced the internal development of states in its own image—exactly as the USA did (it is enough to recall, for example, the role of General Douglas MacArthur in drafting the Japanese constitution).

From this standpoint the authors of NSC 68 obviously left dangling a contradiction when, on the one hand, they declared that the USA, being a free society, does not attempt to remake all other states in its own image but then suggested, on the other hand, that the policy and actions of the USA be directed toward the achievement of fundamental change in the nature of the Soviet system. Or when they demanded that the USSR structure its relations with other countries on the basis of equality and the respect of the countries' rights, while by no means being prepared at the same time to consider the Soviet Union as itself an equal member of the international community.

But this is all still far from what could have really been called striving for world domination either on the part of the Soviet Union or the United States, unless we are to substitute propagandistic clichés for serious analysis.

This conceptual flaw of NSC 68—to wit, attributing to the USSR a plan to establish its hegemony over the world—was made much more severe by the highly serious factual distortion of the actual state of affairs allowed by the authors.

In confirmation of their thesis that the USSR had a plan to establish world domination, starting with Europe, the authors of the document stated that in 1950 the Soviet Union possessed the *capability* to seize the continental part of Western Europe, to enter the oil regions of the Far and Middle East, and even to deliver nuclear attacks on the USA and Canada, not to mention the British Isles. Moreover, for greater persuasiveness, it is said in the document that even if the USA delivered a powerful nuclear attack upon the USSR, (a capability which the USA actually had), that supposedly even after this "the Kremlin would be capable of using the forces it controls to establish hegemony over the majority or all of Eurasia."

This was not only simply exaggerated. It did not correspond at all with reality. When I acquainted the leaders of the General Staff of the armed forces of the USSR with NSC 68's estimate of Soviet military capabilities in 1950, they termed it deliberately false and risible. They could not believe that such an estimate was seriously adhered to by their counterparts from the U.S. Joint Chiefs of Staff, to whom there is reference in the document.

Meanwhile it was precisely this false premise that gave rise to the main recommendation of the authors of NSC 68: the necessity of a forced general buildup of the military power of the USA and its allies. By falsifying their estimates of relative military power in 1950, the authors of NSC 68 apparently had in mind the goal, as is evident from the statement by Dean Acheson, "to so bludgeon the mass mind of 'top government' that not only could the President make a decision but that the decision could be carried out."

And, as is known, they succeeded in this respect. Truman's acceptance of NSC 68, though with some delay, foreordained for many years to come the furious global arms race. This could have been entirely avoided, I think, if only George Kennan's recommendation of "containment" of the Soviet Union by means of principally political and economic methods had prevailed in Truman's second administration, instead of the policy of containment by primarily military means, which is what the acceptance of NSC 68 entailed.

Incidentally, the war that started in Korea in 1950, which, it is said, convinced Truman of the soundness of the analysis and recommendations provided by the authors of NSC 68, in reality was not part of a "Kremlin plan." Stalin seriously doubted the wisdom of the actions of Kim Il-sung, having given them his blessing only after the latter had enlisted the support of Mao Zedong. In other words, the Korean War could not serve as proof of the accuracy of the statements about the Soviet Union's goal of world hegemony.

From my point of view there were also extremely negative consequences for the development of international relations because the authors of NSC 68 did not leave room within the framework of their policy recommendations for serious and successful negotiations between the USA and the USSR either on a general codification of their relations or on the question of arms control. Not expecting superpower negotiations to achieve such a settlement, which would have led to fundamental changes in the Soviet system, the authors of the document tolerated the use of negotiations with the USSR only for purely tactical purposes.

In light of the considerations given above, I believe, now as before, that NSC 68 played a profoundly negative role in postwar history.   ■

NOTES

Bowie

[1]Bowie's title was professor of government, for at Harvard the department that awards higher degrees in political science calls itself the Department of Government and awards its undergraduate degree in government. This is doubly confusing because Harvard also has a John F. Kennedy School of Government, which is a professional school awarding only advanced degrees, these in public administration or public policy. Robert Blackwill, author of another commentary in this book, teaches in the Kennedy School. That being the case, the text here refers to Bowie as a professor of political science, even though he himself takes exception to such labeling, saying perfectly accurately that he is a lawyer and a professor (now emeritus) of government.

[2]David Alan Rosenberg, "The Origins of Overkill," *International Security* 7 (Spring 1983): 21–24.

[3]Paul Y. Hammond, "NSC 68: Prologue to Rearmament," in *Strategy, Politics, and Defense Budgets,* ed. Warner R. Schilling, Paul Y. Hammond, and Glenn H. Snyder (New York: Columbia University Press, 1962), Hammond, "NSC 68," 345–59; NSC 114/3, ". . . United States Programs for National Security," 5 June 1952, *FRUS, 1952–1954,* 2:21–28; NSC 141, ". . . United States Programs for National Security," 19 Jan. 1953, ibid., 209–22; John Lewis Gaddis, *Strategies of Containment,* New York: Oxford University Press, 1982), 359.

[4]*FRUS, 1952–1954,* 2:577–97.

[5]"Notes on a Meeting at the White House [with General Eisenhower]," 31 Jan. 1951, *FRUS, 1951,* 3:453–56; McGeorge Bundy, *Danger and Survival: Choices about the Bomb in the First Fifty Years* (New York: Random House, 1988), 259–60; Richard Immerman, "Confessions of an Eisenhower Revisionist," *Diplomatic History* 14, no. 3 (Summer 1990): 332–34.

[6]From NSC 68, part IX-D and Conclusions.

[7]25 Sept. 1952, *FRUS, 1952–1954,* 2:142–56.

[8]*FRUS, 1952–1954,* 2:205.

[9]John Foster Dulles, "A Policy of Boldness," *Life* 32 (19 May 1952): 146–600.

[10]*FRUS, 1952–1954,* 2:580–81.

[11]Memorandum by the Joint Chiefs of Staff, 17 Dec. 1954, *FRUS, 1951–1954,* 2:828; "Memorandum of Discussion at the 229th Meeting of the National Security Council," 21 Dec. 1954, ibid., 833–34.

[12]"Policy for Security and Peace," *Foreign Affairs* 32 (April 1954): 353–64.

[13]Gaddis, *Strategies of Containment,* 159–61; Bundy, *Danger and Survival,* 287–305, 325–34.

Kaysen

[1]Kaysen explains elegantly his view of how the cold war did come to an end in "Is War Obsolete?," *International Security* 14, no. 4 (Spring 1990): 42–64.

[2]Fred I. Greenstein, *The Hidden-Hand Presidency: Eisenhower as Leader* (New York: Basic Books, 1982), is the flagship work. In any edition published since the mid-1980s, Richard E. Neustadt's classic *Presidential Power* (New York: Free Press, 1991), assays this "Eisenhower revisionism." When Kaysen's essay is neither pure history nor commentary on current affairs, it makes sallies into this controversy, essentially of the 1960s, about how best to organize the policy process.

[3]Bruce Cumings, *The Origins of the Korean War. Vol. II: The Roaring of the Cataract, 1947–1950* (Princeton: Princeton University Press, 1990), esp. 528–624.

Kornienko

[1]From Georgi M. Kornienko, "U Istokob 'Xolodnoï Voïny' " (About the sources of the "cold war"), *Novaya i Noveïshaya Istoriya,* no. 6 (Nov.–Dec. 1990): 105–22.

[2]Translated from the Russian by Timothy Naftali of the Harvard Department of History, with polishing by Professor Rachel May of the Department of Russian, Macalester College.

4

Interpreters of
U.S. Foreign Policy

In this chapter, specialists on U.S. foreign policy offer contrasting explanations of NSC 68. Schools represented include realism, revisionism, neorealism, postrevisionism, and neorevisionism. (Any reader who thinks this a school or two too many should know that aficionados can identify at least another nine.)[1]

Realism

PAUL Y. HAMMOND

Paul Y. Hammond, born in 1929, had been too young to serve in World War II. He took a Ph.D. in political science at Harvard University in 1953. Teaching subsequently at Columbia, Yale, and then Johns Hopkins universities, Hammond was a pioneer in the decision-making analysis that Dean Acheson was to deride. At the Rand Corporation, Hammond later did research for the government. Still later, he returned to teaching as a professor at the University of Pittsburgh.

For context, remember that, when Hammond wrote his forty-thousand-word monograph on NSC 68 in 1962, John F. Kennedy had just become president. In his inaugural address, Kennedy had said, "We shall pay any price, bear any burden, meet any hardship, support any friend, oppose any foe to assure the survival and the success of liberty." In legislation, the chief accomplishment of Kennedy's short presidency was to boost defense spending $650 million in order to speed strategic nuclear missile programs. October 1962 saw the hair-raising crisis over Soviet missiles in Cuba. It was high cold war. Revisionism had scarcely begun to raise its head. While Hammond criticizes NSC 68, he writes strictly as a realist, sure of the wisdom and rightness of the basic policy of containment.

Hammond's Commentary

NSC-68 had much to recommend it. It had avoided . . . entanglement with questions which involved interservice disputes, such as the delineation of service roles and missions or the uses and limits of strategic air power. Moreover, it provided something for everyone and in a way that was palatable. Economic growth is a way to moderate problems of distribution. . . .

[But] NSC 68 had major limitations. It was only a general statement of policy without a definite settlement of its meaning in terms of tangible decisions about budgets, procurement, and forces. Some who read it thought it was a scare document; others, that it justified any international commitments the government wanted to undertake; still others, that it only expressed the prevailing view. None of them were entirely wrong. In addition, NSC 68 was undoubtedly abused as well as used, for the number of people who saw it was strictly limited, yet it was referred to widely as the definitive statement of government policy. . . .

. . . Undoubtedly, much of what was done in the Korean military build-up would have been done anyway. Yet, the existence of NSC 68 at the outset of the war contributed a particular quality to that build-up. From its beginning, and through its most frantic phases, the Korean War remained only a part of the larger picture of national strategy. For the small number of people in the Executive branch who had read it, and for a larger number who knew it by reputation, NSC 68 represented that larger picture.

It is easy for a crisis, particularly war, to break down the separate and conflicting views and interests of government and infuse them with a com-

From Paul Y. Hammond, "NSC 68: Prologue to Rearmament," in *Strategy, Politics, and Defense Budgets*, ed. Warner R. Schilling, Paul Y. Hammond, and Glenn H. Snyder (New York: Columbia University Press, 1962) 361–63, 369–70.

mon purpose. The common purpose, however, may have to be oversimplified. . . . NSC 68 provided a partial substitute within the Executive branch for the oversimplification of objectives in war. Before the Korean War had started, and, of course, without reference to it, a question had been asked and an answer provided which transcended organization perspectives and, when the time for implementation came, consolidated them. NSC 68 became a milestone in the consolidation of perspectives, establishing at least some kind of order of priority and magnitude between economy and security, domestic and foreign commitments, economic and military means, American and allied strength, and short and long-run national interests.

In this respect, it made an important difference. Aided by circumstances, to be sure, the existence of NSC 68 made it possible to move into a general program of rearmament with only a minimum of impedances and fumbling caused by the suspicions and misunderstandings of different agencies. How much the value of NSC-68 derived from the special circumstances surrounding its drafting and implementation, however, is a question which cannot be answered by examining only the one case. Yet it is worth ending this examination with the reminder that NSC 68 was valuable as much because of what—prudently—it did not attempt to do as for the thrust of the argument which it made. . . .

. . . The document itself concentrated upon the analysis and definition of national security goals. The breadth of its scope justified this initial trifling with practical considerations, and so did what NSC 68 achieved in its analysis of national strategy. Without a doubt it was superior to any analysis of national strategy which was involved in the fiscal 1950 defense budgetary process. It was systematic. It was comprehensive. It considered alternative courses of action by weighing their consequences and, in a very general way, their costs. The weight it carried was the weight of rational argument. Its prestige rested on the rational standards which it had visibly met.

But it had met these standards by avoiding practical considerations of two kinds: it had avoided dealing with concrete programs and it had ignored the problem of reconciling what seemed desirable with what was (or was thought to be) possible. As a consequence, until unforeseen events changed the whole frame of reference for policy, it was threatened with irrelevancy. Were it not for the start of the Korean War, its value would, very probably, have been only historical, to mark, but not to effect, a change in the climate of opinion in Washington and, possibly, the integration of the strategic views of several of the opinion elites in the government. ∎

Revisionism
WILLIAM APPLEMAN WILLIAMS

William Appleman Williams's commentary reflects revisionism at its most basic. Its author was a 1944 graduate of the U.S. Naval Academy. After service in the Pacific, Williams left the Navy and took a Ph.D. in history at the University of Wisconsin. Remaining there as a professor, he helped to mold a "Wisconsin school," which was in the forefront of revisionist reinterpretation of the history of American foreign policy.

Williams's first book, published in 1950, concerned the history of Russian-American relations. Even that early, he argued that friction between the two countries had been largely due to an American crusade for capitalism. In 1960 his most influential work, *The Tragedy of American Diplomacy,* appeared. In this long essay, he put most provocatively the basic revisionist thesis that the actual history of U.S. foreign policy was at variance with its idealistic rationales. American rhetoric had championed democracy and self-determination, he contended, but the American government had in reality imposed "open door imperialism" wherever its power could reach.

The brief passage borrowed here is from Williams's 1976 *America Confronts a Revolutionary World.* Not highly nuanced, it may be more representative of Williams as a polemicist than of Williams as a historian. Nevertheless, it shows clearly the view of NSC 68 that followed from revisionist premises.

Williams's Commentary

[The recognition of Israel in 1948] was the beginning of the end of what little remained of the American commitment to the principle of self-determination. That process involved interlocking ironies that can be viewed as the ultimate expression of the contradiction inherent in trying to preserve the present. Secretary of the Navy James V. Forrestal argued strongly against neglecting the Arab right to self-determination within the Open Door System—after all, they had the oil. But at the same time he became the most influential patron of a bright and ambitious foreign service officer named George Frost Kennan, who argued that it was essential to confront Russian totalitarianism

From William Appleman Williams, *America Confronts a Revolutionary World: 1776–1976* (New York: William Morrow, 1976), 175–77.

with unanswerable force on every front because expansionism was the touchstone of the Soviet system.

Kennan was a bureaucratic spokesman of the doctrine espoused by Madison and Jefferson, Congressman Delano and Lincoln, and intellectuals like Frederick Jackson Turner, Brooks Adams, and Woodrow Wilson—to say nothing of Acheson of Yale. Kennan did not know enough history to realize that he was one of them, that his argument was but another version of their argument: if expansion is necessary to the American way, then containment is death. Lincoln followed that logic in developing his doctrine of containing slavery. Adams used the verb "to contain" in 1900 when he proposed a similar policy toward Russia. All Kennan did was to carry the holy doctrine into the 1940s.

Then matters became even more complicated. Forrestal embraced Kennan's argument. But so did Acheson and Truman. The only trouble was that they read it to mean that Israel was the bastion of strength to prevent the Soviets from controlling the Middle East by appealing to and helping the Arabs. That, very simply, meant that Israel became the potential Fort Sumter of the twentieth century.

Acheson viewed Kennan's analysis as a useful footnote to support his own thesis. It *was* true that Kennan's metaphors were more than a bit bourgeois: he talked in middle-class terms about the Soviets as a windup toy that could only be stopped by an American wall. Even so, he also revealed a propensity to speak of deeper matters like civilization. Acheson put it very neatly when he defined the American Present as being "the only kind of world" in which civilization *could* exist.

Thus Acheson used Kennan against other equally intelligent and thoughtful bureaucrats within the State Department. And to fight all others who suggested that it might be useful—even vital—"to reexamine all our policies and all our programs." Acheson gives the game away: there was a very tough argument within the State Department (and with some elements in the Congress) about whether it was historically accurate—*and therefore wise, let alone practical*—to accept the Kennan analysis of Soviet behavior. The doubters advanced impressive arguments that Stalin (and others) sought first and primarily the security to self-determine their own revolution.

Acheson the Yale Man knew The Truth, and so had no patience with such serious and consequential dialogue. He was saving civilization and the individualistic marketplace—the American Christian Present. He considered the debate "a stultifying and, so I thought, sterile argument." And he had the power to pick the winners. Thus the final irony. He chose Kennan's argument even as Kennan began to look for a way to escape the consequences of his inflexible metaphors.

That decision led to a long and elaborate statement of the thinking behind the newest crusade: an American Papal Bull. Known formally as National Security Council Document 68 (NSC-68), it ostensibly remained TOP SECRET for many years; but, as Acheson has admitted, he talked about it so often, and so much of it was leaked to various sympathetic observers, that there was never any mystery about its main themes.

First: the success of the Russian Revolution threatens the American Present.

Second: to preserve that Present, "the nation must be determined, at whatever cost or sacrifice, to preserve at home and abroad those conditions of life."

Third: "this means virtual abandonment by the United States of trying to distinguish between national and global security. . . . Security must henceforth become the dominant element in the national budget and other elements must be accommodated to it."

That outlook led inevitably to war: first in Korea, and then elsewhere. An argument of sorts can be made, of course, for insisting that the South Koreans should be allowed to remain within the Open Door System until they began their own revolution. That is probably the best case that can be offered in behalf of empire. But the crucial point is that Acheson and Truman had no hesitation in using force to dishonor even that imperial ideal.

They were, like Lincoln and Wilson, determined to grab hold of history and make it conform to the American Present. They undertook to *self-determine* all of Korea as an element of the Open Door Present. . . .

We all know the rest of the story. It is not a pleasant tale, and my citizen's soul is weary under the burden of my knowledge of my country dishonoring its once noble commitment to the right of self-determination. I leave it to others to reveal the details of the sagas of the terrible and bloody deeds of the Central Intelligence Agency and the Federal Bureau of Investigation, and to retell and embellish the grisly truths about Iran and Guatemala, Indonesia and Santo Domingo, Italy and Cuba, and Vietnam and Watergate. ∎

Neorealism

SAMUEL F. WELLS, JR.

By the end of the 1970s, revisionism had developed many variations more subtle than Williams's. Also, a natural dialectic had produced critiques of revisionism almost rivaling the revisionist critiques of realism. The following commentary by Samuel F. Wells, Jr., represents what can be called neorealism—analysis akin to Hammond's but informed by revisionist questioning of the premises of U.S. policies. A Carolinian born in 1935, a onetime Marine, and for a long period a professor of history at the University of North Carolina at Chapel Hill, Wells is deputy director of the Washington-based Woodrow Wilson International Center for Scholars.

Most of Wells's essay was published in 1979. The climate of that period affected Wells somewhat as it did Nitze. Indeed, one of Wells's aims was to call attention to similarities between the campaign for NSC 68 and that being waged in 1979 by Nitze's Committee on the Present Danger, and the essay by Nitze in Chapter 2 was written in part as a response to Wells. But Wells was more affected than Nitze by changes in the scholarly climate. There, revisionism was ebbing, and postrevisionism was on a rise.

While Wells's analysis of NSC 68 is more nearly postrevisionist than revisionist, his approach resembles most of all that of Hammond. He offers some sharp criticism of NSC 68, taking Nitze and his collaborators to task for "incomplete and amateurish" analysis of the actual threat and for "sophomoric" presentation of alternatives. Wells argues, however, that there had been a threat and consequent need for a "tocsin." Additional comments, written by Wells in 1992 and appended here, show some subtle changes resulting from changes in climate accompanying the end of the cold war and also from the accumulation of scholarship over the intervening years.

Wells's Commentary

NSC 68 essentially represents a call for increased effort and a tougher stand against the Soviet Union. It is not a dramatic departure for it restates at length the established objectives of American policy as set forth in NSC 20/4 of November 1948. But its tone is more hostile and more urgent than the earlier study, and it contains the new goal of changing the nature of the Soviet system through political pressure backed by economic, psychological, propaganda, and covert activities. . . .

Yet viewed as a call to action rather than policy analysis, NSC 68 is an amazingly incomplete and amateurish study. The authors overdraw the monolithic and evil nature of the Communist bloc. They overlook many nations in the "free world" that have no democratic or responsible govern-

From Samuel F. Wells, Jr., "Sounding the Tocsin: NSC 68 and the Soviet Threat," *International Security* 4 (Fall 1979): 138–39, 141–42, 148–54, 158.

ment. . . . The concluding analysis of courses of action is sophomoric in posing four alternatives which include two straw options (isolation and war), one unacceptable choice (continuation of current policies), and the obviously desired solution (a rapid political, economic, and military buildup). Most serious, the authors deliberately avoided including specific recommendations for program expansion or estimates of cost despite their belief that vastly increased expenditures would be necessary.

The Korean War provided the necessary impetus for the adoption of the programs implicit in NSC 68. . . . If peace had continued under basically similar conditions through 1950, it is likely that the cost of NSC 68 programs would not have exceeded $3 billion annually. What NSC 68 did accomplish was to start senior officials thinking about an increasing Soviet threat and how to respond to it. The real significance of NSC 68 was its timing—the tocsin sounded just before the fire. . . .

[Wells next describes a Committee on the Present Danger organized in 1950 by prominent private citizens to lobby for increased defense spending. He then describes another Committee on the Present Danger, formed in the 1970s to campaign against the defense and arms control policies of the Carter administration, noting that the chief link between the two was "the imposing presence of Paul H. Nitze."]

. . . We are now in a relatively good position to assess that military threat of the early 1950s which was of such concern to the drafters of NSC 68 and the members of the Committee on the Present Danger alike. This process will suggest certain parallels with contemporary events, but one must resist the urge to find clear and simple lessons in the application of judgments from past eras to very different current circumstances.

Neither the drafters of NSC 68 nor the members of the original committee gave precise numerical estimates of the size of the Soviet military threat that they were determined to meet. They did imply estimates of Soviet capabilities in the two most important categories—land-based conventional forces and air-delivered atomic forces. Both groups accepted without apparent qualification the assertion by the Joint Chiefs of Staff that, should a major war break out in 1950, the Soviet Union could immediately "overrun Western Europe, with the possible exception of the Iberian and Scandinavian Peninsulas." Nitze and the State-Defense Policy Review Group also accepted the estimate that in such a war the Soviet Union could hit targets within the United States with atomic weapons. They adopted the CIA estimate that by 1954 the Soviet Union could be expected to have stockpiled 200 atomic weapons, of which one hundred might be delivered with reasonable accuracy on targets within the United States. . . . They were adamant that time was running out on the American atomic deterrent, implying that "in several years" the Soviet Union could reply in kind to an American use of nuclear weapons.

In evaluating the accuracy of these threat estimates for Soviet ground forces, firm conclusions prove elusive. Whether the Soviets did in fact possess the capability to overrun Western Europe is difficult to say. . . . We . . . know that blanket statements by both committees to the effect that the Soviet Union did not demobilize its forces after World War II are simply untrue. . . .

Yet at a minimum the Soviet Union maintained over thirty elite divisions in Eastern Europe after World War II. . . .[1]

One can traverse firmer ground in assessing the Soviet atomic threat as predicted in NSC 68. The estimates of Soviet bomb production (200 weapons by 1954) were probably far too high, but it is impossible to validate this belief with data currently available. The facts are much clearer about the Soviet capability to deliver the available bombs. The authors of NSC 68 asserted: "The Soviet Union now has aircraft able to deliver the atomic bomb." In the spring of 1950 that was true only in the extreme case of the Tu-4 (Bull)—the Soviet copy of the B-29—making a one-way "suicide" mission to the United States. . . .[2]

The prediction of a Soviet capability to deliver 100 bombs effectively against U.S. targets by 1954 was equally unrealistic. The Russian bomber force in that year still deployed mainly the Tu-4. . . . The first Soviet intercontinental bomber was the Tu-95 (Bear), which created quite a sensation and led to claims of an American "bomber gap" after it appeared at the May Day parade in 1955. Both the Bear and the MYA-4 (Bison), a pure jet bomber first deployed in 1956, apparently developed "technical and operational shortcomings" which limited their deployment. . . .[3]

The principal Soviet military buildup occurred after the Korean War had set in motion a massive expansion of U.S. forces. By 1955, the Red Army had grown to 5,763,000 men from a total of 2,874,000 in 1948. . . . Starting in 1950, the Soviet leadership launched a major equipment modernization for the European theater. . . .[4]

This summary evaluation of Soviet capabilities . . . in the period from 1947 to 1955 does not pretend to be definitive, but it does provide the basis for substantially narrowing the range of analytical uncertainty. . . .

We cannot easily criticize Americans of 1950 for desiring greater security. They were for the first time simultaneously facing the challenge of world leadership and the prospect of their homeland soon becoming vulnerable to nuclear attack. Yet when the response to the North Korean invasion took a form which threatened our Soviet competitor with a cordon of overseas air bases and over 1,800 bombers capable of delivering nuclear weapons, and when this threat engendered increased armament in Russia, we can conclude that U.S. action was self-defeating. There is good reason to believe that the massive American buildup in the Korean War era provided a ready excuse for Soviet leaders to initiate new programs of their own. . . .

[Writing in 1992, Wells adds:]

Recent evidence calls even more sharply into question some of the fundamental assumptions contained in NSC 68. Recent disclosures from the records of the Chinese Communist party indicate that the Chinese were much more involved in events leading to the Korean War than we had previously thought. The Chinese Communist politburo had ordered the return between July 1949 and the spring of 1950 of about 60,000 Korean-nationality troops that had been serving with the People's Liberation Army (PLA). As a result of conversations with North Korean leader Kim Il-sung, Chinese officials probably were aware of his goal to reunify Korea by force in the near future. After the war began, China provided staff support to the North Korean military command and moved more than 250,000 troops to take up reserve positions on the Chinese-Korean border. There is some evidence that the Chinese leadership was inclined to intervene in Korea before the United Nations forces made their landing at Inchon on September 15, 1950. The decision to intervene came at a politburo meeting on October 1–2, and the first organized contingents of Chinese "volunteers" crossed the Yalu River into North Korea on October 19, 1950.[5]

Evidence from similar sources, reinforced by new Russian interviews, indicates that the Soviet Union was more cautious and less in control of this series of events than believed earlier. Stalin and his advisers were quite suspicious of Mao Zedong, and this marked lack of confidence proved to be an obstacle during Mao's long visit to Moscow from December 1949 to mid-February 1950 when the Sino-Soviet treaty was signed. It is now known that the treaty had several secret articles containing harsh terms providing the Soviets with military basing and transportation rights in northeastern China and that the Chinese very much resented these concessions. When Mao decided to intervene in Korea, Stalin promised significant air support of the Chinese troops involved in the fighting. But when the time came to implement the plan of cooperation, the Russian leader backed out and after bitter discussion with Chinese representatives would agree only to provide air support of Chinese territory to help prevent retaliatory attacks on the People's Republic of China. Mao never forgot or forgave this reversal of a commitment and saw Stalin as excessively cautious and far too concerned with possible American reactions.

Further disclosures from China and Russia, and someday from North

Korea, will undoubtedly change our understanding of these events. But at this point we can make a tentative estimate of the importance of NSC 68 in shaping U.S. policy in the early years of the cold war. Its primary achievement was to provide a warning about Soviet challenges that might require a significantly higher defense effort. This alert had prepared many officials to respond quickly and decisively when the North Korean invasion occurred. Yet one should point out that the unexamined assumptions of this study led to serious subsequent policy errors. The belief that the North Korean attack was a Soviet-sponsored probe of Western will contributed mightily to decisions to cross the 38th parallel and attempt to unify Korea by force as well as to the massive buildup of military power in Western Europe and the capability for the Strategic Air Command to attack any point in the Soviet Union. This mind-set also caused officials to overlook indications of tensions between Soviet and Chinese leaders that would break into the open only in 1960. The authors of NSC 68 should not be held responsible for these misguided assumptions, for they were very widely shared in top political circles throughout the United States and Western Europe. From our vantage point today, NSC 68 should be seen as a crucial document in national security policy. It functioned very successfully as a tocsin to alert the policy community to an impending danger, yet as guidance for future program choices it proved to be excessively shrill in its tone. ∎

Postrevisionism

JOHN LEWIS GADDIS

Of postrevisionist historians, John Lewis Gaddis is the best known and most influential. Born in Cotulla, Texas, in 1941, he was educated at the University of Texas at Austin, receiving a Ph.D. in history there in 1968. For most of the time since, Gaddis has taught at Ohio University, where he is also director of the Center for Contemporary History.

Gaddis's first book, *The United States and the Origins of the Cold War, 1941–1947* (New York: Columbia University Press, 1972), was an outgrowth of his doctoral dissertation. It portrays security concerns and domestic concerns coming together to push the United States toward an anti-Soviet policy. This policy, Gaddis argues, had neither the inevitability assumed in conventional patriotism nor the expansive purposefulness assumed by revisionists. Choice had been driven by some sense of necessity, but there had been choice. Alternatives could have been chosen.

In *Strategies of Containment* (New York: Oxford University Press, 1982), Gaddis appraises the options open after the original decision. What appears here is an excerpt from that book. In it, Gaddis touches glancingly on strategic choices being made at the time of his writing by the new Reagan administration. Mostly, however, his context is the realist-revisionist debate. He argues that there had been a deep difference between two alternative forms of the basic anti-Soviet policy. Gaddis interprets Kennan as having called for selective, discriminating resistance to Soviet expansion, relying minimally on military threats and hardly at all on explicit or implicit threats to use nuclear weapons. NSC 68 Gaddis reads as prescribing resistance everywhere and anywhere, with military force and the nuclear threat in the forefront. He characterizes the Kennan strategy as "asymmetrical," Nitze's as "symmetrical."

Gaddis's Commentary

The differences between Kennan's conception of United States interests and that of NSC 68 are not immediately apparent. The document proclaimed as the nation's "fundamental purpose" assuring "the integrity and vitality of our free society, which is founded on the dignity and worth of the individual." It went on to announce "our determination to create conditions under which our free and democratic system can live and prosper." It associated American interests with diversity, not uniformity.... And it appeared to rely on the balance of power as the means of ensuring that diversity: the opening paragraph recalled with apparent approval the international system that preceded World War I. . . .

But there the similarity ended. Kennan had argued that all that was necessary to maintain the balance of power, and thereby safeguard diversity, was to keep centers of industrial-military capability out of hostile hands. Unfriendly regimes elsewhere, though not to be desired, posed little threat to global stability so long as they lacked means of manifesting their hostility. NSC 68 took a very different point of view: . . . "the assault on free institutions is worldwide now, and in the context of the present polarization of

From John Lewis Gaddis, *Strategies of Containment: A Critical Appraisal of Postwar American National Security Policy* (New York: Oxford University Press, 1982), 90–98, 104–6. (Footnotes in the original text referring to NSC 68 have been omitted.)

power a defeat of free institutions anywhere is a defeat everywhere."[1] The implication was clear: Kennan's strategy of defending selected strongpoints would no longer suffice; the emphasis rather would have to be on perimeter defense, with all points along the perimeter considered of equal importance.

NSC 68's endorsement of perimeter defense suggests several major departures in underlying assumptions from Kennan. One of these had to do with the nature of effective power in international affairs. Kennan had taken the view that only industrial-military power could bring about significant changes in world politics, and that as long as it was kept in rough balance, international stability (though not necessarily all exposed positions) could be preserved. But Kennan himself had been forced to acknowledge, by 1949, that things were not that simple. Insecurity could manifest itself in psychological as well as physical terms, as the Western Europeans' demands for American military protection had shown. And psychological insecurity could as easily develop from the distant sound of falling dominoes as from the rattling of sabers next door. This was the major unresolved dilemma in Kennan's thinking—how could the self-confidence upon which his strategy depended survive the making of distinctions between peripheral and vital interests? As far as the authors of of NSC-68 were concerned, it could not.

From their perspective, changes in the balance of power could occur, not only as the result of economic maneuvers or military action, but from intimidation, humiliation, or even loss of credibility. The Soviet Union, Nitze reminded his colleagues, made no distinction between military and other forms of aggression; it was guided "by the simple consideration of weakening the world power position of the US." . . .[2]

The implications were startling. World order, and with it American security, had come to depend as much on *perceptions* of the balance of power as on what that balance actually was. And the perceptions involved were not just those of statesmen customarily charged with making policy; they reflected as well mass opinion, foreign as well as domestic, informed as well as uninformed, rational as well as irrational. Before such an audience even the appearance of a shift in power relationships could have unnerving consequences; judgments based on such traditional criteria as geography, economic capacity, or military potential now had to be balanced against considerations of image, prestige, and credibility. The effect was vastly to increase the number and variety of interests deemed relevant to the national security, and to blur distinctions between them.

But proliferating interests could be of little significance apart from the means to defend them, and here NSC 68 challenged another of the assumptions that had informed Kennan's strategy of containment: the perception of limited resources, which had made distinctions between vital and peripheral interests necessary in the first place. On this point there had been no divergence of viewpoint between Kennan and the administration. President Truman had continued to insist on holding down defense expenditures in order to avoid either higher taxes or budget deficits. . . .

What NSC 68 did was to suggest a way to increase defense expenditures without war, without long-term budget deficits, and without crushing tax burdens. . . . "One of the most significant lessons of our World War II experience," NSC 68 pointed out, "was that the American economy, when it operates at a level approaching full efficiency, can provide enormous resources for purposes other than civilian consumption while simultaneously providing a higher standard of living."

. . . To its earlier assertion that there *should* not be distinctions between peripheral and vital interests, NSC-68 had now shown with seductive logic that there *need* not be. . . .

. . . For the authors of NSC 68, American interests could not be defined apart from the threat the Soviet Union posed to them: "frustrating the Kremlin design," as the document so frequently put it, became an end in itself, not a means to a larger end.

But just what was the Kremlin design, and how did perceptions of it reflected in NSC-68 differ from Kennan's? "The fundamental design of those who control the Soviet Union and the international communist movement," the document argued, "is to retain and solidify their absolute power, first in the Soviet Union and second in the areas now under their control. In the minds of the Soviet leaders, however, achievement of this design requires the dynamic extension of their authority." This much Kennan would have found unexceptionable. Nor did Nitze and his colleagues see Soviet expansion as motivated primarily by ideological considerations; like Kennan they saw Marxism-Leninism as more the instrument than the determinant of Soviet policy: "the Kremlin's conviction of its own infallibility has made its devotion to theory so subjective that past or present pronouncements as to doctrine offer no reliable guide to future action." Rather, Soviet hostility stemmed simply from the inability of a totalitarian system to tolerate diversity. . . .

The authors of NSC 68 also agreed with Kennan that this inability to live with diversity was a weakness, certain eventually to create problems for the Kremlin, but they differed with him as to how soon. Kennan took the position that the U.S.S.R. was already overextended; that it was finding it difficult to control areas it had already absorbed; and that the resulting strains, revealed vividly in the Titoist heresy, offered opportunities the United States could exploit. NSC 68 took a more pessimistic view. Soviet expansion, it argued, had so far produced strength, not weakness; whatever the liabilities of Titoism they were more than counter-balanced by the victory of communism in China, the Soviet atomic bomb, and Moscow's continued military build-up at a time when the United States was rigorously limiting its own comparable expenditures. Given this situation, it seemed imprudent "to risk the future on the hazard that the Soviet Empire, because of over-extension or other reasons, will spontaneously destroy itself from within."

Neither Kennan nor NSC 68 questioned the Russians' superiority in conventional forces or their ability, in time, to develop sufficient atomic weapons to neutralize the American advantage in that field as well. Rather, their conflicting assessments of the existing power balance hinged on the issue of whether or not the USSR would deliberately risk war. Kennan, reasoning from an evaluation of Soviet intentions, argued that disparities in military power could be tolerated because the Russians had little to gain from using it. The Soviet leadership was cautious, prone to seek its objectives at minimum cost and risk without reference to any fixed timetable. The United States could therefore content itself with an asymmetrical response—reinforcing its own strengths and those of its allies, but with no effort to duplicate Soviet force configurations. NSC 68, emphasizing Soviet capabilities, argued that the Russians had not provoked war so far only because they had lacked the assurance of winning it. Once their capabilities had expanded to the point where they could reasonably expect to win—NSC 68 estimated that this would occur in 1954, when the Russians would have enough atomic bombs to devastate the United States—then the intentions of Kremlin leaders, if Washington did nothing in the meantime to build up its own forces, might well be to risk war, probably in the form of a surprise attack.

Until then, the most significant danger was that of war by proxy. Kennan himself had come to acknowledge the possibility that the Soviet Union might authorize limited military action by its satellites, but such maneuvers would be designed, he thought, precisely to achieve Soviet objectives without setting off a general war. Since not all of its interests were equally vital, the United States could still choose whether and how to respond: "world realities have greater tolerances than we commonly suppose against ambitious schemes for world domination."[3] NSC 68, on the other hand, saw "piecemeal aggression" as an instrument of war, aimed at exploiting the Americans' unwillingness to use nuclear weapons unless directly attacked. Operating from the very different assumption that interests were indivisible, it warned that any failure to respond could lead to "a descending spiral of too little and too late, of doubt and recrimination, [of] ever narrower and more desperate alternatives." The result would be a series of "gradual withdrawals under pressure until we discover one day that we have sacrificed positions of vital interest."

Even without war the Soviet Union could use its armed forces . . . to erode the position of the United States and its allies. . . . The objective was "to back up infiltration with intimidation." It was true that the United States itself had greater military forces than ever before in peacetime, but the measure of effectiveness in such matters was comparison with present adversaries, not past economies. When balanced against increasing Soviet military power and the commitments the United States had undertaken to contain it, "it is clear that our military strength is becoming dangerously inadequate." If Kennan shared this concern, he said nothing about it; his sole recommendations for increasing peacetime military forces during this period were confined to the development of elite, highly mobile, compact units, capable of responding quickly and effectively to limited aggression, but in no way designed to counter Soviet capabilities he was convinced would not be used.[4]

At the heart of these differences between Kennan and the authors of NSC 68 was a simple inversion of intellectual procedure: where Kennan tended to look at the Soviet threat in terms of an independently established concept of irreducible interests, NSC 68 derived its view of American interests primarily from its perception of the Soviet threat. Kennan's insistence on the need to deter hostile combinations of industrial-military power could have applied as well to the adversaries of World Wars I and II as to the Soviet Union. No comparably general statement of fundamental interests appeared in NSC 68. The document paid obeisance to the balance of power, diversity, and freedom, but nowhere did it set out the minimum requirements necessary to secure those interests. Instead it found in the simple presence of a Soviet threat sufficient cause to deem the interest threatened vital.

The consequences of this approach were more than procedural: they were nothing less than to transfer to the Russians control over what United States interests were at any given point. To define interests in terms of threats is, after all, to make interests a function of threats—interests will then expand or contract as threats do. By applying pressure in particular areas Kremlin leaders could, if they were astute enough, force the United States and its allies to expend resources in parts of the world far removed from Kennan's original list of vital interests. The whole point of NSC 68 had been to generate additional means with which to defend existing interests. But by neglecting to define those interests apart from the threat to them, the document in effect expanded interests along with means, thereby vitiating its own intended accomplishment. . . .

. . . Unlike Kennan, NSC 68 ruled out diplomacy as a means of altering the Soviet outlook: a negotiated settlement, it argued, could not take place until the Soviet system itself had changed. To be sure, public opinion in the West would require that the United States and its allies appear willing to discuss agreements with the Russians; a sound negotiating position, in this sense, was "an essential element in the ideological conflict." But "any offer of, or attempt at, negotiation of a general settlement . . . could only be a tactic." . . .

. . . Moreover, if, as NSC 68 argued, all interests were now vital, then future negotiations could take place only on the basis of Soviet capitulations. Short of that, Moscow's willingness or lack of willingness to negotiate became irrelevant. . . .

NSC 68 was, then, a deeply flawed document, in the sense that the measures it recommended undercut the goals it was trying to achieve. A military buildup might enhance American security if American interests remained stable, but NSC 68 expanded interests. Fragmentation of the communist world might be a desirable objective, but treating communists everywhere as equally dangerous was not the way to achieve it. A more moderate Soviet attitude toward the outside world was certainly to be welcomed, but a negotiating posture that required Soviet capitulation could hardly hasten it. What all of these anomalies reflect is a failure of strategic perception: an inability to relate short-term to long-term considerations, to coordinate actions with interests. ∎

Post-Postrevisionism
LLOYD GARDNER

Born in 1934, Lloyd Gardner did his graduate work at the University of Wisconsin, partly with William Appleman Williams. His first book, *Economic Aspects of New Deal Diplomacy* (Madison: University of Wisconsin Press, 1964), arraigned the pre–World War II policies of Franklin Roosevelt not for misguided idealism but for narrowly selfish pursuit of business advantage. In *Architects of Illusion: Men and Ideas in American Foreign Affairs, 1941–1949* (Chicago: Quadrangle Books, 1970), Gardner made a major contribution to cold war revisionism, describing key U.S. policymakers as intent on ensuring that capitalism triumphed.

As Wells builds upon but does not depart from the early realism of Hammond and others, so Gardner in his essay here assimilates all the thinking and research of recent decades yet preserves the essential framework of Wisconsin school revisionism. The commentary here suggests where revisionists now stand, looking back at the cold war as a closed episode.

Gardner's Commentary

With the sudden end of the cold war and the collapse of the Soviet Union, the certainties policymakers lived with for four decades have all but disappeared. In their place, two tentative interpretations of the meaning of recent world events have gained prominence. The first holds that American policy from the Truman Doctrine to the Reagan arms buildup brought about the downfall of the Soviet system, permitting the construction of a genuine new world order. The second posits that the Soviet threat was always exaggerated, as in NSC 68, and that the rapid disintegration of Kremlin power and authority points up the semihysterical nature of American cold war policy—and its ultimate folly in Vietnam.

If the first suggested interpretation shares certain notions, despite its realist tough-minded conclusions, with Wilsonian idealism, the second, despite its revisionist overtones, places heavy emphasis upon balance-of-power military considerations. Neither is truly helpful in understanding the outlook of the men who wrote NSC 68, nor the circumstances under which the document came into being.

At that time, it should be noted, Truman's advisers were considering whether or not to build the "super," the H-bomb, both to calm popular fears about the Russian explosion of an "atomic device" in late 1949 and to ensure that they would never have to negotiate cold war issues except, as Dean Acheson would put it, from a "position of strength." It had become clear that the containment doctrine needed revising and fleshing out for the long haul. What resulted was a nearly open-ended charter for intervention and covert activities worldwide, and what is most remarkable about those deliberations is that the Russian military threat, even with the A-bomb now in Stalin's hands, looms largest in NSC 68 as an increase in the political threat "to our system":

> It adds new strains to the uneasy equilibrium-without-order which exists in the world and raises new doubts in men's minds whether the world will long tolerate this tension without moving toward some kind of order, on somebody's terms.

Atomic war might become a necessity, if the United States had no other choice but to defend its interests "at any of several vital pressure points."

Devoting more resources to defense spending was essential so as to lessen the danger of war by miscalculation. But the heart of the problem—as seen by the authors of NSC 68—was the breakdown of world order. As Acheson put it on many occasions, the politburo would never deliberately provoke a war with the United States, "unless they are absolutely out of their minds." Instead, Communist leaders would seek to make their "design" prevail through subversion.

Also on the minds of American policymakers was the closely related question of political legitimacy. The fundamental challenge of the Bolshevik revolution, the frequently mentioned long-term "design" in NSC 68, had never been Russian military power, but rather the threat it posed to the political and economic institutions that had flourished during the pax Britannica and that were the legacy now of American leaders. The rise of fascism and its triumph in Germany, the eroding impact of the Great Depression, and the devastation of World War II had all contributed to a malaise of doubt and uncertainty about the future of capitalist democracy. The Soviet Union's ability to withstand these shocks had lent communism a degree of credibility as a plausible alternative to capitalism and political democracy.

Militarily, the West was never on the defensive in the cold war; philosophically was a different matter, especially before Khrushchev's famous revelations about Stalin and the "cult of personality" at the 20th Party Congress in 1956. The democracies had not shown up well in confronting fascism, with Munich the nadir of Western "appeasement" efforts to avoid war. The intranational political struggles of the 1930s had never really ended during the war, with the "left" leading the struggle against German occupation and "collaborationist" regimes in several countries. On top of these difficulties came the added pressure of decolonization and the portentous upheaval in China.

The most dangerous enemy, it almost seemed, was not the Red Army but the Moscow Foreign Language Printing House, for the distributors of Marxist-Leninist writing constituted a new "fifth column," weakening the will of war-weary citizens to resist Soviet-sponsored political turmoil and Russian intimidation. At the time of the Bolshevik revolution, it will be recalled, Western leaders feared that Lenin's exposure of the "secret treaties" among the Allies would discredit not only the war but the traditional hold national leaders exerted over the citizenry by invoking patriotism. Now, it was feared, Russia would exploit not Allied secrets but the open failures of the prewar years.

The Soviet Union, reported the American ambassador to Russia, General Walter Bedell Smith, in late 1947, had exploited all the non-Marxist-Leninist opportunities opened to it by World War II, filling the vacuum in Eastern

Europe with the Red Army, and was now reverting to its "fundamental policy, the irreconcilability of Socialism and Capitalism." The principal task for the West, therefore, was to get across to the masses of Western Europe as well as the rest of the world the realities of life under the Soviet totalitarian system:

> If the majority of the workers and peasants of Western Europe realize what their plight would be under a Soviet controlled regime they would not be so susceptible to Soviet propaganda claims. They would put their shoulders to the wheel to bring about the economic recovery fostered by the Marshall Plan and the Kremlin inspired "revolutionary situation" would vanish into thin air.[1]

Success could not be assured, however, without first grasping the essential point that this was a global ideological crisis. If firm action was not taken to hold back the Soviet threat, it would not end in Eastern Europe. First there would be a Soviet-controlled Europe. "Following this, inevitably, the territory from the North Cape to Dakar and from the Bering Straits to the Dutch Indies will be painted red on the map, while we remain alone to face a menacing and powerful hegemony."

The contrast was between a divided West, still suffering from past mistakes and facing the challenge of decolonization, and the single-minded purposefulness of Soviet communism. Ambassador Smith's concerns were restated in NSC 68 in these words:

> Since everything that gives us or others respect for our institutions is a suitable object for attack, it also fits the Kremlin's design that where, with impunity, we can be insulted and made to suffer indignity the opportunity shall not be missed, particularly in any context which can be used to cast dishonor on our country, our system, our motives, or our methods.

The United States was at a serious disadvantage in responding to these assaults in kind, according to the authors of NSC 68, for the Kremlin recognized no moral standard except "that which serves the revolution." It is always necessary in documents of this sort to cast one's enemy outside the bounds of civilized behavior, but in this instance the authors were ready to introduce what, in effect, became a charter for American subversion of Communist regimes—eventually to be defined only by reference to the Soviet "design."

By the time John Foster Dulles took over as secretary of state in 1953, distinctions between direct actions against the Soviet Union and frustrating the "design" had become nonexistent. And this was reflected in a most remarkable dialogue before the Senate Foreign Relations Committee. Asked by Senator Henry Jackson to explain the term "international communism" in 1957 when the administration requested congressional authority to allow the president to use military force in the Middle East, the so-called Eisenhower Doctrine, Secretary Dulles answered that international communism was a term well known to Congress because it used it frequently. Then the following colloquy ensued:

SENATOR JACKSON: We want to know what it means in connection with this legislation.
SECRETARY DULLES: It means the same thing here, Senator, exactly as it meant and means in the Mutual Security Act.
SENATOR JACKSON: What did it mean in the Mutual Security Act?
SECRETARY DULLES: Congress passed the act and I assume knows what it meant.
SENATOR JACKSON: You folks in the executive branch administer it. What does it mean?

Dulles extricated himself from this unpromising dialogue with an attempt to come to terms with the rationale for American cold war policy, seven years after NSC 68:

SECRETARY DULLES: Well, international communism is a conspiracy composed of a certain number of people, all of whose names I do not know, and many of whom I suppose are secret. They have gotten control of one government after another. They first got control of Russia after the First World War. They have gone on getting control of one country after another until finally they were stopped. But they have not gone out of existence. International communism is still a group which is seeking to control the world, in my opinion.[2]

To thwart the Communist "design" would eventually require Dulles's successors to confront the implications of his testimony. The Soviet challenge was real. It was ironic, however, that the more Washington used the "design" as a rationale for intervention, and hence the more impressive it made the Soviet presence in world politics appear, the less respect its policies commanded at home and abroad. Conservatives blamed policymakers for failing to end the threat, while liberals decried cold war simplicities. The world of NSC 68 became the world of James Bond and Rambo.   ■

NOTES

[1]Michael H. Hunt, "The Long Crisis in U.S. Diplomatic History," *Diplomatic History* 16, no. 1 (Winter 1992): 136.

Wells

[1]Thomas W. Wolfe, *Soviet Power and Europe, 1945–1970* (Baltimore: Johns Hopkins University Press, 1970), 10n, 32–40; Ernest R. May, colloquium presentation, 21 June 1979, Woodrow Wilson International Center for Scholars, Washington, D.C.; Raymond L. Garthoff, *Soviet Military Policy: A Historical Analysis* (New York: Praeger, 1966), 23; Malcolm Mackintosh, *Juggernaut: A History of the Soviet Armed Forces* (New York: Macmillan, 1967), 270–76.

[2]Robert P. Berman, *Soviet Air Power in Transition* (Washington, D.C.: Brookings Institution, 1978), 24–26; Wolfe, *Soviet Power and Europe,* 40–41, 180; Robert P. Berman and John C. Baker, "Backfire Plagues SALT," *Arms Control Today* (Jan. 1979), 4–5; Congressional Quarterly, *Congress and the Nation,* 285.

[3]U.S. Air Force, Strategic Air Command, "The Development of the Strategic Air Command, 1946–1973" (Offutt Air Force Base, Nebr.: SAC Headquarters, 1974), 47; Wolfe, *Soviet Power and Europe,* 47–49, 186.

[4]Wolfe, *Soviet Power and Europe,* 10, 38–41; Garthoff, *Soviet Military Policy,* 44, 134–54; Mackintosh, *Juggernaut,* 275–76, 278–80, 284.

[5]Chen Jian, "The Sino-Soviet Alliance and China's Entry into the Korean War," Working Paper No. 1, Cold War International History Project, Woodrow Wilson International Center for Scholars, Washington, D.C., 1992.

Gaddis

[1]The wording here suggests that Kennan's strategy might have been considered appropriate for less trying times but that the balance of power had swung so far in favor of the Soviet bloc that no further losses could be tolerated.

[2]Paul Nitze memorandum, "Recent Soviet Moves," 8 Feb. 1950, *FRUS, 1950,* 1:145.

[3]George Kennan to Dean Acheson, 6 Jan. 1950, ibid., 132. See also George Kennan to Charles Bohlen, 15 Mar. 1949, *FRUS, 1949,* 5:593–94.

[4]See George F. Kennan, *Memoirs: 1925–1950* (Boston: Little, Brown, 1967), 311–12.

Gardner

[1]Walter Bedell Smith to Secretary of State George Marshall, 5 Nov. 1947, *FRUS, 1947,* 4:606–12.

[2]From Lloyd Gardner, ed., *American Foreign Policy, Present to Past* (New York: Free Press, 1974), 194.

5

American Interpreters
of American History

In this chapter, NSC 68 appears in widening contexts: first that of U.S. political history, then U.S. intellectual history, then U.S. cultural history.

U.S. Political History

ALONZO L. HAMBY

Born in 1940, Alonzo Hamby earned a Ph.D. in history from the University of Missouri in 1965. He is a professor at Ohio University and a colleague there of John Lewis Gaddis. His works include *Beyond the New Deal: Harry S. Truman and American Liberalism* (New York: Columbia University Press, 1973) and *Liberalism and Its Challengers: F.D.R. to Reagan* (New York: Oxford University Press, 1985).

While students of U.S. foreign policy sometimes take economic factors into account, they tend to focus on the international economy—foreign markets, foreign investments, and the like. Presidents, Hamby reminds us, usually pay most attention to the domestic economy—to employment levels, inflation rates, and such. Presidents think also of their domestic programs and of parties, patronage, and elections. Hamby urges thinking about how

NSC 68 appeared to Harry Truman in light of his preoccupations at home. Why, he asks, was Truman initially so resistant? What alternatives could the president have explored to escape the corner toward which the document pushed him? Why did he, in the end, accept it lock, stock, and barrel? (Or, if your view is more that of Bowie, Kaysen, or Gaddis, hook, line, and sinker?)

Hamby's Commentary

NSC 68 was presented to President Truman on April 7, 1950. It gathered dust on his desk for nearly six months. Truman was no procrastinator; he worked hard at his job and took pride in a capability to make hard decisions expeditiously. What happened to this one? Truman's *Memoirs* are no help; they do not even mention the then-classified document. Numerous historians who have written on the issue likewise fail to provide much help; some fuzz things up rather badly by implying implicit presidential approval from the beginning.

It seems clear, however, that Truman's initial approval extended only to the document's fundamental conceptual framework of a long-term struggle between American freedom and Soviet totalitarianism. The president shrank from committing himself to the expensive means that NSC 68 advocated, and he instituted a process of having them studied and debated to death within the administration. Not until September 30, three months into the Korean War, did he finally endorse the paper and thereby give it meaningful policy effect.

Truman was a cold warrior and a hard-eyed realist about the uses of military power; what most likely gave him pause were the domestic consequences of implementation. He knew that these would impact on the American economy, on his domestic program, and on the Democratic party in ways that would be mostly unfavorable. The hang-up, in short, was "political," in the broad sense of that word.

The economics of the thing entailed all sorts of unfavorable political prospects. Although the United States was just coming out of the recession of 1949, its economy was basically at full employment. How could the defense program be tripled in a few years without an inflationary impact? NSC 68 skirted the question, but Truman must have had vivid memories of how the politics of inflation (manifested not in official statistics but in a flourishing black market and chronic consumer shortages) had damaged the

Democratic party during World War II. The disastrous Democratic congressional defeat of 1946, largely a product of inflation-fueled dislocations and discontent, was, one may be certain, indelibly etched in his mind.

A related issue, which tied neatly into inflation fears, was how to pay for a defense buildup. NSC 68 suggested two ways (both placed far down in the list of measures that would follow implementation): (1) "reduction of federal expenditures for purposes other than defense and foreign assistance, if necessary by the deferment of certain desirable programs"; (2) "increased taxes." It is hard to guess which proposal would have been less appetizing to the president.

Higher taxes surely would be necessary, if only as an inflation-control measure. Truman, moreover, had never fully accepted Keynesian economics of any variety. His ideas on budgetary management had been formulated during ten generally grim years of local government administration in which raising funds through debt had been a difficult process and the goal had always been to balance income with outgo. He was flexible enough about his belief in a balanced budget to accept a deficit during the 1949 recession, but he felt far greater pride in the surpluses he had run previously. He would not shrink from higher taxes to pay for a necessary military buildup, but he assuredly had no illusions that such a policy would help him and his party.

"Deferment of certain desirable programs" could be interpreted only as a euphemism for abandonment of much of the administration's Fair Deal domestic program, including such objectives as public housing, federal aid to education, national health insurance, and the Brannan Plan (not simply an agricultural program but also the linchpin of a domestic political strategy to bring together farmers and urban labor). Leon Keyserling, the new chairman of the Council of Economic Advisers, would attempt to ameliorate the issue by arguing that the potentialities of economic expansion would make a choice unnecessary. Truman may ultimately have been persuaded, but it is certain that such was not his first impulse.

NSC 68 as a whole raised the specter of a militarized economy with a conspicuously malnourished civilian sector, short on such middle-class essentials as new automobiles and quality housing. (Anyone who doubts the immediate and pervasive character of such fears would be well advised to take a look at the consumer buying panic and consequent run-up in the consumer price index that followed hard upon the outbreak of the Korean War.) The political consequences were obvious.

If the politics connected with possible to probable economic developments presented a daunting prospect, so did the implications of NSC 68 for the politics of national security. Through mid-1949, the Truman administration had ridden on a political tide of successful Communist containment. True, there was already a small reservoir of the disenchanted among those upon whom the Democratic party had counted—Polish-Americans and other Eastern European ethnics who had watched with dismay as the iron curtain had come down over the nations of their origins, a fair number of politicized Catholics who wanted to roll back Communist advances.

By and large, however, containment had been a political asset for the Truman administration. The Truman Doctrine, the Marshall Plan, the Berlin airlift, NATO—all displayed an active administration protecting the nation against a foreign menace and doing so with minimal domestic cost or dislocation. In the minds of many Americans, Henry Wallace's Progressive insurgency validated Truman's depiction of himself and his party as purposeful and successful in the fight against Communist expansionism. The Republican party, moreover, seemed still divided between discredited isolationist impulses and a me-too internationalism.

NSC 68 all but trashed this political landscape. It suggested that the administration's earlier actions, far from being a not very painful triumph in erecting a permanent structure of containment, were at best a prelude to years of expense and sacrifice. Suddenly all the money spent on postwar European relief, the Marshall Plan, the rearmament of Europe would be just a not very large down payment. How did one sell this proposition to the American people without forfeiting their confidence? And what politician would even want to attempt the pitch if it seemed at all avoidable? Worse yet, this big, possibly indigestible bite of bad news would come on top of news of the "loss of China" and the Soviet A-bomb.

In April 1950, moreover, Truman would have been acutely aware that NSC 68 might underscore another political vulnerability—the administration's internal security policy and practices. At the beginning of 1949, it had been possible to dismiss most of the charges of Communist penetration of Washington as political hot air of the smelliest sort. By April 1950, Alger Hiss had been convicted (and Dean Acheson had quixotically refused to turn his back on him). Other former State Department employees had been indicted. Julius and Ethel Rosenberg were under arrest for atomic espionage. They would eventually be convicted and executed. Previous disconnected and ill-conceived charges of Communist sympathizers in the Truman administration had been easily dismissed. It was not so easy now. Some of the questions that might be asked were legitimate. If, for example, a drastic rearmament program were necessary because of the Soviet A-bomb, had lax safeguards against atomic espionage facilitated the Soviet nuclear program?

Other questions—more often outright accusations—might not be legitimate in the cold light of historical evaluation, but they were equally powerful at the time. And by April 1950, the opposition had produced an inquisitor of unparalleled tenacity and irresponsibility to make the charges—Senator Joseph R. McCarthy of Wisconsin. Could not McCarthy assert that NSC 68 revealed the bankruptcy of earlier cold war policy, that it advocated an expensive crash effort to compensate for the softness, perhaps downright disloyalty, of Alger Hiss, unnamed scores of officials who had willfully or otherwise failed to meet the challenges of international communism, and their protector, Dean Acheson?

In April it was still possible to hope that McCarthy could be dealt with and soon forgotten. The outbreak of the Korean War would dash that prospect, creating an atmosphere in which varying practitioners of the politics of anticommunism could join McCarthy in a reorientation of the political dialogue. Among them were Senators Pat McCarran of Nevada and Karl Mundt of North Dakota and Representative Richard M. Nixon of California. McCarran, a Democrat, would sponsor legislation forbidding Communists to come to the United States even as tourists. Mundt and Nixon would cosponsor a bill outlawing the Communist party.

It is hard to imagine in fact that Truman would ever have signed off on NSC 68 without the Korean War. The likely political price of its implementation before the North Korean attack must have been grim to contemplate. Korea served as a kind of mini–Pearl Harbor, seeming to demonstrate that Communist military aggression was a real threat, presumably in Europe as well as on a small Asian peninsula. By thus creating a sense of national crisis, it made large-scale rearmament a much more feasible proposition politically.

When Truman gave his approval to NSC 68 on September 30, however, he surely expected the war to be over in a matter of weeks. He could not have realized that in the end it would inflict much of the political pain he hoped to avoid—higher taxes, economic controls, a shattered domestic program. By the end of the year, the United States was at war with China, and the sense of national crisis deeper than ever. At that point, if NSC 68 had not already existed, it would have had to be invented.   ∎

U.S. Intellectual History
BRUCE KUKLICK

Born in 1941, Bruce Kuklick received his Ph.D. from the University of Pennsylvania in 1968. His thesis became his first book, *The United States and the Division of Germany: The Clash with Russia over Reparations* (Ithaca: Cornell University Press, 1972), a monographic contribution to cold war revisionism. His most recent book is on baseball—*To Every Thing a Season: Shibe Park and Urban Philadelphia, 1909–1976* (Princeton: Princeton University Press, 1991), but his paramount interests are in intellectual history, as illustrated by his two-volume history of American thought (the second published before the first): *Churchmen and Philosophers: From Jonathan Edwards to John Dewey* (New Haven: Yale University Press, 1985) and *The Rise of American Philosophy: Cambridge, Massachusetts, 1860–1930* (New Haven: Yale University Press, 1977).

As a specialist on the history of American religion and philosophy, Kuklick asks of NSC 68: What historic *American* ideas does it embody? If one thinks of NSC 68 as a major state paper, what links it with *The Federalist Papers,* George Washington's farewell address, or Woodrow Wilson's call for war "to make the world safe for democracy"? Kuklick suggests that the document may not be properly understood unless seen in light of the Reformed Protestantism pervading the institutions where Acheson, Nitze, and other key figures were educated.

Kuklick's Commentary

Many historians have seen NSC 68 as simply the rationalization of the American desire to rearm after World War II. According to some analysts, the report exaggerated the menace of the Soviet Union and continued the scare tactics the foreign policy elite had been using since the elaboration of the Truman Doctrine in 1947. The end result was an assertive, some say aggressive, internationalist diplomacy that was perhaps more bellicose than it otherwise need have been. NSC 68, on this account, was part of a public information program showing a dangerous contempt for reasoned discussion about the commitments the United States should make abroad. Dean Acheson himself allowed that the policymakers who drew up the paper were not writing a Ph.D. thesis and that arguments had to be made clearer than truth.

A document of this sort would not appear to be much of a candidate for study by intellectual historians. Yet the report, I believe, is a major American state paper, worthy of close textual scrutiny. Such state papers are not necessarily political philosophy, but over three hundred years they have expressed a consistent vision of a certain kind of social order and the relation of this order to other nations around the world. They form an impressive tradition rooted in the ideas of Reformed Protestantism and the Enlightenment. From the early seventeenth century, moreover, their authors have had a predictable connection to the political culture that the state papers defend.

In 1630 John Winthrop, a principal organizer of the Massachusetts Bay Company, delivered a famous sermon aboard the flagship *Arbella* about the experiment the Puritans were about the launch in the New World. Winthrop envisioned America as the setting for a peculiar covenanted polity that provided for individual rights and communal order. Though small and inconsequential in the seventeenth century, this society, said Winthrop, would be like a city on a hill, with the eyes of all the people upon it. The Puritans had a deep sense of their own righteousness and a compulsion to battle the human propensity to evil that they saw around them. But part of the power of the new order was supposed to be its power to convert other people by the influence of its own glowing example. One small candle, said the Puritans, could light a thousand.

By the time of the Revolution, suspicions about human motives were still reflected in documents like *The Federalist Papers*. The notion of the special American political society, however, now accentuated more the individual liberties that Americans possessed. The unconscionable abrogation of these rights made the Revolution inevitable and desirable, and a few years later their preservation warranted the drawing up of a new national constitution.

These eighteenth-century ideas of freedom appear repeatedly in NSC 68. The paper cites the Declaration of Independence, the Constitution, and *The Federalist*. At the same time the conflict between America and the Soviets is clearly, for the authors of NSC 68, one between the good and the depraved, between true religion and satanism. Though NSC 68 calls for a military buildup, its authors simultaneously note that "the prime reliance of the free society is . . . the strength and appeal of its ideas." Americans must "bear witness" to their values. Military victory over the evil empire was ultimately rejected. Rather, the goal was to "light the path to peace and order." America must "project" its "moral and material strength" into the Soviet system and internally transform that system.

The synthesis of righteousness, pride in *patria,* and sense of the evil in other polities, as well as the belief in the spiritual potency of American ideas, places NSC 68 in a long line of similar documents. It has, that is, nearer antecedents than Winthrop's "Model of Christian Charity" and the Declaration of Independence. Abraham Lincoln's second inaugural address, in 1865, both justified a crusade against the moral cancer of slavery and stressed that mere military triumph was not sufficient—after the Civil War the South was to be rehabilitated. Woodrow Wilson's declaration of war against Germany in 1917 affirmed once more the point of the struggle against the forces of darkness and of the reconfiguration of the psychology of the evildoer. In its reasoning and commitments, George Kennan's "X" article of 1947 was a near kin to the 1950 paper. And NSC 68 was followed by John Kennedy's inaugural address, proclaiming the all-pervasive dangers to the United States and the end of remaking the globe in the image of our way of life. Similar ideas pervaded George Bush's less eloquent rationales for war against Iraq in 1991.

Some commentators have protested that this tradition is much too narrow to represent the diversity that is essential to a full understanding of what the United States is really about. Yet in fact a small elite with a long record of holding power and a monopoly on communication has dominated American public life for over three centuries. The intellectual historian can find rich topics for investigation in exploring the rhetoric and ideas of documents like NSC 68 and their links to other expressions of the American political creed. Nonetheless, intellectual historians must also look to the social background of the authors of these documents and the cultural ambience that nourished them. From Winthrop to the Founding Fathers to Lincoln to Wilson to Kennan to Acheson to Bush, those authors have found comfort and truth in the narrative world of Reformed Protestantism—even Kennedy the Roman Catholic. They have often been men of great privilege and have frequently been the sons of the great universities of the East Coast.

Those institutions—Harvard, Yale, and Princeton chief among them—were founded to educate a learned Calvinist ministry and to carry sacred views into the profane world. They have done their job well and are the point at which the intellectual historian can locate the intersection between the ideas and the milieu in which they became relevant to American foreign policy.

I must conclude by suggesting the fundamental importance of the role of intellectual history in understanding foreign policy. Criticism of "the arrogance of power" and the narrow social stratum of the "foreign policy establishment" has been common. Other critics have argued that the rhetoric covered up less attractive ideas, hidden intentions that have actually shaped American behavior. These critiques are undeniably appealing. Nonetheless, at the end of the twentieth century, if we look at the long Soviet-American encounter—as NSC 68 did in its era—much can be said in favor of the independent causal significance of American ideals and even of their comparatively positive, not to say metaphysically benign, character. ∎

U.S. Cultural History

EMILY S. ROSENBERG

The last purely American context in which we view NSC 68 is that of American cultural history. Our guide, Emily S. Rosenberg, was born a year before the end of World War II. She did doctoral work at the State University of New York at Stony Brook during the years when the hottest public issue was the Vietnam War. She is now a professor of history at Macalester College in Minnesota. Her book *Spreading the American Dream: American Economic and Cultural Expansion, 1890–1945* (New York: Hill and Wang, 1982) links cultural and economic history to the expansion of American influence in the twentieth century. An essay, "Walking the Borders" (in *Explaining the History of American Foreign Relations,* ed. Michael J. Hogan and Thomas G. Paterson [Cambridge: Cambridge University Press, 1991], 24–35), suggests the relevance of cultural analysis, particularly gender analysis, to the writing of international history.

In the following essay Rosenberg applies to NSC 68 "discourse analysis," as developed by the French historian-philosopher-critic Michel Foucault. Accepting Acheson's view of NSC 68 as intended "to . . . bludgeon the mass mind of 'top government,' " Rosenberg asks what accounted for its persuasiveness. She finds the answer in what Foucaultistes term "discursive strategies": ways of deploying words or combinations of words to defend or overcome threats to customs or institutions. The words of NSC 68, Rosenberg argues, organized an unfamiliar and frightening world in familiar categories: urgent peril, traditional purpose, "we" and "they."

While Rosenberg's perspective has something in common with that of Kuklick, she pays particular attention to the document's organization of symbolic forms. She also emphasizes linkages between its discursive structure and the institutional growth of a new and unprecedented "informational" campaign.

Rosenberg's Commentary

NSC 68's impact on military spending, the nuclear buildup, and economic policy is, by now, familiar to those who study the cold war. Less examined has been its cultural power. A cultural analysis of this document involves examining the construction and organization of its symbolic forms within its particular sociohistorical context. Building on the work of the French theorist Michel Foucault, such an analysis seeks to probe the dominant strategic "discourse" that emerged in the late 1940s, elaborating the linkages between institutions that embody power and the symbolic codes that constitute "knowledge" or "truth."[1]

Updating the familiar genre of the American jeremiad, NSC 68 uses three principal discursive strategies: an implied narrative, warning that inaction in foreign policy could bring imminent destruction; an appeal to the authority of history; and a binary framework of symbolic representation. Together, these strategies try to establish a single point of view from which the new postwar world is "mapped" and national security choices are understood.

First, the document posits urgent peril that demands immediate action. "The issues that face us are momentous" and "will not await our deliberations." A sense of unparalleled crisis permeates the text. "The risks we face are of a new order of magnitude." Because the issues dare not be pondered at leisure or length, debate and diversity must be sacrificed. "A large measure of sacrifice and discipline will be demanded of the American people. They will be asked to give up some of the benefits which they have come to associate with their freedoms."

Such calls for discipline to save civilization built upon familiar narratives of World War II and of religious and secular jeremiads before that, tapping cultural themes that were already in place. Unlike the crisis of World War II, however, the postwar one would be ongoing, perhaps even perpetual. "For a free society there is never total victory, since freedom and democracy are never wholly attained. . . . But defeat at the hands of the totalitarian is total defeat." Victory can never be won, and sacrifice is unending; only defeat is final.

Second, the document locates its recommendations with historical tradition. The "fundamental purpose" of the United States, NSC 68 asserts, is "laid down" by the Constitution. The policies advanced in NSC 68 amount to a revolutionary departure in the role of the state and the conduct of American foreign relations in peacetime. Rapid militarization, formalized foreign alliances, extensive economic assistance, huge federal budgets, secrecy, and propaganda are all part of NSC 68's agenda, but these were measures that most Americans rejected, associating them only with wartime emergency or explicitly with practices of "enemies."

Simply put, the central dilemma in NSC 68 is how to advocate "freedom" by greatly enlarging the state's capacity for coercion. By casting unpopular departures within historical authority (the Constitution), NSC 68 helps obscure the break with the past and emphasizes continuity of tradition and purpose. Those who sought a new approach to America's international dealings, like so many previous revolutionaries, wisely cast proposals within the context of conservative ends and unfathomably evil enemies.

Finally, NSC 68 relies on binary opposites to construct its view of the postwar world. By use of the word *we* the document encourages readers to adopt a "we" versus "them" perspective. "We" and "them" generate mirror-opposite and mutually exclusive definitions and symbols that proliferate symbiotically throughout the text. NSC 68 offers no alternatives to the opposing categories "we" and "them," "freedom" and "slavery," "good" and "evil," "individual" and "mass." The phrase "tolerance and lawfulness" helps construct and is constructed out of oppositeness to "fanatic, expedient, and absolute." A "system of values which animates our society" finds binary pairing against "the ideology which is the fuel of Soviet dynamism." "Values" and "ideology" consistently provide antipodal anchors for the document's symbolic system. These binary constructions of meaning strip human experience of nuance, shading, relational shifts, or complexities. Only absolutes, certainties, and mutually exclusive categories remain. Bipolar military structures of the cold war era had semiotic counterparts in binary systems of meaning.

NSC 68 thus employs a familiar technique of militant nationalism: trying to forge a national consensus through creation of a symbolic "other" with mirror-opposite characteristics. Again, anchoring national identity and purpose within the symbolic characteristics of an evil "other" fits comfortably with earlier habits of thought in American culture. Dominant racial ideology (surfacing, for example, in the Indian Wars) had a similar binary structure of symbols and meanings. American propaganda during World War II (for example, Frank Capra's *Why We Fight* film series) was rooted in the images of a good-evil dichotomy. The symbolism in the Truman Doctrine speech of 1947 clearly foreshadowed the cold war binaries of NSC 68. The document's power derives not from any original formulations but from its adroit reworking of the established rhetoric of American nationalism.

Binary constructions, in addition to the invocation of crisis and tradition, skillfully lead the document's audience into the vantage point of its authors. These techniques seek to construct a single point of vision as "reality." The symbolic system is so stark and compelling that a potential critic must struggle to rearrange the terms of discussion in order to find ground from which to dissent. Policy "alternatives" presented at the end of NSC 68 are merely stage devices to suggest diversity and option where, in fact, powerful discursive strategies have already directed a singular perception. Unable to find standing *within* the framework of this document, critics would have to remap the world before engaging in debate. As Michel Foucault's work demonstrates, the power to shape the symbolic systems of language and meaning is the power over "knowledge" and "reality."

One may object to the emphasis on NSC 68's cultural significance by arguing that, because it remained top secret, seen by only a few insiders and not declassified until 1975, the document can have had little relation to the broader culture of the cold war era. But, as Acheson testifies, public statements came very soon to be based on "this leading embodiment of Government policy" and "preached" it to the public.

NSC 68, moreover, provided both the rationale and the discursive strategies for an unprecedented "information campaign" to counter the Soviet "propaganda offensive." Though agencies of the United States had mounted vigorous "informational" campaigns during both world wars, the campaigns had been dismantled almost as soon as the wars were over. A 1948 article entitled "Propaganda and a Free Society" commented, probably correctly, that "it is possible that more Americans approve of the use of the atom bomb in defensive warfare than approve the use of propaganda to forestall war."[2]

While Nitze was crafting NSC 68, Edward Barrett, the assistant secretary of state for public affairs, was preparing a document entitled "Recapturing the Propaganda Initiative." It called for a vastly enlarged foreign informational program, especially a significant strengthening of the Voice of America. Brought to the National Security Council as NSC 59/1, the plan was approved by Truman in March 1950; in May, after seeing NSC 68, Truman publicly announced as a major new departure a "Campaign of Truth." During the summer of 1950, as Acheson stumped the country repetitively proclaiming the premises of NSC 68, a once-reluctant Congress passed a large appropriation for the Campaign of Truth, now heralded as a "Marshall Plan in the field of ideas."[3]

After 1950, informational programs grew apace, not only within new agencies such as the United States Information Agency (USIA), formed in 1953, but also as a regular part of other national security bureaucracies. The Central Intelligence Agency, for example, began counteracting Soviet "peace conferences" by clandestinely financing international conferences by the Congress for Cultural Freedom. Both the European Recovery Program (ERP) and NATO had separate budget lines for developing bilateral propaganda campaigns. Paralleling these government-financed efforts were new global initiatives by private-sector information and entertainment companies (movie studios, newspapers, magazines).

Developed at the same time, NSC 68 and the Campaign of Truth were mutually reinforcing. The new propaganda offensive gained punch and money from NSC 68's strong formulation of cold war dangers. The ideas in NSC 68 gained wider dissemination and greater effect because of the new mechanisms funded as part of the Campaign for Truth. NSC 68 and the institutions of postwar cultural diplomacy were part of the same strategic discourse.

Two points should be made in passing. First, this analysis does not imply that the symbolic system of NSC 68 ever became so dominant that it squeezed out all opposing ways of seeing the world and created a single "anti-Communist consensus." The very need for blacklists and other formalized systems of cultural coercion during the 1950s shows that the dominant formulations of cold war "truths" were continually contested. The dynamic between power and knowledge, as Foucault has also emphasized, remains fluid. Even the most powerful discursive forms, in any sociohistorical context, still leave room for ambiguity, challenge, and reformulation.

Second, a cultural analysis does not imply that NSC 68 offers mere rhetoric, covering up real intentions or interests. Neither does it imply that NSC 68's view of the world was "wrong" or a product of "false consciousness." Most cultural analysis rejects the very notion of a structure of real interests existing separate from a superstructure of ideas and rhetoric. Through discourse, knowledge and power are structurally linked; they are not separate realms.

For the cold war era, NSC 68 successfully encoded the fundamentals of the structure of knowledge within which treaties, missiles, and aid packages were debated. It advanced discursive strategies that provided the long-lasting cultural and strategic references of the cold war. Indeed, the world presented in NSC 68 and then "preached" to the public in the 1950s became, as Acheson says, "clearer than truth." ∎

NOTES

Rosenberg

[1] Two useful introductions to different modes of cultural analysis are John B. Thompson, *Ideology and Modern Culture: Social Theory in the Era of Mass Communication* (Stanford: Stanford University Press, 1990), and Frank Lentricchia and Thomas McLaughlin, *Critical Terms for Literary Study* (Chicago: University of Chicago Press, 1990), particularly the contribution by Paul A. Bové, "Discourse."

[2] Ralph Block, "Propaganda and a Free Society," *Public Opinion Quarterly* 12 (Winter 1948–49): 677–86.

[3] See Edward W. Barrett, *Truth Is Our Weapon* (New York: Funk and Wagnalls, 1953).

6

A World Historian and a
Social Scientist

How does NSC 68 appear if we back far off and look at it either in the context of world history or in that of international relations theory? The two essays in this chapter attempt to answer that question.

Modern World History

WALTER MCDOUGALL

The Alloy-Ansin Professor of International Relations at the University of Pennsylvania, Walter McDougall was born in 1946 in Washington, D.C. He served in an artillery unit in Vietnam, reaching the rank of sergeant. In 1974 he took a Ph.D. in history at the University of Chicago and then taught for thirteen years at the University of California at Berkeley.

McDougall's approach to history resembles that of his teacher William H. McNeill, the author not only of monographs and biographies but of panoramic studies of the history of disease and military force and of "the rise of the West."[1] McDougall's best-known book is *The Heavens and the Earth: A Political History of the Space Age* (New York: Basic Books, 1985), which won a Pulitzer Prize.

McDougall asks of NSC 68: What are counterparts in other areas and periods of human history? What themes in the document echo themes to be found in great state papers of the past such as Friedrich von Gentz's memoranda for Metternich or Sir Eyre Crowe's memorandum of 1907 analyzing the growing rivalry between Britain and imperial Germany?

McDougall's Commentary

To describe NSC 68 as merely the sort of internal review of national security policy churned out annually by bureaucracies and parliaments is to kill imagination with category. If such documents are now routine, it is because the National Security Council itself provided such excellent examples of how to produce them. That is not to say that prior governments never put to paper their fundamental national values, the apparent threats to those values from abroad, their perceptions of an enemy's ideology, intentions, and capabilities, and the resultant inferences for policy. Others produced documents covering comparable ground. To name a few: British Prime Minister William Pitt in the Seven Years War; Alexandre Hauterive and Friedrich von Gentz, policy advisers to, respectively, revolutionary France's Foreign Minister Prince Talleyrand and Austria's counterrevolutionary Foreign Minister Prince Metternich; Admiral von Tirpitz, champion of a world role for the Germany of Kaiser Wilhelm II; President Woodrow Wilson; Nazi Germany's Führer, Adolf Hitler, and the Imperial Japanese General Staff. But none combined philosophical discourse, strategic analysis, call to arms, and operational program in a single memorandum.

NSC 68 is of particular interest as a revelation of the American foreign policy elite's understanding of the Soviet Union and its justification for the unprecedented peacetime mobilization and global deployment of American military power. It is of general interest inasmuch as its authors allude, in just twenty thousand words, to six of the most enduring themes in history, themes that echo Pericles' orations in the agora of Athens.

The first such theme is geopolitical, the age-old rhythm between balance of power and hegemony, between sea power and land power. "For several centuries," the authors observe, "it had proved impossible for any one nation to gain such preponderant strength that a coalition of other nations could not in time face it with greater strength." But now, in the post-1945 world, that balance was at risk. The destruction of Germany and Japan, the wasting of the French and British empires, and the Communist victory in China raised the specter of Soviet domination of the Eurasian landmass, an outcome "strategically and politically unacceptable to the United States." Few assumptions were more embedded in the Anglo-Saxon mind than that even the sea powers could not long survive in freedom and prosperity should some continental empire command the resources of "the world island" (Eurasia). For fifty years scholars had debated the political implications of the very shape of the earth, its arrangement of seas and continents. Navalists like A. T. Mahan had judged sea power ultimately decisive in geopolitical conflict. But Halford Mackinder and Andreas Haushofer suggested the opposite: modern communications and transport now made it possible for one state to conquer a "heartland" empire and mobilize resources superior to those of the rest of the world.[2] In 1941 Hitler nearly did so, and the authors of NSC 68 could only shudder to imagine the consequences had he succeeded. In 1950 it behooved the United States, at the very least, to deter Stalin from attempting a Eurasian hegemony, to keep open the world's sea lanes and commerce, and to preserve a balance of power.

But more was seemingly at stake. For ever since Leopold von Ranke in the late nineteenth century first theorized on the *meaning* of the rivalry of the Great Powers, Europeans and Americans alike judged that the balance of power, by sheltering the independence of states, also made possible the delightful profusion of national cultures, each with its own genius, and so ensured the continuance of all that made life diverse and progressive.[3] Geopolitical competition was not just a meaningless cycle of kingdoms of Ozymandias, but the process by which humans remained creative in the arts, sciences, and technology. It so happened that the current pretender to empire was Communist, but even if it were not, the geopolitical threat it posed had to be opposed. Lately the Allies had fought, like Athens, Sparta, and Corinth, among themselves. Now the Persians had crossed the Hellespont, and the West must unite, or see its civilization perish.

A second, more prosaic theme sounded in NSC 68 was that of the dilemma presented to free peoples by the necessity of an arms race. Before World War I, Liberal British Foreign Secretary Sir Edward Grey, who abhorred armaments, nevertheless promised Theodore Roosevelt that he "would build to preserve Britain's naval advantage over Germany until one of the two powers [and Grey believed it would be Germany] collapsed financially."[4] Not a pretty option, and after the First World War it was common currency that arms races not only were ruinous but provoked the very wars they were meant to deter. The history of the 1930s seemed to teach the opposite lesson, while the advent of nuclear weapons placed a premium on discovering a third choice between "the anxiety arising from the risk of atomic war" and "substantial further expansion of the area under the domination of the

Kremlin." That third choice seemed, inevitably, to be deterrence. Now, historians may argue that Stalin never considered an invasion of Turkey or Western Europe. But his "premature" success in breaking the U.S. nuclear monopoly suggested that America's power to deter was severely damaged and prompted the review that became NSC 68. If the balance of power were to be upheld without war, which nuclear weapons made unthinkable, then the Western alliance must make up for the Soviet nuclear arsenal.

But at what cost? The "great equation" (as Eisenhower called it) between economic and military power is the third theme raised by NSC 68, and one as old as ancient Rome, which by the fourth century was no longer able to pay the legions on its far-flung frontiers. Paul Kennedy argues that Great Powers habitually overreach, erode their own economic base through military expenditures, and so in time become unable to resist more competitive newcomers.[5] After 1945 the equation was obvious in the fates of the Nazi and Japanese empires, which failed, despite brilliant blitzkrieg operations, to muster resources proportional to their strategic reach. The first issue raised by President Truman regarding NSC 68 was the "effect of these Conclusions upon the budgetary and economic situation," and Eisenhower warned that the only way the United States could lose the cold war was by spending itself to death. Yet how could economic considerations be allowed to constrain policy if, as the authors maintained, "the survival of the free world is at stake"? They took comfort in the fact that the U.S. economy was four times the size of the Soviet and echoed Grey's hope that the adversary would crack first. But even if it did, what damage might be done in the meantime to American society? In choosing to race the Soviets in armaments, the authors of NSC 68 risked the very thing they sought to avoid: the turning of Athens into a Sparta.

It is said that to defeat the enemy you must become the enemy, and the ideological warfare called for in NSC 68 raises a fourth hoary theme in human conflict: the subtle marriage of the sword and the spirit. Leftist critics of U.S. policy may exaggerate the depravation of American values and institutions through its "mirror imaging" of Soviet nuclear terror, espionage, and propaganda. But NSC 68 did call for all that—and how else, *short of war,* could the West triumph? Napoleon said that "the moral is to the material as three is to one," and Clausewitz, the renowned writer on military strategy, taught that the purpose of combat is to break the enemy's will.[6] The cheapest way of doing so, and certainly the one most appealing to an open society, was to fight in the arena of ideas and morale, with psychological weapons. Eris, who sows discord in the enemy's camp, can be more powerful than Mars. Jesuits knew that when they infiltrated Protestant courts in the seventeenth century. Jacobin clubs and monarchical agents practiced disinformation and subversion in the wars of the French Revolution, and the Soviets were masters at injecting self-doubt through fear and fear through self-doubt. The authors of NSC 68 predicted that "labor unions, civic enterprises, schools, churches, and all media for influencing opinion" would be "prime targets" of Communist activity. But the West might use the same weapons to exploit the sullen disaffection of the "captive nations," Russians included. The essential nonviolence of NSC 68 is evident in its expectation of victory "as a result of internal forces in Soviet society."

Fifth, the specific conflict between capitalism and communism was itself only the latest manifestation of the age-old conflict between the market principle and the command principle in the organization of labor and capital. Throughout most of recorded history, in all regions of the world, the command principle (what historian William H. McNeill terms "macroparasitism") has been the norm.[7] Free exchange of goods and services according to a price mechanism occurred only sporadically and within limits defined by the policy, or executive reach, of political authority. Only in the last four or five hundred years, in Western Europe and its overseas offspring, has the market emerged as the principal regulator of economic behavior. Even then, the market's precarious reign was constantly beset by waves of neomercantilism, regulation, corporatism, or more or less dictatorial socialism. The greatest enemy of the market is war, for then an extreme and undeniable public good demands subordination of civil society. But the ideology, rhetoric, and apparent behavior of the Soviet Union under Lenin and Stalin indicated that the Western states were at war, if only a cold one, and that the Soviets' war aims were global and nonnegotiable. Hence the dilemma for the authors of NSC 68: Yes, the United States and its allies could readily outcompete the USSR, but to do so meant going, in large part, on a war footing and thus violating the market principles that (presumably) made their economies stronger in the first place. If the assessment in NSC 68 were correct, the emergency of World War II was not over, and the American people faced the necessity of *imitating* Soviet command methods in order to *defeat* Soviet methods!

Some leftist historians argue that this was a false dilemma, that corporate, military, and political elites encouraged the anti-Communist frenzy so as to expand the military-industrial complex and smash progressive politics at home. According to this "primacy of domestic policy" (a theory derived in the first instance to explain German imperialism before 1914), rightist regimes pursue expansionism abroad so as to suppress, or distract attention from, class conflict at home.[8] The Soviets, by contrast, claimed to follow a primacy of foreign policy; that is, their domestic discipline and defense spending were a function of the imperialist threat from abroad. But the authors of NSC 68 implied that nearly the opposite was the case, that Stalin swallowed Eastern Europe and declared unending conflict with the "imperialist camp" in order to *justify* totalitarianism and shore up his rule at home, whereas Americans were asked reluctantly to tolerate a militarized economy at home in order to meet the Soviet threat abroad. By the 1980s, of course, the cold war burden had so worn down the Soviets that they had to let their empire go away and struggle to introduce market methods, while the exhausted Americans found themselves no longer competitive in the world market economy. A final irony of this latest "war" between the market principle and the command principle is that Soviet scholars of the Brezhnev years insightfully chose 1950 as the date when the United States adopted many "Soviet-style" methods, especially government-financed and -directed research and development.[9] They even attributed American technological successes to this very adoption of command principles, whereas advocates of the free market pointed to 1950 as the beginning of America's decline, and for the same reasons!

A sixth historical theme raised by NSC 68 is the still more comprehensive conflict in history between the Individual and the Collective. "The free society," states NSC 68, "values the individual as an end in himself," while behind the iron curtain the individual exists only as a unit of the collective. Of course, the collective is a myth: in reality the individual is functionally a slave to the members of the ruling party. This conflict between the dignity of the individual and those "in high places" who claim to rule for the good of the whole is as old as Socrates' duel with the Athenian authorities, as old as the Jewish struggle against Babylon, Greece, and Rome, as old as the clash between Jesus of Nazareth and the Jewish and Roman authorities. In modern times the struggle is more often secular, and almost always, it seems, the champions of freedom become tyrants in their turn: Cromwell, Robespierre, Lenin. The authors of NSC 68 called Soviet governance by its true name—slavery—and determined to resist in the name of human dignity. Did they fail to anticipate the danger that the United States, in its fear, zeal, and righteousness, might itself become an enemy of freedom? Yes, and no. No, they did not anticipate the full virulence of the McCarthy era, the expansion of domestic and foreign surveillance, the Vietnam War and resulting domestic violence, and the unprecedented taxes and inflation that would erode the freedom of every working American. But yes, they did understand that the United States itself might betray a victory in the cold war by seeking, or just seeming, to impose a pax Americana. Hence the goal of their grand enterprise must be, and must be *perceived* to be, "a world society based on the principle of consent" among America's allies and the "former subject peoples" alike: a new world order. The peoples of the Soviet bloc were not enemies, but the most powerful potential allies in the struggle against the

Collective. This distinction between bolshevism and Bolsheviks was first drawn by Secretary of State Robert Lansing in 1919. The former, he said, was simply "a popular state of mind growing out of the war and past abuses. It is compounded of demoralization and protest."[10] But the latter were people committed to imposing a militant dictatorship over other people. In separating out the individuals of the Soviet bloc and naming their lust for freedom the greatest threat to the Bolshevik apparatus, the authors of NSC 68 *personalized* the cold war.

For otherwise, the great themes of geopolitics, balance of power, economic and ideological conflict, and the dilemma of arms racing might have seemed but airy abstractions. Instead, the authors addressed the most concrete and immediate of all issues: the lives and dignity of individuals, even in the Soviet Union. In this, and in its surprising humility, rests the fundamentally moral character of NSC 68. Yes, an American-led Western alliance might turn back the barbarians. But it offered no utopia, no Collective, of its own. "For a free society there is never total victory, since freedom and democracy are never wholly attained, are always in the process of being attained." The false idealist is precisely the one who promises ideals. The real idealist knows that ideals, by definition, are transcendental. Critics of America's cold war posture point up the fanaticism, inordinate fears, exploitation, greed, waste, and folly that proliferated under the patriotic cloak of "national security." But in so doing, they only prove the truth of NSC 68. Measured by its own standards, the Soviet hierarchy was infallible. Measured by *its* own standards, American leadership was subject to every creaturely foible. And the cause at stake was to preserve those standards of decency, tolerance, freedom, justice, peace, and wisdom against which free individuals themselves must inevitably fall short.

"A bad cause never fails to betray itself." So wrote Madison in *Federalist Paper* No. 41. "That it may please thee to forgive our enemies, persecutors, and slanderers, and to turn their hearts." So prays the litany of the Book of Common Prayer. And so it was that the authors of NSC 68 rejected preventive war as an option and placed their faith instead in the "existence and persistence of the idea of freedom" within the enemy camp itself. As Eisenhower put it ten years later, "The spiritual powers of a nation—its underlying religious faith, its self-reliance, its capacity for intelligent sacrifice—these are the most important stones in any defense structure."[11] For forty years Americans did sacrifice, and not for their own comfort and pelf, but that other nations might be reborn. That is why NSC 68 was, for better or worse, a sublime expression of the Judeo-Christian culture it purposed to defend. ■

International Relations and Foreign Policy Theory
DEBORAH WELCH LARSON

Deborah Welch Larson, a professor of political science at UCLA, looks at NSC 68 in the context of relevant political theory. Born in 1951, Larson did her undergraduate work at Texas Christian University. She received a Ph.D. from Stanford University in 1983, having worked with the distinguished student of decision making Alexander George and with Lee Ross, a psychologist who studies errors and biases in human thinking. Larson's best-known work is *Origins of Containment: A Psychological Explanation* (Princeton: Princeton University Press, 1985).

Larson's Commentary

Social science theory may indirectly shape state actions by establishing an intellectual climate from which policymakers derive their assumptions. NSC 68, the call to arms for the cold war, bears distinguishing trademarks of realist thought, the dominant school in international relations theory in the postwar period.[1] But its emphasis on ideology as a factor in foreign policy far exceeds the narrow focus of realism on power. As such, NSC 68's analytical shortcomings reflect not only the blind spots of realism but inherent biases and errors in the way people think.

Realism challenged and ultimately supplanted American idealism, which had been the leading philosophy of international relations both before World War I and during the period of U.S. isolationism in the 1930s. Idealists believed that increasing trade and contacts between states would make war unprofitable and therefore obsolete. The First World War discredited the idealists' belief in an underlying harmony of interests between states, while Hitler's aggression disproved the idea that collective security as embodied in the League of Nations could prevent war. As refugees from Nazi Germany, realists such as Hans Morgenthau and Arnold Wolfers came to the United States with a mission—to persuade Americans to abandon the illusions of idealism and recognize that conflict between states is inevitable, peace a temporary interlude, and ideals merely a sop to public opinion. Anything less would endanger national security—a new term.[2] According to realists, international relations is a struggle for power between states. Morgenthau argued that a prudent statecraft must therefore try to preserve a balance of power with potential enemies.

During the 1970s when the United States and the Soviet Union experienced a brief détente in their relationship, the new field of international political economy emerged in political science.[3] Political economists attacked the realist assumption that states pursue only military power. Like traditional idealists, political economists suggested that growing economic interdependence between the industrialized states made the resort to military force increasingly unthinkable. As domestic publics had increasingly high expectations for government management of the economy, national leaders faced new problems of trying to maximize national wealth in the face of increasingly complex interconnections of the world economy. Also challenging the realists' narrow focus on power were political scientists who studied foreign policy decision making within governments.[4] According to a psychological perspective, how national leaders respond to the international environment depends on their beliefs and perceptions of other states.[5]

The Soviet invasion of Afghanistan in 1979 and President Reagan's defense buildup in the 1980s stimulated a realist resurgence by seeming to prove that military power was still the most important currency in world politics. Neorealism, as exemplified by its founders, Kenneth Waltz and Robert Gilpin, is more self-consciously social scientific than is traditional realism, which grew out of traditional European theory on statecraft and the balance of power.[6] Out of a desire to imitate the simple, elegant theories of neoclassical economics, neorealists deduce propositions from the simple assumption that states at minimum try to preserve themselves and at maximum strive to increase their relative power.

Consistent with realism, NSC 68 praises the balance of power for making it "impossible for any one nation to gain such preponderant strength that a coalition of other nations could not in time face it with greater strength." That equilibrium was now endangered, NSC 68 averred, by the polarization of power between the United States and the Soviet Union and the "fanatic faith" of the Soviets.

NSC 68 contrasts the fundamental purposes of the United States and the Soviet Union, the conflict between values and ideas, before analyzing Soviet military capabilities and intentions. It is striking how the authors invoke basic values such as freedom as if these abstract concepts had any relationship to concrete policy. Thus, NSC 68 states that "the objectives of a free society are determined by its fundamental values and by the necessity for maintaining the material environment in which they flourish." The importance NSC 68 attributes to values is consistent with psychological theory rather than realism or international political economy. Psychological theory holds that the most important values and beliefs are located at the center of each person's belief system, connected to many other derived convictions, opinions, and tastes.[7] In contrast, realists contend that national leaders invoke values such as freedom and self-determination as a cloak for the real issue of international relations, the struggle for power. International political economists would maintain that NSC 68 refers to the challenges of maintaining freedom and democracy in order to legitimize and rationalize American economic hegemony. Thus, for example, the document's reference to a more integrated economic program for Western Europe with U.S. involvement implies that these states should orient their economies to serve the economic needs of the United States. An international political economist would view NSC 68 as signaling the assumption by the United States of responsibility for maintaining global economic stability and a multilateral free trade system.

The authors of NSC 68 inferred that the Soviets had aggressive intentions because they possessed "armed forces far in excess of those necessary to defend [their] national territory." In other words, the authors of NSC 68 judged that the Soviets would not assume the financial burden of maintaining a large conventional army unless they somehow hoped to gain by attacking the free world. Such a conclusion does not follow if we adopt a psychological perspective. The Soviets may not have viewed their army as superfluous in light of the numerous enemies they faced and the previous two invasions from Germany, or the Soviets may not have regarded any amount of military strength as excessive for defense. Instead of being an inescapable deduction from the size of the Soviet army, I propose that this inference about Soviet aggressive intentions reflects the tendency for people to believe that costly or risky behavior reveals the actor's real motives.

NSC 68 contended that "the assault on free institutions is world-wide now, and in the context of the present polarization of power a defeat of free institutions anywhere is a defeat everywhere." Neorealist Kenneth Waltz would agree that there are no unimportant or peripheral states in a bipolar world. Each superpower must be concerned about the other's actions throughout the world in a self-help system where each state must look out for its own security. The problem with the neorealists' argument is that no great power can defend unlimited commitments without bankrupting itself. As traditional realists such as George Kennan and Walter Lippmann realized, a state's leadership must rank and prioritize various areas of the world in terms of their intrinsic as well as strategic value.[8] Not only does NSC 68 fail to set priorities, but it neglects to mention the cost of the recommended programs relative to other policy alternatives. International political economists would find this a rather striking omission, given their belief that states seek economic development and prosperity.

Realists put aside concerns for the health of the economy on the grounds that military capabilities are the underlying basis of power in an anarchic world. With no higher authority able to make binding decisions, force is the final arbiter of disputes between states. States seek economic welfare in order to attain international political power. Thus, NSC 68 observes that "economics in the Soviet world is not an end in itself. The Kremlin's policy . . . is to utilize economic processes to contribute to the overall strength, particularly the war-making capacity of the Soviet system." International political economists would object that states play many games simultaneously. For international trade and investment issues, military force is irrelevant. Indeed, as the case of the former Soviet Union illustrates, military expenditures can prevent a state from achieving the economic productivity and technological development essential to playing a role as a great power.

According to NSC 68, the United States must be prepared to pay any price because "the fundamental design" of the Soviets "is to retain and solidify their absolute power, first in the Soviet Union and second in the areas now under their control." NSC 68 referred numerous times to the Kremlin's "design," a coherent strategy to dominate the world. Yet the authors of NSC 68 present no proof that the Kremlin had a master plan for world domination. Where could such a belief come from? A psychological approach would argue that the source of this idea lies less in overt Soviet behavior than in the minds of U.S. policymakers. People attribute greater logic and coherence to others' behavior than actually exists. We seek to impose meaning on our experience by finding patterns even in random data such as the flip of a coin.[9]

NSC 68 argues strongly that the source of Soviet expansionism is the nature of the Soviet domestic system. Waltz would object that a state's domestic system is not the cause of war or peace, because wars have occurred throughout history despite variations in the character of states.[10] For a realist, it is not a state's domestic system that matters but its foreign policy, which is the only legitimate object of concern. How can we explain NSC 68's neglect of external sources of Soviet policy? I would first look at psychological experiments which show that we overestimate the role of internal goals, needs, and traits in causing behavior. According to psychological theory, people usually attribute others' actions to personality characteristics, while neglecting situational pressures that would lead anyone to behave the same way. If similar psychological processes characterize our thinking about states, then we will exaggerate how much the other state's behavior reflects the enduring character of the regime while overlooking the very real fears and pressures to which the state may be reacting.[11]

Given the domestic sources of Soviet foreign policy, NSC 68 predicts that "we can expect no lasting abatement of the crisis unless and until a change occurs in the nature of the Soviet system." NSC 68 repeatedly refers to the "Kremlin" rather than Joseph Stalin, implying that the individual identity of Soviet leaders does not matter and that a change in leadership would not change Moscow's "design." But decision-making theorists know that individuals matter. Unlike previous Soviet leaders, Gorbachev responded to Soviet inferiority by accommodating the West rather than by trying to match American arms expenditures.

NSC 68 portrays a Soviet Union immune to external influence by any other means than the logic of superior power. The Soviets would accept no agreements with the West unless they foresaw an advantage from acting in bad faith. Traditional realists would object that to exclude diplomacy as an instrument of influence is to forget what international politics is all about. A psychological perspective would add that NSC 68 overlooks the unintended consequences that arise when we fail to consider how others view our behavior. In this case, the U.S. military buildup stimulated by NSC 68 contributed to Soviet militarism and isolation.   ∎

NOTES

McDougall

[1] William H. McNeill, *The Rise of the West: A History of the Human Community* (Chicago: University of Chicago Press, 1963); *Plagues and Peoples* (Garden City, N.Y.: Doubleday, 1976); *The Pursuit of Power: Technology, Armed Force, and Society since A.D. 1000* (Chicago: University of Chicago Press, 1982).

[2] A short summary of these geopolitical theories appears in Paul M. Kennedy, "Mahan *versus* Mackinder: Two Interpretations of British Sea Power," in *Strategy and Diplomacy, 1870–1945* (London: Allen and Unwin, 1983), 41–86.

[3] See Ranke's "Die grossen Mächte" (1833), translated as "The Great Powers" in *Leopold von Ranke: The Formative Years,* ed. Theodore von Laue (Princeton: Princeton University Press, 1950), and Lord Acton, "Beginning of the Modern State" (1906), in *Essays in the Liberal Interpretation of History,* ed. William H. McNeill (Chicago: University of Chicago Press, 1967).

[4] William Reynolds Braisted, *The United States Navy in the Pacific, 1897–1909* (Austin: University of Texas Press, 1958), 189.

[5] Paul M. Kennedy, *The Rise and Fall of the Great Powers: Economic Change and Military Conflict from 1500 to 2000* (New York: Random House, 1987).

[6] Napoleon, cited by Robert Debs Heinl, ed., *Dictionary of Military and Naval Quotations* (Annapolis: U.S. Naval Institute, 1966), 196. On breaking the enemy's will, see Carl Maria von Clausewitz, *On War,* vol. 1, bk. 1, chap. 2, cited in Roger Ashley Leonard, *A Short Guide to Clausewitz on War* (London: Weidenfeld and Nicolson, 1967), 60ff.

[7] McNeill, *Pursuit of Power.*

[8] See Eckhardt Kehr, *Economic Interest, Militarism, and Foreign Policy,* trans. Grete Heinz, ed. Gordon A. Craig (Berkeley: University of California Press, 1977).

[9]See William Zimmermann, *Soviet Perspectives on International Relations, 1956–1967* (Princeton: Princeton University Press, 1969).

[10]Robert Lansing, 1 Dec. 1919, *FRUS, 1920,* 3:331.

[11]"Radio and Television Address to the American People on Science in the National Security," 7 Nov. 1957, *Public Papers of the Presidents: Dwight D. Eisenhower, 1957,* (Washington, D.C.: Government Printing Office) 789–99.

Larson

[1]Hans J. Morgenthau, *Politics among Nations: The Struggle for Power and Peace,* 6th ed. (New York: Knopf, 1985); Arnold Wolfers, *Discord and Collaboration: Essays on International Politics* (Baltimore: Johns Hopkins University Press, 1962); John H. Herz, *Political Realism and Political Idealism* (Chicago: University of Chicago Press, 1951).

[2]Wolfers, *Discord and Collaboration,* 148.

[3]Robert O. Keohane and Joseph S. Nye, *Power and Interdependence* (Boston: Little, Brown, 1977).

[4]Alexander L. George, *Presidential Decisionmaking in Foreign Affairs: The Effective Use of Information and Advice* (Boulder, Colo.: Westview, 1980).

[5]Robert Jervis, *Perception and Misperception in International Politics* (Princeton: Princeton University Press, 1976).

[6]Kenneth Waltz, *Theory of International Politics* (New York: Random House, 1979); Robert Gilpin, *War and Change in World Politics* (Cambridge: Cambridge University Press, 1981).

[7]Milton Rokeach, *Beliefs, Attitudes, and Values* (San Francisco: Jossey-Bass, 1968).

[8]See John Lewis Gaddis, *Strategies of Containment* (New York: Oxford University Press, 1982).

[9]Hazel Markus and R. B. Zajonc, "The Cognitive Perspective in Social Psychology," in *The Handbook of Social Psychology,* vol. 1, *Theory and Method,* ed. Gardner Lindzey and Elliot Aronson (New York: Random House, 1985), 192.

[10]Kenneth N. Waltz, *Man, the State, and War* (New York: Columbia University Press, 1954).

[11]Deborah Welch Larson, *Origins of Containment: A Psychological Explanation* (Princeton: Princeton University Press, 1985).

7

Foreign Scholars

This chapter backs even farther away than the previous one, looking at NSC 68 from standpoints outside the United States. The first view is that of a historian at Cambridge University in the United Kingdom. Next come observations from a German political scientist and from three historians, one Norwegian, one Russian, and one Chinese.

What makes these commentaries noticeably different from those in earlier chapters is a common emphasis on the American political system. The earlier commentaries by Americans, whether officials or scholars, all took the American system for granted. They focused then on questions such as whether the choices made in 1950 were right or why alternative choices were not made or what can be learned from a document like NSC 68 about American ways of thinking. Most of these commentaries by non-Americans reflect what might be called "political determinism." In effect, they say that the peculiarities of American democracy made NSC 68 and the policies associated with it almost inevitable.

The United Kingdom
ZARA STEINER

College lecturer and fellow in history at Cambridge University's New Hall, Zara Steiner was born in the United States in 1928 and educated at Swarthmore College and Harvard University. She has another degree from St. Anne's, Oxford, and has had her academic base in the United Kingdom since the mid-1960s.

Steiner's best-known works concern British foreign policy: *The Foreign Office and Foreign Policy, 1898–1914* (London: Cambridge University Press, 1969) and *Britain and the Origins of the First World War* (London: Macmillan, 1977). She edited *The Times Survey of Foreign Ministries of the World* (London: Times Books, 1982). She is currently writing a volume in the Oxford History of Modern Europe series, tentatively entitled *The Reconstruction of Europe, 1919–1941.*

Particularly in comparison with the earlier essay by Walter McDougall, Steiner's commentary suggests some of the subtle differences that, as of the 1990s, separate British perspectives from American, even when the observers are wholly cosmopolitan in background and outlook: Steiner sees NSC 68 less as a document to be bracketed with the Eyre Crowe memorandum than as an example of the extravagant argumentation made necessary by the American political system.

Steiner's Commentary

NSC 68 is one of the post-1945 documents most frequently cited by British students of American foreign policy. It has become emblematic of the rising tension between the United States and the Soviet Union and of the American globalization and militarization of the cold war. Because of the successive waves of revisionist writings that have threatened to make the study of cold war origins an exercise in American historiography and the present preoccupation of British scholars with the European and, in particular, the British contribution to the early history of this struggle, it has become essential in teaching this subject to place NSC 68 in its historical and bureaucratic framework. Following the arguments developed by Samuel Wells in his still influential 1979 article, "Sounding the Tocsin: NSC 68 and the Soviet Threat" and by John Gaddis in *Strategies of Containment* (see pages 136 and 141, respectively, in this book), one distinguishes between the early policies of containment and the new course outlined in NSC 68 by concentrating on that sequence of events that led to the demands for a "much more rapid and concerted build-up" of American strength to frustrate Soviet "world designs." It has to be shown how the explosion of the Soviet atomic bomb, coupled with recent events in Europe, the "loss of China," and the start of the McCarthy hunt for Communists in the government heightened the sense of vulnerability in the face of a perceived Soviet drive for world domination. It was in response to the intense debate over the advisability of building a fusion bomb that the president ordered this overall review of national security policy. Disputes between and within executive departments over the nature of the Soviet threat, divisions over atomic stockpiling and the thermonuclear bomb, and the bitter conflicts over the defense budget go far in explaining the way the small ad hoc committee of State and Defense officials presented their case for an enlargement of the American national security effort with a new emphasis on its military component.

Critical to the background of these discussions was President Truman's belief, even after the Soviet atomic explosion, that the country could not afford to spend more than $13.5 billion for defense purposes. A highly secret document intended for the president was deliberately framed to create political support for an expensive and ongoing program intended to frustrate Russian designs. Like George Kennan, committee members thought that the United States was relying too heavily on atomic weapons for deterrence. While supporting the decision to build the thermonuclear bomb, the committee rejected a resort to preventive war with the use of atomic weapons as both infeasible and morally repugnant. Unlike Kennan, the committee assumed that the Soviet Union could and would use the considerable means at its disposal to implement schemes for worldwide dominion. The emphasis in NSC 68 was on the buildup of military strength rather than on the alternative means of deterrence. To marshal support (and the committee looked beyond the president) for this extensive and expensive program, it was necessary to convince government and the people that "the cold war is in fact a real war in which the survival of the free world is at stake."

Some contemporaries, as well as later commentators, were critical of these recommendations. There has been little recent dissent from John Gaddis's judgment that NSC 68 was a "deeply flawed document" that "undercut the goals it was trying to achieve." Both the Soviet threat and its capabilities were considerably exaggerated and the weaknesses in the Russian position understated. It is true that some historians have argued that there were sound reasons for the alarmist views of Soviet intentions expressed not only in NSC 68 but also in the British Chiefs of Staff reports of the same period. But there is, as yet, no archival evidence to suggest that Stalin was preparing to launch an attack or that the Soviet Union would have had the capacity to bomb the United States by 1954. By defining American interests solely in terms of an undifferentiated and worldwide Soviet threat ("a defeat of free institutions anywhere is a defeat everywhere"), it became difficult if not impossible to distinguish between America's vital and secondary interests. The global view of the Soviet threat committed the country to a massive defense effort on a world scale.

It was only after the outbreak of the Korean War, which conformed in so many respects to the scenario outlined in NSC 68, that the president approached Congress for the sums needed both for the war and for the military buildup recommended in the report. Without the Korean conflict, it is highly doubtful whether these large supplemental appropriations would have won approval. Support was short-lived. The stalemate in Korea and the absence of any Soviet moves in Europe led to an erosion of congressional and public backing. Military budgets were cut during the Eisenhower years, though it was Vietnam that finally buried the undifferentiated globalist view of American interests.

This brings us to the heart of the matter. NSC 68 was more than the product of immediate concerns. It was the culmination of a long-term effort to secure the resources needed to back an ambitious foreign policy. The interest in NSC 68 goes beyond its part in the escalation of the first cold war. The rhetorical techniques used in the document—the exaggeration of the enemy's threat and capabilities, the Manichean division of the world, the appeal to specifically American values and traditions—are not unique to this paper but are found, for example, in some of Franklin Roosevelt's pre-1941 speeches and in the Truman Doctrine. The Nitze committee used the terminology of war ("the risks we face are of a new order of magnitude, commensurate with the total struggle in which we are engaged") to achieve support for a high-cost and long-term policy intended to avoid war. It is not easy to create the public sense of threat or danger that alone justifies the mobilization of the country's extensive resources in peacetime. My Cambridge colleague John Thompson sees this need to create and maintain the political base required to convert the country's economic strength and military potential into actual power for use on the world stage as the key perennial problem faced by all American policymakers.[1]

One must explain to a foreign audience the peculiar nature of the American foreign policy process that makes recourse to such rhetorical devices necessary, not a simple task in a country where Parliament takes only the most limited role in policy formulation and which is noted for its pragmatic approach to foreign affairs. One does not need to be a Cassandra to argue that the techniques of evocation and ideological identification embodied in NSC 68 will outlive the ending of the cold war and will continue to be used as long as the United States remains a great power. ∎

Germany
HELGA HAFTENDORN

A German political scientist, most of whose scholarship focuses on German foreign policy and defense policy after World War II, Helga Haftendorn was born in Erfurt in 1933. She received her first advanced degree in 1960. After a number of years in the Research Institute of the German Society for Foreign Policy in Bonn, she became a professor both at the Armed Forces University in Hamburg and at the Free University of Berlin. She knows the United States well, having been a visiting professor at American universities and a visiting fellow at American research institutes. She has also been president of the International Studies Association, which, though an international organization, is made up primarily of American scholars specializing in international relations.

Despite these associations, Haftendorn, like Steiner, has a view of NSC 68 that is European rather than American. Steiner sees the document as but one example among many of a type of extravagant argumentation made necessary by the American political system. Haftendorn takes a similar view but goes on to suggest that, given that system, the drafting and adopting of NSC 68 may have been a necessary prelude to subsequent U.S. policy choices generally applauded by critics of the document, particularly choices that cemented the Atlantic alliance.

Haftendorn's Commentary

The debate that led to the drafting of NSC 68 went by largely unnoticed in Germany. However, papers and journals in the young Federal Republic registered Dean Acheson's address to American business leaders on February 16, 1950, in which the secretary of state was reported to have called for a "total diplomacy" vis-à-vis the Soviet Union.

What made the headlines in the spring of 1950 was the Schuman Plan, the French foreign minister's proposal for the creation of a single authority to control the production of steel and coal in both Germany and France, open to other countries as well. The other item was German rearmament, whether as a contingent to a European army, as had been proposed by former British Prime Minister Winston Churchill at Strasbourg, or as a contribution under the twelve-nation North Atlantic Treaty signed a year earlier in Washington. In contrast to developments in the Soviet zone, where a strong paramilitary force was set up, the Western allies publicly still insisted on German demilitarization while their military experts as well as German Chancellor Konrad Adenauer in Bonn considered some West German rearmament inevitable.

Most Germans of the time could not have agreed more with NSC 68's evaluation of Soviet capabilities and intentions. The Czech coup of 1948 had but happened on their very doorstep, and the Berlin blockade of 1948–49 had victimized their fellow citizens in the old German capital. Besides, millions of Germans were still traumatized by the horrors of Soviet wartime occupation, by the expulsions from the Eastern territories of the former German Reich, and by the experience of living under Communist rule in East Germany. They certainly shared the document's pessimistic appraisal of the military balance and were concerned that West Germany would be an easy prey to Communist aggression. However, they probably would have differed in their economic outlook. Comparing the economic situation in West Germany with that in the Eastern zone made them much more optimistic about the vitality of the capitalist world economy and its indefinite superiority.

Reading NSC 68 forty years later, most Germans would hesitate to accept the black-and-white picture comparing Communist Russia and the "free world." They would be more discriminating as to those Western measures (such as the currency reform of June 1948) that had also contributed to the division of Germany and the rise of the cold war. Likewise, they would have difficulty accepting the language of the document; it would strike them as too melodramatic and as alien as some of President Reagan's pronouncements would be more than three decades later.

A German would now also take a deeper look both at the international situation and at the domestic environment in which the document was written. Neither the impact of the "loss of China" nor that of the loss of the nuclear monopoly on political elites in the United States should be underrated. Given the impression that these two events, among others, created at the time that communism was on the rise worldwide while the power of the United States was declining, Paul Nitze's stark language was to convince the administration, Congress, and the public that it was time to reverse the trend and to muster political resolve as well as economic resources to prevent the West from slipping vis-à-vis the Soviet Union.

Did NSC 68 make a difference for Germany? Not by itself: not without the North Korean attack on South Korea on June 25, 1950. This act of aggression not only vindicated the dire prognoses of the planning staff document but also gave it bureaucratic weight and congressional endorsement. Because the political preconditions and the economic consequences of its recommendations had been examined, the American decision to intervene in Korea was facilitated. It also paved the way for the eventual admission of West Germany to NATO, rearmed and sovereign, with the occupation statute rescinded. To some extent, NSC 68 laid the ideological ground and provided the political cement for the North Atlantic alliance that endured for a decade.

However, with the advent of the first signs of détente in the 1960s, this version of containment strategy lost credibility and was replaced by one with much greater emphasis on diplomacy, negotiation, maintenance of stability, and concurrence among the Western allies.   ∎

Norway
GEIR LUNDESTAD

Professor of history at the University of Tromso in Norway and director of Norway's Nobel Institute, Geir Lundestad, born in 1945, is one of Scandinavia's premier Americanists. In addition to the book from which the following selection is excerpted, Lundestad's works in English include *America's Non-Policy towards Eastern Europe, 1943–1947* (New York: Columbia University Press, 1975); *America, Scandinavia, and the Cold War, 1945–1949* (New York: Columbia University Press, 1980); and *East, West, North, South: Major Developments in International Politics, 1945–1986* (Oxford: Oxford University Press, for the Norwegian University Press, 1988).

Lundestad's commentary here is focused not on NSC 68 per se but on the general question of why U.S. military spending shot up after 1950, leveled off, rose again in the 1960s, fell in the 1970s, then moved up again in the Reagan years. His answer to this question echoes Steiner's and Haftendorn's comments. Lundestad, however, provides elaboration, detailing features of the American Constitution and of American political culture conducive to rhetoric that strikes Haftendorn as "melodramatic and alien" and to behavior that, in other European eyes, can seem erratic.

Lundestad's Commentary

Countries have to change policies because the international environment changes. It would be a strange policy indeed which had remained unchanged

From Geir Lundestad, *The American "Empire" and Other Studies of U.S. Foreign Policy in a Comparative Perspective* (Oxford: Oxford University Press, for the Norwegian University Press, 1990), 135–41.

in spite of the changes in the political and strategic map of the world since 1945. But why should this factor result in wider pendulum swings in America than in other countries?

Part of the answer could well be that the United States has enjoyed greater freedom of action than most other countries. Its location in the Western hemisphere—plus the British Navy—made it possible for the United States to choose isolationism. After the Second World War its new position as by far the world's strongest power formed the material background for the informal American "empire."[1] The Europeans, on the other hand, simply had to involve themselves in each other's affairs. Isolationism was not a real option. After 1945, neither was empire. . . .

America acted while Europe reacted The counterpart of the American policy swings could perhaps be found in what might be called European dependency swings. Whatever Washington did was bound to result in some European criticism, at least in part as a result of Europe's dependence on the United States. Thus, in periods of East-West tension the Europeans tended to see America as overly rigid and ideological. Then, when Washington and Moscow cooperated, fears quickly arose that the superpower duo would operate at the expense of European interests. This had been de Gaulle's criticism going all the way back to the alleged division of Europe at Yalta in February 1945, but in milder forms this kind of response could be found also outside France. (Similar dependency swings could be said to exist in other policy areas as well. American leadership was fine, but there also had to be consultation. Too much consultation, however, showed a lack of leadership. When the dollar went down, that could be bad for Europe. It could also be bad when it went up.)

On the defense side, some of the fluctuations in American spending were due to commitments (e.g. Korea, Vietnam) which the United States arguably undertook at least in part as leader of the "free world." Since the Americans did this, the Europeans could do less than they might otherwise have had to. This, then, can help explain some of the "highs" on the American side and also some of the "lows" in the form of the defense cuts after the commitments had ended.

Then, a whole host of other factors have been seen as contributing to the wider swings on the American side. Party politics have been mentioned as one such factor. The definition of what constituted American national interests was undoubtedly influenced by the existence of and rivalry between the two parties with their different geographical, class, and ethnic bases. But, on the other hand, ideological differences between the major parties are rather smaller in the United States than in most other democracies.

Three slightly different institutional explanations would seem to be more important. First is the so-called presidential "predecessor" argument. As John Gaddis has written, ". . . incoming administrations tend to define their geopolitical codes, not by an objective and dispassionate assessment of what is going on in the outside world, but by a determination not to repeat what they see as their immediate predecessor's errors."[2] Every president has his own foreign policy. Regardless of what course Washington comes to pursue, the newest "new" policy is always here to stay because, it will be argued, it is most directly in tune with the deepest desires of the American people. Often the road to the very political top is also different in the United States from what it is in Western Europe. Most European leaders have served in several national offices before they become president or prime minister. . . . Experience probably tends to reduce swings. On the other hand, too much should not be made of this factor in that many of these "predecessor" changes have been primarily cosmetic, and have had more to do with presentation than substance.

The second explanation concerns the sharing of power. Arthur Schlesinger, Jr., has focused on one part of this: the ebbs and flows in the struggle for power between the president and Congress. Strong presidents will, sooner or later, provoke a reaction from Congress, and congressional supremacy will, in turn, lead to a resurgence of presidential authority. The interventionism of Theodore Roosevelt and Woodrow Wilson stimulated the congressional isolationism of the 1920s and 1930s. Then, ". . . the memory of the deplorable congressional performance in foreign affairs . . . gave Americans in the postwar years an exalted conception of presidential power." . . .[3]

Another aspect of power-sharing and of other constitutional arrangements is the fact that it is relatively easy to block legislation and appropriations. Strong action has to be taken or at least strong words used to overcome all the domestic obstacles. The result is that, in Joseph Nye's words, "In order to shorten the lags in formulating consensus in our democracy, the political leadership must exaggerate the degree of external threat,"[4] or, for that matter, exaggerate the possibility of cooperation in periods of detente.

There is much to Schlesinger's point, but . . . many swings [occur] *within* presidential congressional swings. Even in the period of executive leadership and relative bipartisanship, from the 1940s to the mid- to late 1960s, the swings of the policy pendulum were pronounced.

Nye's explanation, although important, as a general element probably lets the top political leadership off too lightly. Various administrations have undoubtedly, for tactical reasons, painted the international picture with a broader brush than was done in internal analyses. The public presentation of the Truman Doctrine in 1947, of the ideas behind National Security Document 68 in 1950, and of the prospects for detente in the early 1970s provide three examples among many.

On the other hand, the first two presentations in particular were not really that different from what policymakers actually believed at the time. And there are examples of an administration swinging further out than Congress and public opinion. . . .[5]

The third institutional factor concerns the politicized nature of large sections of the American executive branch, sections which would be staffed by permanent civil servants in most West European countries. The stabilizing influence of the permanent career officials has been particularly strong in Britain (it was exaggerated only slightly in the popular 1980s TV series, *Yes, Minister*). Although the spoils system has been pushed back, many Europeans still find Harold Nicolson's comment that "the American diplomatic service . . . [is] staffed by a constant succession of temporary amateurs . . ." not only witty but, frequently, all too true.[6] The civil servants act as stabilizers vis-à-vis both the politicians and the public while in America the latter two often feed on each other. . . .

An abundance of examples of incompetence on the part of political leaders and their appointees has led many American foreign policy experts (and State Department career officials) to argue that the "experts" should be given more power, that the influence of Congress should be reduced or even, as George Kennan has argued, that a parliamentary system should be introduced in America.[7] Most such proposals are politically unrealistic, to put it mildly. And it is necessary to remember that this is only one of a complex set of factors.

Frank Klingberg has related his extrovert-introvert cycles to swings in many other fields of human behavior: the alternating strength of major political parties, war cycles, business fluctuations, even the rise and fall of civilizations. In Hegelian fashion he argued that "the principle of rhythm" is perhaps a basic law in human society.[8]

Klingberg's pattern of extroversion-introversion generational swings, each about 25 years long, breaks down for the years after the Second World War. More specifically, the swings in American attitudes to the Soviet Union and to defense spending have been much shorter than 25 years.

Although a general theory about rhythms can provide useful insights, I would play down the universality of the swings, seeing them instead as rather more typical of the United States. Then I would relate the rhythm theory to certain American cultural factors and argue that it is here we find perhaps some of the deepest explanations for the swings of American foreign policy. American society, it can be contended, in many ways adheres to one overall ideology, and Americans are quite satisfied with the fundamental structure of their political system. But it is also possible to argue that the country is built on conflicting cultural subvalues. The exact mix between these values will vary from person to person, but, to a larger extent than in most other countries, the basic conflict can probably be found even within most U.S. citizens. In some periods certain values will be emphasized, in other periods the opposite values will tend to dominate.

One such pair of cultural values is moralism vs. pragmatism.[9] On the moralist side (again to simplify matters vastly), just as in 1862 the United States could not remain half free, half slave, so in 1917 and in 1941 Washington concluded that the world could not remain half free, half slave. After the Second World War the crusade against communism was based on a similar dichotomy.

On the pragmatic side, Americans used to feel (they are probably not so sure any more) that they were the world's leading "how-to-do-it" people. If one approach does not work, you try something different. Since most Americans are not terribly patient—U.S. athletes have traditionally been better sprinters than marathon runners—they will not wait long for the desired results. This impatience in itself provides an additional explanation for the swings. Aspiring politicians cater to this mood: "If you elect me, the problem will go away." This attitude has probably been even more pronounced in American-West European than American-Soviet relations, since the differences with Moscow are recognized as much deeper than any with the West Europeans.

A second pair of cultural values is optimism vs. pessimism. As citizens of God's own country, most Americans take it for granted not only that the United States is the "best" country in the world, but also that it is bound to prevail in the long run. That old Army Corps of Engineers slogan, "The difficult we do immediately; the impossible takes a little longer," has become part of the national creed. There is a solution to every problem. Europeans are less certain. America's foreign policy optimism has not been tempered by foreign occupation, nor even by invasions or defeats. . . .

At the same time, pessimism or, perhaps, rather a strong sense of vulnerability is often expressed. America is a fragile experiment and can be threatened so easily, either by infiltration from within (McCarthy's communists in the State Department) or by attack from without—Pearl Harbor in 1941 or, according to the extreme version of Reagan's early "window of vulnerability" rhetoric, a Soviet first strike out of the blue. So, while the United States will win, threats are to be found everywhere.

Many other similar pairs of values could be mentioned: power (in the sense of how many troops you have) vs. ideas (often expressed in the form of a world community of interests); change (America as the world's most revolutionary country) vs. stability (the United States as the prime defender of the status quo); good vs. evil, war vs. peace.[10]

The last two of these pairs would seem particularly important. There is a deep-rooted feeling in America (though not only there) that peace is the normal condition. Certainly wars and conflicts interrupt the normal, ideal state of affairs, but somehow the expectation remains that once the enemy is defeated—and its surrender should be unconditional—"normalcy" will be brought back. As Henry Kissinger has argued, "Our deeper problem was conceptual. Because peace was believed to be 'normal,' many of our great international exertions were expected to bring about a final result, restoring normality by overcoming an intervening obstacle."[11] The United States itself—and most democracies, for that matter—is considered almost constitutionally incapable of aggressive action. Thus in the postwar world only the Soviet Union stood between America and this world of "sweet reason and peace." Or, as Ronald Reagan phrased it in 1980 in a simplistic restatement of this belief: "Let us not delude ourselves. The Soviet Union underlies all the unrest that is going on. If they weren't engaged in this game of dominoes, there would not be any hot spots in the world."[12]

Either there is peace or there is war (or at least serious conflict). If the Soviet Union is an "evil" power, then the United States has to respond accordingly. If the Soviet Union is a "good" country, as was believed by so many during the Second World War and during the heyday of détente, then conflicts will disappear. The world is black or white, seldom gray. Americans apparently feel uncomfortable with the idea of cooperation in some fields and conflict in others. This underlying dichotomy of black or white would appear be an important explanation for the violent shifts of mood in the United States. ∎

Russia

VLADISLAV ZUBOK

Born in 1958, Vladislav Zubok received a Ph.D. in 1983 from the Institute for the Study of the U.S.A. and Canada in Moscow. An early celebrant of glasnost, he coordinated teach-in seminars in 1988–89 on the theme "Blank Pages of Soviet History." Since 1990 he has headed a project gathering oral history on the cold war from former Soviet officials. For most of the time since 1990, however, he has been in the United States as a visiting professor or visiting scholar, exposing Americans to Russian "new thinking" about the cold war. For a sense of the differences between "new" and "old" thinking, compare the following essay with that of Georgi Kornienko on page 125.

Zubok gives an account of how, after declassification in 1975, NSC 68 took on a new life in the Soviet Union. As Nitze had cited Marxist-Leninist texts as proof of a Soviet master plan to enslave the world, so *Pravda, Izvestiya,* and other Soviet journals cited NSC 68 as a capitalist master plan for world conquest. In ultimate irony, Soviet leaders used NSC 68 to argue for increases in *their* military spending.

Zubok's Commentary

Looking at the precipitous unraveling of the Soviet Union, political scientists and historians cannot escape two questions. First, does the fact that the Soviet Union collapsed so miserably demonstrate that the "Soviet threat" in the past was grossly exaggerated?[1] If so, then perhaps NSC 68 merely fed anti-Communist hysteria. It may even have helped Kremlin rulers to stay in power and mobilize the nation for an unbridled arms race by substantiating their croaking about an "imperialist threat." Second—alternatively—was the Soviet collapse due to American "toughness"? Did unflinching opposition to Soviet expansion, supported by huge and costly military forces, contribute to the collapse of the Soviet empire? In that case, NSC 68 and its reincarnation in the early Reagan years may be judged right and effective.

Authoritarian empires can be crushed, as Hitler's was, by war waged to "unconditional surrender," or they can be worn down until fatigue and overextension make them prey to an economically stronger adversary. NSC 68 rejected the first approach, seeing war with the Soviet Union as a global catastrophe. Yet neither did NSC 68 prescribe the second course. It called on the Western world to mobilize to forestall a presumed *Soviet* global offensive.

NSC 68 was an unquestionable success in 1950–52 in its effects on the United States and its major allies. The American military, especially nuclear, buildup alleviated domestic fears about a possible further expansion of the Soviet Union through open military aggression. It converted NATO into a formidable force on Western European soil and removed the fear of Soviet intimidation. By cementing the unity of the Western world and shielding its prosperity, this buildup may have made victory over totalitarianism more nearly inevitable.

Whether or how much the Soviet Union was affected by NSC 68 policies remains unclear. It is unlikely that Stalin knew of the document, though he could have learned of it from spies such as Donald Maclean and Kim Philby. It probably made no difference. The Kremlin always paid attention to actions more than to pieces of paper. According to Khrushchev, the American military buildup frightened Stalin. But did it deter him from anything?

The authors of NSC 68 believed that the successful atomic test and Communist victory in China had boosted Stalin's confidence to new heights and spurred him to launch a political and perhaps military offensive in hope that the rest of Eurasia would fall like overripe fruit. But new evidence demonstrates that Stalin in early 1950 showed anything but a high level of confidence.

Soviet probings in Europe between 1946 and 1949 had met firm resistance. Communist revolutions in Germany, Italy, and France, predicted by Stalin, had not happened. Khrushchev recalled that the politburo was disappointed that "the powerful economy of the United States prevented the devastated economies of the European countries from reaching the point of a revolutionary explosion."[2]

On the other hand, contrary to Stalin's expectations, communism triumphed in China and began to spread around Southeast Asia. Stalin and Mao Zedong were rivals from the beginning. Any keen reader of *Pravda* could notice that Chinese leaders were never addressed as "Dear Comrade" but rather as "Mr. Mao" and "Mr. Chou" and that Stalin was not eager to meet them face to face. From records of Stalin's negotiations and correspondence with North Korean leader Kim Il-sung (as yet unpublished correspondence), one gets an impression that Stalin gave his reluctant nod to an attack on South Korea only when he realized that the Chinese Communists would support Kim with or without him. He did not want to be "less revolutionary" than Mao.

From Prague archives in 1968 came a report of Stalin's meeting in 1951 with Communist leaders of Eastern European countries and warning them that a war might start soon. Did Stalin, as some say, want to get the U.S. conventional forces tied up in the Far East, while pondering an offensive against Western Europe? There have so far been no further revelations from Eastern European or Soviet archives. However, another plausible reading of Stalin's remark is as evidence that he feared a possible U.S. nuclear "bolt from the blue."

What all this means is, of course, not that Stalin was a peaceful defensive creature but that U.S. policymakers, by hypothesizing a Soviet offensive threat, may have missed possibilities for exploiting "seeds of decay" within the Communist world. The expansion of Western military forces spurred Stalin toward a further drive to correct the "correlation of forces." His measures included accelerated programs to produce nuclear and thermonuclear weapons and long-range bombers, deployment of air defense systems to stop a U.S. air strike, a worldwide campaign for "peace and disarmament," and the remarkable suggestion in 1952 to create a neutral unified Germany. So under the impact of NSC 68, the Soviet leader shored up his imperial positions and augmented his military might, with effects evident for an entire decade.

The militarized form of containment embodied in NSC 68 could not prevent expansion of Soviet influence in the Middle East in the mid-1950s or, later, the communist regime in Cuba. Nor did it make the Soviet regime "behave" in a way more acceptable to Washington. It did not deter the Soviets from repressions in Berlin in 1953 or slaughter in Hungary in 1956. An atmosphere of intense dangerous confrontation strengthened reactionary elements in Communist ruling elites and weakened reform-minded elements.

Almost forty years later, however, NSC 68 itself figured, unintentionally and ironically, in a coda of the declining Soviet empire. The document was declassified and published. Paul Nitze, identified as its chief author, led opposition to SALT II. The United States began a new military buildup, and Nitze became a prominent figure in the Reagan administration. In the Kremlin, NSC 68 was carefully analyzed for clues to the behavior of the "Reaganauts," parallels with "competitive strategies," and explanations for the emergence of the space-based defense system SDI.

These readings of the document fully betrayed the worst-case mentality of Soviet officials who had started their careers under Stalin and had the cold war in their blood. Most Soviet commentaries on NSC 68 ignored its cautions against "pre-emptive war." For many Party analysts, KGB generals, and top military officers, NSC 68 served as proof of a long-laid American master plan for the destruction of the Soviet state and society and subversion of its vital institutions. They argued that the United States would never accept the Soviet Union as a legitimate superpower, or nuclear parity as an acceptable status quo. Other highly placed Soviets saw behind the "facade" of the declassified document a dark plot to unleash a new arms race with the aim of exhausting the weaker Soviet economy, making worthless previous Soviet investments in defense, and—finally—winning the global contest with the USSR without a war.

These perceptions affected Soviet domestic politics by inspiring the politburo once again to seek a vigorous leader—first Andropov and then, after a hiatus, his protégé, Mikhail Gorbachev. As it happened, fears of economic exhaustion and technological preemption provided a crucial argument to reform-minded Communist officials in 1983 and then in 1985 helped them push through an idea of "acceleration" of industrial-technological development in the Soviet Union. That was how Gorbachev's "perestroika" was initiated, with fatal consequences for the whole Soviet empire and the old elite. As a live document in the early 1950s, NSC 68 may have prolonged the cold war. As a dead, declassified paper in the 1980s, it may have contributed to ending it.

To say that NSC 68 probably prolonged the early cold war is not to say that, in 1950, there existed a viable, less militarized alternative. In the late 1960s, in much more straitened circumstances, the Soviet government made a choice similar to that of the United States in 1950. With Sino-Soviet tension at a peak, the "cultural revolution" in progress, and China just having become a nuclear power, Soviet leaders panicked before images of millions of Chinese soldiers pouring into the Soviet Far East. Only one analyst predicted confidently that the Chinese would not attack, arguing that Chinese leaders drew from past experience, particularly the Korean War, the lesson that Chinese soldiers were no good at fighting abroad. Soviet leaders ignored this analyst. They construed their choice as one between initiating a nuclear war and building up an enormous military machine in the Far East to offset a possible offensive by Chinese conventional forces. Like Americans in 1950, the Soviets chose the second alternative. Only with the wisdom of hindsight do we know that the analyst was right and that the expenditures were squandered. Only with the wisdom of hindsight can we say that Americans in the 1950s overestimated the Soviet threat and perhaps squandered *their* resources.

In 1950 domestic and international forces coalesced to make the logic of NSC 68 irresistible and any less militarized alternative to it highly problematic. To argue that there was an alternative after the Korean War began is to misread the shaping forces of the period's history. But to attribute to NSC 68 more ingenuity than it really had, or more influence than it really exercised, is no less than to misread the shaping forces of our own era's history.   ■

People's Republic of China
SHU GUANG ZHANG

Born in Nanjing and educated in the People's Republic of China, Shu Guang Zhang was sent to the United States in 1983 for advanced study in international relations. He took an M.A. in political science and a Ph.D. in history at Ohio University, studying with John Lewis Gaddis. He has remained in the United States, teaching currently at Capital University in Columbus, Ohio. He has, however, maintained close contact with historians in China, and the following essay reflects in some degree the thinking of other Chinese scholars of his generation.

Zhang's Commentary

NSC 68 played an important role in shaping the development of Sino-American confrontation in the 1950s. So far, however, Chinese scholars have viewed the document as nothing but more evidence of U.S. hostile intention toward China. More important, they have admired the sagacity and farsightedness of Mao Zedong's theoretical concept of the "intermediate zone"—the framework within which the Chinese Communist leader understood the cold war.[1]

Mao's central argument was that although the United States and the Soviet Union were confronting each other, they were separated by "a vast zone which includes many capitalist, colonial and semi-colonial countries in Europe, Asia, and Africa." The chairman of the Chinese Communist party (CCP) calculated that "before the US reactionaries have subjugated these countries, an attack on the Soviet Union is out of the question."[2] The cold war period, in his view, was one in which the United States would fight for this vast intermediate zone. General war with the USSR would come only after the United States had consolidated its foothold in countries within the zone.[3]

To Chinese scholars, Mao's "intermediate zone" argument makes sense. Along that line, they have viewed the Truman Doctrine, the Marshall Plan, the rehabilitation of Germany and Japan, the U.S. occupation of South Korea, and especially American military assistance to the Chinese Nationalists (Kuomintang or KMT) as strong evidence of U.S. focus on this "intermediate zone." NSC 68, they have argued, merely synthesized the Truman administration's aggressive policy and laid a foundation for further U.S. expansion. Often pointing out the hostile tone of NSC 68, Chinese scholars have asserted that the Truman administration's national security document slammed shut the door to a possible Chinese-American rapprochement.[4]

As for the CCP leaders, they believed that the United States, because of its rivalry with the Soviet Union, would not tolerate a Communist regime in China and thus would try all possible ways to overthrow it. As pointed out by Zhou Enlai, the longtime CCP foreign minister, the CCP leadership was convinced that a military conflict with the United States was inevitable.[5] In late October 1949, Mao expressed urgent concern about possible American armed intervention from either the Korean peninsula, the Taiwan Strait, or French Indochina. He ordered deployment of the best troops of the Fourth Field Army (including three regular armies) along railroads in Henan province, within easy reach of Shanghai, Tianjin, and Guangzhou as the "contingent" forces of national defense in case of U.S. military action from any one of the three directions.[6]

In retrospect, it seems that the Chinese Communists exaggerated U.S. strategic interests in the Far East. The CCP leadership did not have a full and correct understanding of U.S. intentions toward its rule in China. Mao's "intermediate zone" concept was, in fact, inadequate to lead to a full understanding of the cold war situation and was misleading in its forecast of the future American-Soviet relationship.[7]

Unfortunately, the Chinese scholars would not acknowledge the possibility that Beijing authorities might have misjudged Washington's intentions toward China and, in particular, mistaken U.S. defensive moves as offensive actions. Thus, they will not concede that NSC 68, although it mistakenly extended U.S. responsibility for global security, aimed in Asia merely at containing perceived Soviet expansion and hence at maintaining the status quo. They have insisted that this national security document indicates Washington's determination to strive for dominance in regions of East and Southeast Asia. It is taken as proof that China was justified in acting to contain U.S. expansion in Korea, the Taiwan Strait, and Indochina.[8]

It is also important to point out that the authors of NSC 68 did not make an adequate assessment of regional problems. They exaggerated the power of the Kremlin in "directing" local Communist movements. What is missing in the text of NSC 68 is recognition that local Communist leaders might manipulate the Soviet Union into defending and promoting their own interests. In late 1949 and early 1950, Mao succeeded in securing a military alliance with the USSR. Kim Il-sung managed to have Moscow supply military materials and advisers. And Ho Chi Minh, though he had no luck in winning Stalin's support, persuaded Beijing to back his struggle first against the French and later against the United States.[9]

A more serious problem is that the authors of NSC 68 overlooked Soviet aspirations for expansion in "soft spots." New evidence indicates that Moscow never took the initiative to increase its influence in East Asia. The Kremlin agreed upon a military alliance with Beijing in February 1950 only after being vigorously pushed by Mao and Zhou. The Soviet leaders merely made a commitment to China's defense with no intention to have the Chinese

Communists "spearhead" their expansion. Moscow did dispatch a jet division of its air force to Shanghai in March 1950, and this was invited by Mao to defend East China's coast against KMT air raids. There is no evidence that this Soviet air force would be used to attack Taiwan, nor any proof that the USSR wished to turn that island into its military base. Stalin never pressured Beijing to intervene in Korea. He only asked the CCP leaders to allow Kim Il-sung to form an exile government in Manchuria after it began to seem likely, in the autumn of 1950, that U.S. forces would rout the North Koreans in South Korea and possibly occupy all of North Korea. Moreover, after the Chinese intervened to check the Americans and the Chinese People's Volunteers (CPV) began to drive U.S.-UN forces into total retreat, Stalin strongly resisted the urgings of Kim and the Soviet ambassador in Pyongyang that Chinese forces should go on to liberate all of Korea. Instead, he supported CPV Commander in Chief Peng Dehuai's decision simply to establish a line at the 38th parallel. The massive American military buildup during the Korean War seems to have convinced the Kremlin of the importance of strengthening Soviet-Chinese military cooperation in East Asia.[10]

Why did the drafters of NSC 68 fail to see these facts? American Soviet-centrism, combined with Chinese Asia-centrism, contributed to the development in Asia not only of a separate cold war but of hot wars as well. Beijing's and Washington's ethnocentrism or ignorance of cultural differences regarding national security played a major role in causing misperception and miscalculation of each other's intentions and actions. Each acted according to its own logic while paying little attention to the logic of the other; each attempted to understand the other from its own stand and dealt with the other by following its own code of behavior. Viewing each other in dark light, Communist China and the United States became trapped in a series of military conflicts. As we look back, it is worth asking whether the history of the cold war might have continued to be a history of confrontation in Europe if American policymakers and Chinese policymakers had had clearer perceptions and better understanding of one another. ■

NOTES

Steiner

[1] John A. Thompson, "The Problem for United States Foreign Policy," *Diplomacy and Statecraft* 2, no. 3 (Nov. 1990): 65–80.

Lundestad

[1]Geir Lundestad, "Empire by Invitation? The United States and Western Europe, 1945–1952," *The Society for Historians of American Foreign Relations Newsletter* 15, no. 3 (Sept. 1984): 1–21, esp. 1–3.

[2]John Lewis Gaddis, "Strategies of Containment," *The Society for Historians of American Foreign Relations Newsletter* 11, no. 2 (June 1980): 11.

[3]Arthur M. Schlesinger, Jr., "Congress and the Making of American Foreign Policy," *Foreign Affairs* 51, no. 1 (Fall 1972): 94. See also Arthur M. Schlesinger, Jr., *The Imperial Presidency* (Boston: Houghton Mifflin, 1973), esp. chap. 9.

[4]Joseph W. Nye, *The Making of America's Soviet Policy* (New Haven: Yale University Press, 1984), 6–7.

[5]William Schneider, "Public Opinion," in Nye, *Making of America's Soviet Policy,* 11–35. See also Daniel Yankelovich and John Doble, "The Public Mood: Nuclear Weapons and the USSR," *Foreign Affairs* 63 (Fall 1984): 33–46; Joseph Fitchett, "Soviets Upgrading Weapons," *International Herald Tribune,* 12 Jan. 1990, 1.

[6]Sir Harold Nicolson, *Diplomacy* (Oxford: Oxford University Press, 1969), 120. See also Kenneth N. Waltz, *Foreign Policy and Democratic Politics: The American and British Experience* (Boston: Little, Brown, 1967), 133–39.

[7]Nye, *Making of America's Soviet Policy,* 329–54, esp. 348–54; George F. Kennan, *American Diplomacy, 1900–1950* (Chicago: University of Chicago Press, 1951), 82.

[8]Frank J. Klingberg, "The Historical Alternation of Moods in American Foreign Policy," *World Politics* 2 (Jan. 1952): 260–68, esp. 262–63.

[9]John W. Spanier, *Games Nations Play: Analyzing International Politics* (New York: Praeger, 1972), 325, 327–28.

[10]For interesting comments on some of these pairs, see Knud Krakau, "American Foreign Relations: A National Style?," *Diplomatic History* 8 (Summer 1984): 253–72, and Stanley Hoffmann, *Gulliver's Troubles: Or, the Setting of American Foreign Policy* (New York: McGraw-Hill, 1968), pt. 2, esp. 177–78.

[11]Henry A. Kissinger, *White House Years* (Boston: Little, Brown, 1979), 61.

[12]Quoted in Robert Dallek, *Ronald Reagan: The Politics of Symbolism* (Cambridge: Harvard University Press, 1984), 141.

Zubok

[1]On this point, see Strobe Talbott, "Rethinking the Red Menace," *Time,* 1 Jan. 1990.

[2]*Khrushchev Remembers: The Glasnost Tapes,* ed. Jerrold Schechter and Vyacheslav Luchkov (Boston: Little, Brown, 1990), 100–101.

Zhang

[1]See Liu Tongshun, ed., *Zhanhou Shijie Lishi Changiban* (An annotated history of world affairs since the end of World War II), (Shanghai: Renmin Press, 1985), 2:36–42; Wang Jianwei, "An Analysis of American Policy toward China around the Formation of the People's Republic of China" (M.A. thesis, Fudan University, Shanghai, 1985), 3–8; Shi Yinghong, "The Truman Administration's Policy toward New China: A Historical Review of the Period from Hostilities to War" (Ph.D. thesis, Nanjing University, Nanjing, 1988), 132–39. See also Zi Zhongyun, *Meiguo Duihua Zhengce de Yuanqui yu Fazhan, 1945–1950* (The origins and development of U.S. policy toward China, 1945–1950) (Chongqing: Chonquing Press, 1987), 1–79.

[2]Mao Tse-tung, "Talks with the American Correspondent Anna Louise Strong" (Aug. 1946), *Selected Works of Mao Tse-tung* (Peking: Foreign Languages Press, 1966), 99.

[3]He Di, "The Development of CCP's Policy toward the United States from 1945 to 1949," *Lishi Yanjiu* (Historical studies), no. 3 (June 1987): 18–19.

[4]Liu, *Zhanhou Shijie Lishi Changiban,* 41–42; Zhang Baijia, "Comment on the Seminar of the

History of Sino-American Relations in 1945–1955, October 1987," *Lishi Yanjiu,* no. 3 (June 1987): 40–42.

⁵Yao Xu, *Cong Yalujiang dao Banmendian* (From the Yalu River to Panmunjon) (Beijing: Renmin Press, 1985), 21–22.

⁶Mao to Lin Biao, commander in chief of the Fourth Field Army, 31 Oct. 1949, *Jianquo Yilai Mao Zedong Wengao, 1949.9–1950.12* (Mao Zedong manuscripts since the foundation of the People's Republic: September 1949–December 1950) (Beijing: Zhongyang Wenxian Press, 1988), 1:107.

⁷Shu Guang Zhang, "Deterrence and Chinese-American Confrontation, 1949–1958" (Ph.D. thesis, Ohio University, 1990), 64–65.

⁸Yao Xu, "The Brilliant Decision to Resist U.S. Aggression and Air Korea," *Dangshi Yanjiu* (Studies of CCP history), no. 5 (1980), 12–13.

⁹Zhang, "Deterrence and Chinese-American Confrontation," chap. 9.

¹⁰Ibid., chaps. 2–5.

8

Afterword

At this point, you know a great deal about NSC 68, and you have seen many different answers to the questions posed in the Introduction: What was the nature of the document? How logical was it? What made it persuasive? What did it accomplish?

If this book has served its purpose, however, you have found these questions increasingly complex and increasingly hard to answer. And other questions have arisen. For the path of the book is patterned on the path of historical research—from interpretations to sources and back again. And the essence of historical research is questioning. To historians, as to scholars in most fields, answers are most interesting when they open up new puzzles.

At the end of this book, you can mull questions that would have been hard to mull at the beginning. These include not only extensions of the earlier questions but also some more speculative: What if? So what?

The former—counterfactual questions—concern the history that did not unfold. Would Truman have accepted NSC 68 had there been no Korean War? Would U.S. defense spending have gone so high? Without NSC 68 *and* the Korean War, might the United States have remained a comparatively demilitarized nation and society? Nitze argues that, had the United States not followed the prescription of NSC 68, the Soviet Union might well have bullied Western Europe into some form of submission. Many others in this book disagree with Nitze. Some contend that, without NSC 68, containment might have succeeded much earlier and the cold war could have ended sooner, with vastly less expense.

No one can answer any of these questions with certainty. But that does not make them frivolous or useless. The answer to a counterfactual question cannot be put to tests of evidence. There can be no hard evidence of something that did not happen. The answer to a counterfactual question can, however, be put to very rigorous tests of plausibility.[1]

It seems comparatively unlikely, for example, that U.S. defense spending would have tripled in 1951 absent both NSC 68 and the Korean War. It seems comparatively more likely that, with NSC 68 but without the Korean War, the U.S. defense budget would have been larger in 1951 than in 1950.

To explain why the second proposition is more plausible, one has to articulate premises—about processes and shaping forces within the American political system. To side with Nitze or with his critics, one needs to articulate premises about the fundamental mechanics of the cold war—indeed, about the fundamental mechanics of international relations. One *has* to make choices among propositions argued by revisionists and postrevisionists. One also has to make choices within the range of theories sketched by Deborah Larson.

You come to these questions now—at the end of the book—because they are, unfortunately, questions that depend upon specific knowledge. Speculation about what might have happened requires knowing the details of what did happen. And that speculation can roam freely only if your knowledge comes from basic sources—contemporaneous documents and testimony from eyewitnesses. Otherwise, you are a prisoner of the scholars who have picked from those sources whatever fits *their* premises.

If counterfactual questions are second-order questions because they require close knowledge of actual evidence and how it has been interpreted, then instrumental or "So what?" questions are third-order. They require, in addition, a rich context.

A person who has studied a particular episode may raise questions about its alleged lessons. An expert on Munich can make many points that undermine the simple lesson to avoid "appeasement." To cite just one: Hitler did not see the 1938 Munich agreement as a triumph. On the contrary, he was furious at the outcome. He thought the British and French had outmaneuvered him and denied him the war he wanted. When war actually came in 1939, the British and French were better armed.[2]

Analysis of alleged lessons of history, however, calls for knowledge beyond that of the particular episode. The logic of lesson-drawing depends on comparisons. During the cold war, the Munich analogy had power because of the supposition that the Soviet Union was like Nazi Germany. Compromises with Hitler were said to have fed his appetite for aggression. It followed that compromises with Stalin and his successors would do likewise. To have challenged the Munich analogy effectively would have involved not only reciting its details but also pointing out differences between the post–World War II Soviet Union and Hitler's Third Reich. It would also have called for understanding some of the psychological functions served by historical analogies (and other metaphors).

What lessons are to be taken—or should not be taken—from the history of NSC 68? Should one infer, as do the Europeans here, that the way to get something done in the U.S. government is to create an exaggerated sense of threat? Is it rather the case, as the introductory chapter of this book implies, that the operational lessons have more to do with timing and bureaucratic coalition building? And what other history should be brought in for comparison if the reason for studying the case is concern that the U.S. government in the present day should do something it is not doing about, say, education or energy or the environment or health or Latin America or Africa?

Is a document like NSC 68 desirable, perhaps necessary, for a powerful nation seeking consistency in foreign policy? Are Kennan and Bowie and Gaddis right in describing NSC 20/4 and NSC 162/2 as better models because they are more flexible, less doctrinaire, and less prescriptive? Are revisionists and critics of NSC 68 such as Kuklick and Rosenberg right in implying that any such document will be likely to distort national priorities because it will come from, and reflect the interests of, governing elites resistant to domestic change?

To have a cut at such questions, you need knowledge not only of NSC 68 but of documents with which it might be compared, including those from other countries and periods cited by McDougall. You also need clarity about what you believe to be the relevant patterns in history. How have national priorities been set? By whom? Why?

In short, thinking about NSC 68 illustrates the problems and delights of thinking about anything in the past. There are no answers in the back of the book. There are only questions.

NOTES

[1]See Nelson Goodman's wonderful *Fact, Fiction and Forecast* (Cambridge: Harvard University Press, 1955) or the posthumous collection of Hans Reichenbach, *Laws, Modalities, and Counterfactuals* (Berkeley: University of California Press, 1976).

[2]Hitler's disappointment is extensively documented in Gerhard L. Weinberg, *The Foreign Policies of Hitler's Germany: Starting World War II, 1937–1939* (Chicago: University of Chicago Press, 1980). Counterfactual questions concerning war in 1938 are thoughtfully explored in Williamson Murray, *The Change in the European Balance of Power, 1938–1939* (Princeton: Princeton University Press, 1984), with a conclusion that more or less supports the moral of "nonappeasement."

APPENDIX A

Chronology of the Cold War, 1944–1954

1944

October: Communists take over Yugoslavia. Red Army halts advance just as non-Communist Poles revolt in Warsaw and are decimated by the Germans.

November: Franklin Roosevelt elected to a fourth term, with Harry Truman as vice president.

1945

January: Yalta Conference, apparent high point of Soviet-Western cooperation.

March: Soviet-backed Communists take effective control of Rumania.

April: Roosevelt dies; Truman becomes president; San Francisco Conference creates United Nations.

May: European war ends.

July: Potsdam Conference—friction between East and West, but conferees confirm the partition of Germany into four zones of occupation—American, British, French, and Soviet.

August: U.S. drops atomic bombs on Hiroshima and Nagasaki; USSR enters Pacific war; Japan surrenders.

September: Foreign ministers' conferences—increasing East-West friction.

November: Communists take over Albania.

1946

February: George F. Kennan's "Long Telegram."

March: Churchill's "iron curtain" speech in Fulton, Missouri. Communists take full power in Bulgaria.

November: Sweeping Republican electoral gains; Democratic majorities replaced by Republican majorities in both houses of Congress.

1947

January: General George C. Marshall becomes secretary of state, appoints Kennan head of a new Policy Planning Staff.

February: Soviets definitively reject U.S.-sponsored Baruch Plan, proposing eventual UN control of atomic weapons.

March: Truman Doctrine.

June–July: Marshall Plan—U.S. program for economic recovery aid accepted by Western European nations, rejected by the USSR and all nations in its orbit.

July: National Security Act creates independent Air Force, a secretary of defense and a Joint Chiefs of Staff organization to coordinate defense policy, a National Security Council to coordinate defense policy with diplomacy, and a Central Intelligence Agency to provide information and analysis. Kennan's "X" article appears in *Foreign Affairs*.

1948

January: Communists take complete power in Hungary.

February: Communist coup in Czechoslovakia.

March: Congress fully funds Marshall Plan; Western European states sign Brussels Treaty, pledging mutual defense against USSR.

April: U.S.-backed Christian Democrats decisively defeat Soviet-backed Communists in Italian elections. Communist Yugoslavia breaks with the USSR. Soviets agree to accept a non-Communist but neutral government in Finland.

May: Western powers change currency in western Germany, shutting off Soviet ability to buy western German goods with currency of their own printing.

July: Berlin blockade and airlift.

November: Truman wins surprise victory as president; Democrats regain the majority in both houses of Congress. NSC 20/4 outlines official policy of containment.

1949

January–March: Truman unveils Fair Deal program; appoints Louis Johnson secretary of defense; signals intent to hold down defense spending; acquiesces in Marshall's desire to retire and appoints Dean Acheson secretary of state.

April: North Atlantic Treaty signed; NATO created; West Germany obtains comparative autonomy subject to control by Allied high commissioners.

May: Soviets end Berlin blockade.

August: State Department white paper explains total victory of Communists in China as a result of weakness of Chinese Nationalists, but large segments of the U.S. public blame the Roosevelt and Truman administrations for having "lost China."

September: Truman announces that Soviets have tested an atomic device.

December: Acheson makes Kennan counselor of the State Department, appoints Paul Nitze head of the Policy Planning Staff.

1950

January: Truman announces decision to proceed with a hydrogen bomb; as corollary, authorizes general review of national security policy, which will eventuate as NSC 68. Alger Hiss convicted of perjury.

February: Senator Joseph McCarthy charges that State Department is full of Communists.

April: NSC 68 presented to Truman; he orders that it be kept under wraps and be studied by officials likely to oppose increases in military spending.

June: Outbreak of Korean War; UN General Assembly demands North Korean withdrawal; under UN mandate US forces go to the rescue of South Korea.

July: Senate committee reports that McCarthy's charges are groundless.

September: Truman approves NSC 68, orders its full implementation. Successful UN landings at Inchon, South Korea; UN forces under General Douglas MacArthur commence conquest of North Korea.

November: In House and Senate elections, critics of McCarthy lose badly while candidates endorsed by him are generally successful.

December: Chinese intervention in Korea sends UN forces into precipitate retreat. General Dwight Eisenhower named NATO supreme commander; U.S. promises four combat divisions for European defense.

1951

January: Defense budget, following guideline of NSC 68, increased threefold.

March: Frontier in Korea stabilizes near former North Korea–South Korea boundary.

April: Truman fires MacArthur, precipitating several-month hearing on policy of avoiding all-out war in Asia.

June: At Soviet initiative, truce negotiations commence in Korea; fighting does not stop.

1952

November: Eisenhower elected president; Republican majorities in House and Senate.

1953

March: Stalin dies.

July: Armistice in Korea.

October: NSC 162/2—the Eisenhower New Look replaces NSC 68.

1954

January: John Foster Dulles's "massive retaliation" speech.

April: Dulles *Foreign Affairs* article tones down January speech, fleshes out public articulation of New Look.

APPENDIX B

Some Public Opinion Polls, 1948–1951

	1948							1949					
	June	July	Aug.	Sept.	Oct.	Nov.	Dec.	Jan.	Feb.	Mar.	Apr.	May	June
Truman as president													
Approve	39												
Disapprove	47												
Russia wants peace[a]													
Yes								16					22
No								72					60
War likely in													
one year				57									
five years										41			
ten years												15	
25–30 years													
In cold war, U.S. is													
winning							17						
losing							15						
US defense spending[a]													
too high													
too low													
Biggest U.S. problem													
avoiding war													
unemployment													
inflation													
government waste													
housing													
strikes													
communism in U.S.													
Joe McCarthy does													
more harm													
more good													
Korean War will last													
1–6 months													
6 months–1 year													
1 year plus													

	1949						1950						
	July	Aug.	Sept.	Oct.	Nov.	Dec.	Jan.	Feb.	Mar.	Apr.	May	June	July
Truman as president													
Approve	57			51				45		37			
Disapprove	26			31				40		44			
Russia wants peace[a]													
Yes		50					18						
No							70						
War likely in													
one year											22		
five years													
ten years													
25–30 years													
In cold war, U.S. is													
winning										16			
losing										23			
US defense spending[a]													
too high									15		7		
too low									23		63		
Biggest U.S. problem													
avoiding war				16	14						40	21	
unemployment				12	6						10	4	
inflation				11	9						15	5	
government waste				9	7						?	9	
housing				5	4						3	4	
strikes				6	18						4	3	
communism in U.S.				7	3						8	5	
Joe McCarthy does													
more harm											29		39
more good											39		41
Korean War will last													
1–6 months													23
6 months–1 year													44
1 year plus													14

	1950					1951						
	Aug.	Sept.	Oct.	Nov.	Dec.	Jan.	Feb.	Mar.	Apr.	May	June	July
Truman as president												
Approve		43				36		26	28		24	
Disapprove		32				49		57	57		61	
Russia wants peace[a]												
Yes				9								
No				81								
War likely in												
one year				29								
five years												
ten years												
25–30 years												
In cold war, U.S. is												
winning							9					
losing							30					
US defense spending[a]												
too high												12
too low						73						82
Biggest U.S. problem												
avoiding war												
unemployment												
inflation												
government waste												
housing												
strikes												
communism in U.S.												
Joe McCarthy does												
more harm												
more good												
Korean War will last												
1–6 months			33									
6 months–1 year			37									
1 year plus			14									

[a] Wording of question changed over time; responses may not be comparable.
Source: George H. Gallup, *The Gallup Poll: Public Opinion, 1935–1971,* 3 vols. (New York: Random House, 1972).

Suggestions for Further Reading

Chapters 1 and 2 discussed historical writing about the origins and early course of the cold war. A few thoughtful works illustrating differing approaches to the period of NSC 68 deserve mention here. One that offers an updated version of prerevisionist orthodoxy is Robert J. Maddox, *From War to Cold War: The Education of Harry S. Truman* (Boulder, Colo.: Westview, 1988). One looking at the whole twentieth century from an essentially revisionist standpoint is Thomas J. McCormick, *America's Half-Century: United States Foreign Policy in the Cold War* (Baltimore: Johns Hopkins University Press, 1989). The latest thoughts on the period from the foremost postrevisionist scholar, John Lewis Gaddis, are in two collections of essays: *The Long Peace: Inquiries into the History of the Cold War* (New York: Oxford University Press, 1987) and *The United States and the End of the Cold War: Implications, Reconsiderations, Provocations* (New York: Oxford University Press, 1992).

The most thorough and comprehensive survey is Melvyn P. Leffler, *A Preponderance of Power: National Security, the Truman Administration, and the Cold War* (Stanford: Stanford University Press, 1992). Not easily labeled, Leffler's work draws on all schools of cold war historiography. Its center of gravity, however, lies somewhere between revisionism and postrevisionism.

As pointed out in Chapter 1, two concerns gave rise to NSC 68. One was the shaky condition of postwar Europe. The other was the decline in U.S. military strength. For background on the first, see Robin Edmonds, *Setting the Mould: the United States and Britain, 1945–1950* (New York: Oxford University Press, 1986); Robert A. Pollard, *Economic Security and the Origins of the Cold War, 1945–1950* (New York: Columbia University Press, 1985); Michael J. Hogan, *The Marshall Plan: America, Britain, and the Reconstruction of Western Europe, 1947–1952* (New York: Cambridge University Press, 1987); Thomas A.

Schwartz, *America's Germany: John J. McCloy and the Federal Republic of Germany* (Cambridge: Harvard University Press, 1991); William Taubman, *Stalin's American Policy: From Entente to Détente to Cold War* (New York: W. W. Norton, 1982); or the collection of essays edited by Olav Riste, *Western Security: The Formative Years, 1947–1953* (New York: Columbia University Press, 1985).

For background on U.S. defense policy as related to NSC 68, the fundamental works are Samuel P. Huntington, *The Common Defense: Strategic Programs in National Politics* (New York: Columbia University Press, 1961), and Warner R. Schilling, Paul Y. Hammond, and Glenn H. Snyder, *Strategy, Politics, and Defense Budgets* (New York: Columbia University Press, 1962), which includes Hammond's monograph on NSC 68. On nuclear issues in particular, the outstanding studies are Herbert York, *The Advisors: Oppenheimer, Teller, and the Superbomb* (San Francisco: Freeman, 1976), and McGeorge Bundy, *Danger and Survival: Choices about the Bomb in the First Fifty Years* (New York: Random House, 1988).

On American domestic politics and public opinion in the period, see Alonzo Hamby, *Beyond the New Deal: Harry S. Truman and American Liberalism* (New York: Columbia University Press, 1973); some of the autobiographies and biographies listed in the next few paragraphs; Stephen J. Whitfield, *The Culture of the Cold War* (Baltimore: Johns Hopkins University Press, 1991); or Paul Boyer, *By the Bomb's Early Light: American Thought and Culture at the Dawn of the Nuclear Age* (New York: Pantheon, 1985).

The literature on individuals is particularly rich. For Truman, there are his *Memoirs,* 2 vols. (Garden City, N.Y.: Doubleday, 1955–1956); Robert J. Donovan, *The Presidency of Harry S. Truman,* 2 vols. (New York: W. W. Norton, 1977–1982); and David McCullough, *Truman* (New York: Simon & Schuster, 1992). On Acheson, his own *Present at the Creation: My Years at the State Department* (New York: W. W. Norton, 1969); Gaddis Smith, *Dean Acheson* (New York: Cooper Square Publishers, 1972); and David S. McLellan, *Dean Acheson: The State Department Years* (New York: Dodd, Mead, 1976). On Kennan, his *Memoirs,* 2 vols. (Boston: Little, Brown, 1967–1972); Walter L. Hixson, *George F. Kennan: Cold War Iconoclast* (New York: Columbia University Press, 1989); David Allan Mayers, *George Kennan and the Dilemmas of U.S. Foreign Policy* (New York: Oxford University Press, 1989); and Anders Stephanson, *Kennan and the Art of Foreign Policy* (Cambridge: Harvard University Press, 1989).

Nitze's autobiography is *From Hiroshima to Glasnost: At the Center of Decision, a Memoir* (New York: Grove, Weidenfeld, 1989). Works about him are Steven L. Rearden, *The Evolution of American Strategic Doctrine: Paul H. Nitze and the Soviet Challenge* (Boulder, Colo.: Westview, 1984); Strobe Talbott, *The Master of the Game: Paul Nitze and the Nuclear Peace* (New York: Alfred A. Knopf, 1988); and David Callahan, *Dangerous Possibilities: Paul Nitze and the Cold War* (New York: HarperCollins, 1990).

Walter Isaacson and Evan Thomas, *The Wise Men: Six Friends and the World They Made* (New York: Simon & Schuster, 1986), is an enthralling collective portrait of Acheson, Kennan, and four of their associates: Charles Bohlen, W. Averell Harriman, Robert A. Lovett, and John J. McCloy.

For Congress during the period of the gestation of NSC 68, the best insights can be found in James T. Patterson, *Mr. Republican: A Biography of Robert A. Taft* (Boston: Houghton Mifflin, 1972), and either Thomas C. Reeves, *The Life and Times of Joe McCarthy: A Biography* (New York: Stein and Day, 1982) or the less vivid but more scholarly *A Conspiracy So Immense: The World of Joe McCarthy* (New York: Free Press, 1983) by David M. Oshinsky.

Arthur Krock, *Memoirs: Sixty Years on the Firing Line* (New York: Funk and Wagnalls, 1968), is the autobiography of a *New York Times* reporter. Ronald Steel, *Walter Lippmann and the American Century* (Boston: Little, Brown, 1980), analyzes the columnist who was an important early critic of containment. Drew Pearson, *Diaries, 1949–1959,* ed. Tyler Abell (New York: Holt, Rinehart and Winston, 1974), suggests the perspective during this period of the nation's premier political gossip columnist.

The best works about or by important non-Americans include Alan Bullock, *Ernest Bevin: Foreign Secretary, 1945–1951* (New York: Oxford University Press, 1983); Konrad Adenauer, *Memoirs, 1945–1953* (Chicago: Henry Regnery, 1965); and Adam Ulam, *Stalin, the Man and His Era* (New York: Viking, 1973).

You can find references to other relevant works in this book's footnotes. If you really want to get a feeling for how historians build their stories, however, don't be content with going just to histories or biographies. Nothing can take the place of looking at original sources such as *The Papers of Harry S. Truman;* the official documents in the State Department series *Foreign Relations of the United States* (from which comes the text of NSC 68); hearings transcribed by various committees of Congress; and newspapers and magazines of the late 1940s and early 1950s. Nothing can so quickly reveal how much challenge there is in reconstructing the past—and how much fun it can be.

Index

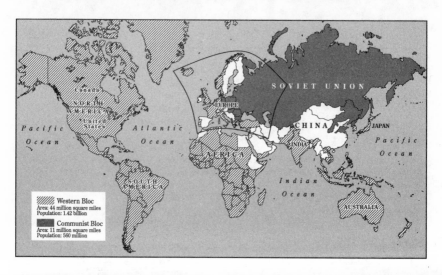

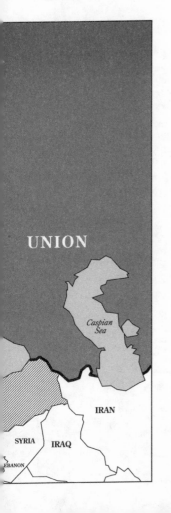

UNION

Caspian Sea

IRAN

SYRIA   IRAQ

EBANON

◀ The Postwar Division of Europe (about 1949)

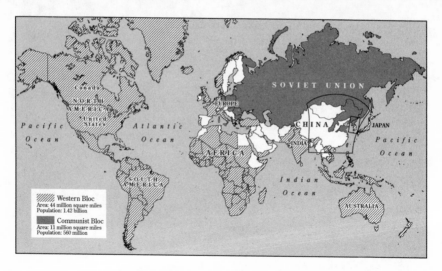

◄ The Western and Communist Blocs (about 1949)

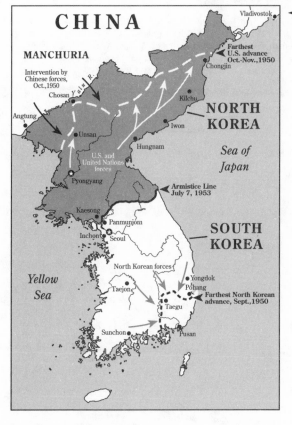

◄ The Korean War
(1950-53)

◄ The Spread of Communism in China (about 1947)

Acknowledgments *(continued from page iv)*

Paul Y. Hammond. *Strategy, Politics, and Defense Budgets* by Warner R. Schilling, Paul Y. Hammond, and Glenn H. Snyder, 1962. © Columbia University Press, New York. Reprinted by permission of the publisher.

George F. Kennan. From *Memoirs: 1950–1963* by George F. Kennan. Copyright © 1967 by George F. Kennan. By permission of Little, Brown and Company.

Geir Lundestad. Excerpted from *The American "Empire" and Other Studies of U.S. Foreign Policy in a Comparative Perspective* by Geir Lundestad, pp. 135–41. Copyright © 1990 by permission of the Scandinavian University Press (Universitetsforlaget).

Paul H. Nitze. Reprinted from Paul H. Nitze, "The Development of NSC 68," *International Security* 4 (Spring 1980), pp. 170–176, by permission of the MIT Press, Cambridge, Massachusetts. Copyright © 1980 by the President and Fellows of Harvard College and of the Massachusetts Institute of Technology.

Samuel F. Wells, Jr. Reprinted from Samuel F. Wells, "Sounding the Tocsin," *International Security* 4 (Fall 1979), pp. 138–139 and 151–158, by permission of the MIT Press, Cambridge, Massachusetts. Copyright © 1979 by the President and Fellows of Harvard College.

William Appleman Williams. Text excerpt from pp. 175–179 of *America Confronts a Revolutionary World: 1776–1976* by William Appleman Williams. Copyright © 1976 by William Appleman Williams. By permission of William Morrow & Company, Inc.

Appendix B, Poll Data. Reprinted from *The Gallup Poll: Public Opinion, 1935–1971* by George H. Gallup. Copyright © 1972 by the American Institute of Public Opinion. Reprinted by permission of Random House, Inc.

Pp. 224–227, world maps. Copyright © 1949 by the New York Times Company. Reprinted by permission.

Page 226, map of China. From Wallbank et al., *Civilization Past and Present*, copyright 1992. Reprinted by permission of HarperCollins Publishers Inc.

Page 227, map of Korea. From Paterson et al., *American Foreign Policy: A History*, copyright 1988, p. 378. Reprinted by permission of D. C. Heath and Company.